THE
BLUE
WALL

THE BLUE WALL

Street Cops in Canada

CARSTEN STROUD

McClelland and Stewart

McClelland and Stewart Limited
The Canadian Publishers
25 Hollinger Road
Toronto, Ontario
M4B 3G2

Canadian Cataloguing in Publication Data

Stroud, Carsten, 1946-
  The blue wall

ISBN 0-7710-8313-0

1. Police – Canada. 2. Criminal investigation –
Canada. I. Title.

HV8157.S77   363.2'0971   C83-098665-0

Printed and bound in Canada
by T. H. Best Company Limited

for
Linda Mair,
Danielle, Jay, Emily,
and
Catherine Amanda Stroud

. . . for tolerance far beyond the call.

Acknowledgments

I can't thank everyone who helped with this book by name, but I can name some of the people without whose support and advice this book would have been quite simply impossible.

Chief John W. Ackroyd, Metropolitan Toronto Police Department; Staff Superintendent William McCormack, Metropolitan Toronto Police Department; Staff Sergeant Julian Fantino, Metropolitan Toronto Police Department; Staff Sergeant Dave Boathby and Sergeant Wayne Oldham, Metropolitan Toronto Police Department; Deke McBrian, Firearms Officer, Metro Toronto Police; Chief Constable R. Stewart, Vancouver Police Department; Inspector W. Baird, Vancouver Police Department; Superintendent H. Starek, Vancouver Police Department; Inspector George Pike, City of Winnipeg Police Department; Detective Sergeant Ray B. Johns, City of Winnipeg Police Department; Staff Sergeant Ivan Klepatz, City of Winnipeg Police Department; M. André de Luca, Directeur de la Police de la Communauté urbaine de Montréal; Royal Leger, Sergent, Police de la Communauté urbaine de Montréal; Jean St. Martin, Sergent-Detective, Communauté urbaine de Montréal; Captain John Burns, Reserve Officer Retired; Marq de Villiers, Executive Editor, *Toronto Life* Magazine.

And the men and women on the forces who are still out there.

Prologue

"There's only one important thing to remember on the street and that is to always know precisely what the hell is really going down."

If you're going to read this book it's worthwhile to bear in mind that the street where the following incidents took place starts just outside our front doors. This street, like all streets, is nothing more or less than the crystallisation of everything you and I want it to be. Or fear that it is. How we feel about our streets in this country can tell us something about ourselves and our neighbours and the world we have made. It may not be something we'd like to hear.

If we have made The Street, then we have also made The Street Cop. Whatever the street cop does, he does it in our names and in accordance with the principles and laws we have caused, through our energy or our apathy, to be instituted and enforced. It follows that his defeats are our defeats, his sins are our sins, and his grace is our grace.

It's not the goal of this book to decide for the reader which is which.

You should also know that although the characters and events depicted in this book are real, certain names, locations, and incidents have been disguised in order to protect the civilians and officers involved from administrative or political harassment. The incidents and emotions described in these stories, are, inevitably, coloured by my own subjective responses. Further, they did not necessarily take place in the cities in which they have been set.

Table of Contents

DEDICATION / v

ACKNOWLEDGMENTS / vii

PROLOGUE / viii

CHAPTER ONE–The Davie Street Beat / 11

CHAPTER TWO–Powder Blues / 43

CHAPTER THREE–Scout Cars in Toronto / 60

CHAPTER FOUR–Area Foot Patrol in Toronto / 79

CHAPTER FIVE–The Piece / 93

CHAPTER SIX–Hold-Up Squad in Montreal / 125

CHAPTER SEVEN–Drug Squad in Vancouver / 139

CHAPTER EIGHT–Casualties / 162

CHAPTER NINE–Hookie-Mal's Run / 188

CHAPTER TEN–Winnipeg Major Crimes Division / 205

CHAPTER ELEVEN–The Line / 223

GLOSSARY / 234

CHAPTER ONE

The Davie Street Beat

They bring the 747's into Vancouver Airport from the north, around the last of the western Rockies where they run into Howe Sound. Under the port wing the mountains are a tilted plain of craggy grey rock, blue-black fir trees, and high valleys snowbound in the passes. As they recede into the interior of British Columbia they climb higher under the wing, building slowly towards the peaks at Rogers Pass and the sheer wall of the Columbia Mountains. To starboard the waters of Howe Sound look deep and cold as fiords but the Gulf Islands are too rounded, their outlines softer, bear-like, under a thick covering of pine and cedar. Out to the west beyond the islands the Pacific Ocean is a flat sheet of beaten silver where the low sun breaks up on the surface.

The jets alter in tone as the plane clears the last of the peaks and cuts over the arc of English Bay. West Vancouver covers the sides of the mountains almost to the tree line, bisected by the Trans Canada, a concrete thread running east to west along the mountains. Further up the slope there are whole sections still buried in snow, but down at sea level it's spring with a vengeance. The City of Vancouver rides a peninsula of granite, shaped like a broad knife held flat, out into English Bay, separated from the highlands of West Vancouver by the crescent of the Burrard Inlet, marked off to the south by the Fraser River. Along the north shore of the peninsula Stanley Park is a dark green diamond covered with Redwoods, column straight and two hundred feet tall. The Lions Gate Bridge runs north into West Vancouver over the First Narrows. Further south False Creek defines the downtown the way the East River cuts Manhattan off from the Bronx. Beyond that the city is a grid of blocks, low brick buildings and new suburban sprawl in a flat span from the Endowment lands in the west all the way to Burnaby in the east. In Burrard Inlet, east of Stanley

Park, hundreds of freighters and small cutters move over the surface trailing white foam like threads of lace torn from a gown. All along the shoreline of Burrard Inlet there are docks and slipways, cranes, barges, elevators, warehouses, shipyards, railroad spurs choked with freight cars and tank cars. On either side of the Inlet, and for eleven miles inland, the business is shipping and trade. There's sunlight on the water here. It hits the office towers in the downtown area behind Stanley Park, but a thunderhead has caught on the peaks above West Vancouver and shreds of raincloud are already sliding down the sides of the mountains and across North Vancouver. Over the Inlet there's a faint mist. The last of the sunlight moves in seventeen yellow ovals over the interior of the cabin as the 747 banks left for the runway. It's raining hard by the time we land.

* * *

I was still trying to get my seat belt locked in when the cruiser pounded over another railroad crossing. My tape recorder flew out of my hand and shattered on the rear window. I felt a sharp sting in my left cheek. I put a hand up to it just as the cruiser skidded around a corner and fired up a hill. The world tilted. I had a glimpse of a huge rooster tail of water flaring out across a sidewalk. In the middle of that wall of water I could just see the flashing red light from our car. In the front seat the radio was crackling with urgent, exhilarated cross-talk.

"Roger o div this is 3434 we're in pursuit of white GM four-by-four northbound repeat northbound on Thurlow last intersection Davie Street require dog car repeat dog car confirm?" "Confirm 3434 this is o div dog car intercept on Thurlow repeat on Thurlow white GM four-by-four two passengers one caucasian male possible 30 years one caucasian female no data now northbound Thurlow – " "Negative that Thurlow this is 3434 he's just gone right onto Dunsmuir copy that all cars!" From the front seat I could hear Beauchamp's gasp. "Jesus Christ!" he looked over at his partner, who had his arms locked against the dashboard as the speeding cruiser took another crossing with four wheels in the air, "Jesus Christ that's *another* one-way the wrong way!" Kreuger, whose young face was pale in the crazy flashing glare of the cars coming at us, looked over his shoulder at me and said, in a reasonable counterfeit of nonchalance considering his age, "This guy's doing an easy hundred from the cross-talk and Thurlow's a one-way street running south. Right now he's got almost the whole o division sector on his ass I hope we catch up with *thos* guys before they get him." I watched the needle in the speedometer rake over the numbers on its way to the end of the dial. Out the right hand window there was nothing but a fog bank where I knew the channel of False Creek cut into the city. We were racing up a gravel road next to the huge dome of BC Place. Somewhere inside it they were building a stand for the Queen to sit on and listen to Trudeau say something portentous. Off to the left the streetlights on Mainland Avenue marked the perimeter of the downtown area. Up ahead another checkered barrier flashed by in the headlights. Beauchamp hadn't turned on the siren yet. "Technically," he said, "we shouldn't be doing this."

"This" was proceeding in hot pursuit of a stolen GM truck. The radio had burst into life just a few minutes before while PC Kreuger and PC Beauchamp and I were patrolling in an unmarked car along the waterfront under the Granville Bridge. Beauchamp and Kreuger were uniform officers of the Vancouver Police. Their assignment this evening was to "show me around" and to keep me out of trouble. We had been on patrol less than fifteen minutes when the chase had started. Beauchamp's instinctive and immediate response had been to jam the pedal into the firewall and hit the flasher. The unmarked car carried a portable flasher that clipped onto the dashboard. Although the rear section of the light was blacked out, the red flare lit up the inside of the cruiser every time it made a circuit. Since Beauchamp was doing over seventy miles an hour up a very bad road in the middle of a rainstorm, the overall effect was quite spectacular. I bounced around in the back seat among the debris of my Nagra with one hand braced into the roofbar and both legs pressed into the rear of the front seat. Beauchamp was trying to anticipate the path of the chase from the staccato commentary coming over the radio. We slammed up another short steep hill and suddenly we were out into a well-lit thoroughfare. People out for an early evening stroll flattened up against a wall as Beauchamp punched the accelerator again. The tail of the car slipped loose, but he corrected neatly, gracefully, and we got halfway up that block before three black-and-whites cut in in front of us. All three cars had their flashers on. In the lead car I could see a large black shape jumping from side to side, silhouetted in the glare of headlamps.

"That's the dog car!" said Kreuger, jubilant, having a wonderful time, "Jesus if you want to have some fun ride with those bastards some night! The dog cars are supposed to lead all chases – Christ Phil hit the siren we're gonna get killed anyway! – what, yeah, anyway, the dog cars they've got these huge bloody German Shepherds – " he paused while the radio crackled up with news. The four-by-four was now headed south on Richards. "We've got him now he'll have to cross us at Smithe or near there come *on* you bastards!" said Beauchamp, his voice tight with excitement and sheer joy. "I love this stuff! You lucked out, man! We hardly *ever* get a decent chase in the downtown area. Nowhere for the poor suckers to go. He's locked in by water on every side, and they'll have the Lions Gate sealed up by now. *Go Go Go Go Go – sheeit!*" he gritted this out as another cruiser flashed out from an alley way, swerved, rocked, cut away and back again until the two cars were less than two inches apart. I looked through the rain-streaked window into the wide staring eyes of another uniformed cop. The other car jerked back and fell in behind us, just clearing our tail-lights as he braked and cut in. "Maybe you should announce us, Mike," said Beauchamp, his eyes locked onto the sidestreet coming up.

"O div this is 3440 officers and observer in pursuit of suspect now proceeding Smithe at Homer other cars also accompanying repeat 3440 now in pursuit!" The set crackled a little, and then broke out again in a rush of voices from other cars. You could tell the speed the cars were doing even over the radio; tires would squeal, engines were winding out, snarling, officers' voices hurried as they crammed as much information into as few words as possible. Here and there a voice came through with a siren in the background. Over the deep bass bark of a large dog, the officer in the lead car suddenly broke in with "I've got him I've got a white four-by-four now headed west repeat west on Smithe from Richards – " the rest of his words were unintelligible, the barking dog sounded as close as his right ear even over the radio. "You don't want to fuck around with those dogs, man. They're crazy. If I were the asshole in that truck I'd just drive it off the edge and into the water. Better to get drowned than eaten alive. *There!* There he is!" Up ahead as we cut through another intersection you could just make out a flash of white paint, jerking from side to side, tail-lights flashing as the driver fought to keep the thing upright as he fishtailed around another corner a block up. At this point there must have been at least seven cars on his bumper, jammed up tight, closing, everyone fired up and wild. The radio crackled up with "This is 3455 I have the vehicle in close pursuit proceeding at speed northbound Hornby at Robson repeat northbound on Hornby at Georgia please intercept at Hastings – " the rest was blocked out by his engine howl and the dog's frantic barking. Beauchamp drove the pedal hard into the floorboards again and I was thrown back against the rear seat. The car in front was less than four feet off our grillwork. The needle on the dial was bouncing off the mark at 85. We stayed on the bumper of the car ahead for another four blocks, until another cruiser forced the four-by-four off the road at a construction site at Hastings and Hornby, or someplace near there, since it was hard to take in all the details standing on your shoulder. We skidded to a stop in a jam-up of police cars in the middle of the intersection. The four-by-four was canted sideways at the bottom of a dirt hill inside the construction site. A young girl was leaning up against the door of a police car. A few yards away a large policeman in a heavy blue reefer was trying to drag a police dog off a man lying sprawled in the dirt. As we pressed forward into the yard, another cop brushed past us with two dogs straining at their leather straps, pink tongues out, white canines glinting in the red lights flashing from the street. Beauchamp and Kreuger turned and slapped each other's upraised hands. I could not feel the gash on my cheek until the rainwater ran into it on the way back to the cruiser.

*　*　*

Beauchamp pulled the cruiser to a stop in an alley way off Davie Street, just west of Denman. Both men were wearing the short blue serge jacket they call The Eisenhower over light blue shirts, navy blue trousers, black boots. They had nightsticks but they usually left them in the car. On the walk out to Davie Street I asked them why.

"Well, the department, that is Chief Stewart, he wants us to carry them more often, especially out here on the Davie Street Beat. Davie is a bad beat. It runs from down here near the shoreline all the way up to Burrard anyway, and most of it is stores and restaurants and bars during the day. But since they decided to run all the hookers out of Granville they end up here. Where you have hookers you have everything else. It's a bad beat and the chief thinks that a stick will keep the trouble down. I don't really like the stick. I don't like to carry it. For one thing, it's a threat, you know, the old policeman with his club. I like to keep my hands free. I'm not a small guy, what am I Mike? maybe six one, one ninety, and Mike is five eleven, maybe two hundred. We don't really need a stick. In a fight they just grab the damn thing and pull it out of your hand and what then, eh? What are you going to do, pull your gun? Only a dork pulls a gun just for a fight. I hardly ever think about the gun, only had it out three, four times. People think the gun is a real big part of the job. But it isn't. It's nothing, really. If you can't fight them on your feet you shouldn't be out here. Anyway, look at this, will you? Davie Street, the boulevard of Broken Dreams!"

We had reached the corner of Denman and Davie Street. On our left the road ran downhill onto Beach Drive and the Seawall Promenade. There were people out everywhere, couples strolling, young kids on skateboards, teens and punkers, girls in parachute pants or tight white jeans, good-looking young boys with Polo shirts, preppies, punkers, straights, gays, everyone in a party mood on the second good weekend of spring. On the Beach road the cars were lined up bumper to bumper waiting to turn east up into Davie Street. The scene reminded me of the Lucas film *American Graffiti*, kids out cruising in muscle cars and station wagons, blipping their engines, snarling and rumbling in a long procession up from the shoreline onto Davie Street. I looked right and east where Davie rose up into the hill. It ran arrow straight, lined with bright shops and fast-food places, Chinese food shops, grills, bars, clothing stores. On the side-streets parallel to Davie the residential areas were mainly high-rise apartments with a scattering of lower brick homes, older block apartments, and some renovated mini-mansions. On the surface, it looked as good a place to spend a Friday night as any on the West Coast; lots of people, fast times, good food, that hot restless edge that you get when you're young and unbloodied.

"Yeah, well, it would be, too," put in Mike, "if it weren't for the hookers." He pointed out a group of young girls standing outside a Becker's store. I hadn't noticed anything special about them. "Take a closer look," Phil said. We walked over to the group. What had been nothing but a collection of young girls on a spring night gradually altered into a gathering of not-so-young women in dark eye-shadow, powder thick as icing on their faces, their bodies presented arrogantly and outrageously in thin silk blouses, low-cut jersey dresses, mini-skirts over white stockings and garter-belts, all of them talking loud and fast at the top of their lungs, most of their attention on the street. One of them saw us coming.

"Hey, hey Phil – I gotta talk to you! Some bastard worked Rita over last night. She's marked up real bad, black eyes and everything! Tony says he's gonna kill the fucker, cut his fucking balls off. You gotta *do* something!" The girl saying this said it at a distance of twenty feet from us. As we got up to her I could see that she was Eurasian, perhaps in her early twenties. Her skin was the colour of cornsilk. Her eyes, dark and shining, were beautifully shaped and tilted slightly upwards. Under the red satin dress her breasts were small and high, obviously braless, and her body was lithe and slender. She had a voice like a tubercular buzzard which she used relentlessly and continually, salting her commentary with expressions as revolting as they were creative. Within five minutes, I couldn't stand her. When Phil Beauchamp reached her, she stepped forward out of the crowd of hookers, all of whom were listening with genuine interest. She was speaking for the professional community. An outrage had been committed. The law must act. Phil, his cap pushed back on his head in a gesture I later knew indicated irritation and boredom, stepped far enough back from the woman so that her breasts were not pressed into his belt.

"Slow down slow down! Who did what to Rita?"

"A John, a fucking John, man! A real slimesucker, too. Her man's *real p-o'd* about it. He's gonna do some serious cutting. She's gonna be off work for some time, her face looks like a dead prune. She'll haveta fuck the blind. You better *do* somethin'. We can't work with this shit goin' on. Tony's got a blade with him, but he says he'll wait for you guys to fix it first. You go talk to him!"

"Where is he?"

"Up at the Olympia, where else? Rita's out on the street, but nobody's stoppin' for her," the hookers all laughed at this, "not even for a freebie." She broke off and looked at me. "Who's this? Another narc? I'm clean, cutie. Wanta check me over?" She stepped back and pulled her top away from her body, exposing her breasts, which were oddly high, too firm, and too regular. I looked over at Beauchamp and Kreuger, who were smiling at the act.

"Come on," Mike Kreuger put in, "let's go find Rita."

"Yeah," Beauchamp laughed, with his attention already a block away, "let's go see Lovely Rita Meter Maid where would I be without you. . . ."

"May I enquire discreetly. . . ."

Kreuger and Beauchamp were different from eastern beat cops, looser, more easy-going, not nearly as military. Beauchamp's hair was long and curly. He looked a little like an aging high-school track star and he walked with a definite roll, as if he spent a lot of time at sea. On the way up Davie Street he joked with people he knew and smiled at people he didn't know. Kreuger was younger, it was still new for him. Every few feet he'd stop and get into an extended talk with the girls on the street, flirting, kidding, gossiping, while Beauchamp and I went on ahead. Beauchamp was not as patient as Kreuger. Under the jock facade he was hiding some genuine career goals.

"I was up for CLU, or so I thought. You know the CLU?"

CLU meant Combined Law Enforcement Unit. What that meant was that the Vancouver Police Department couldn't afford to maintain a broad range of police services on its own. Even a simple forensic lab, with a ballistic branch, was a brutally expensive proposition. Let alone a drug investigation branch. The Vancouver Police Department was one of the only purely municipal police forces in Canada. Their territory was limited to Vancouver south of Burrard Inlet. Just the city itself. North Vancouver, West Vancouver, Burnaby, all of the outlying areas, they belonged to the RCMP. West of Winnipeg, the RCMP provided contract police services on local as well as provincial scales. But since Vancouver was the heroin centre of Canada, a situation that looked as if it was going to worsen now that Reagan had detailed the Coast Guard to assist the DEA in derailing illegal drug traffic off US coastal waters, then the RCMP had to work with Vancouver Police to control heroin and cocaine in the city. Anytime the RCMP has to work with a local force, there will be trouble; friction, jealousies, territorial disputes. The two forces had worked out a joint unit called CLU. Assignment to CLU was a ticket to sergeant's stripes and a fast route out of uniform. Almost every cop I ever met wanted out of the uniform and into plain clothes. Beauchamp was no exception.

"Yeah, I was so sure . . . I tried *not* to believe it, right? The rumour went around for weeks . . . you're on CLU Beauchamp . . . congrats Beauchamp . . . we're gonna *miss* ya, Beauchamp . . . way ta go buddy . . . after a while I got to believe it myself. That's what it's always like in the force. Just when you buy the story, *bang*. Tonight, before we went to pick you up, even my duty sergeant says hey Phil, I guess you're leaving soon for the CLU . . . and then the Staff Sergeant calls me in and says 'sorry Beauchamp you're just too good a man to lose' and *bang* no CLU. I'm back on this goddamned street listening to these sluts whine and listening to the pimps brag. Gets to you, after a while. Mike, he still thinks these bitches are listening to him, he still thinks he'll talk one of them off the street, out of the life . . . if that's not a dream, I don't know what is!"

The traffic got thicker as the street rose higher. In the west the tourmaline was gone from what had been an excessively beautiful sunset, even for Vancouver, the sun breaking out under a heavy load of thunderheads, lighting up the grey wool with a hot pink glow. On the street everyone looked at the cops, everyone smiled, no one seemed to be nervous, or to show any of the eastern mistrust of policemen.

Beauchamp and Kreuger made it a point to be approachable. Their progress up Davie Street was something like a visit to their home towns, to streets lined with friends, people they knew and liked. If it hadn't been for Beauchamp's bitter comments about the hookers and their pimps, I would have thought that the two beat cops actually liked the street people.

"It's not that I *like* them," Mike Kreuger said, while Beauchamp was answering a tourist's query at the side of the street, "it's just that some of these girls are so bloody young. This one − " he indicated a blonde girl leaning against a railing, one knee artfully raised enough to show anyone passing in a car that she wasn't wearing anything under the mini-skirt, "that kid's fifteen according to her ID but I'd bet she's thirteen if she's a day. Thirteen, and she makes her living giving blow jobs to businessmen in their cars. Most of the men who come down here don't want anything else. No involvement. No time. No fuss. Just cruise along Davie Street until there's no cop and something you like is available. Pop her into the car − split for Stanley Park or just a local alley, down goes the zipper, up pops roscoe, down goes the little girl. They *like* the little girls, too, the ones who look like children. *That* part I can't even begin to understand. Not even if I walk this miserable street until I die. I'm a normal guy, at least my wife thinks so. I like women just as much as anyone. But I like women with hips and breasts and flesh, women with something going on in their faces, you know, some sign of a life being lived, a few marks, just to prove she's been there. Full-grown, right? Canada's Finest! But to imagine myself turned on by a chick who's thirteen, tiny, skinny, a baby, I don't see it, I don't see what the hell it's all about. But christ do these older guys pay for it. That kid back there, she'll turn, if she's lucky, maybe three, four tricks tonight, earn fifty, maybe a hundred if it's a half-and-half, for each trick. She could make two fifty, three hundred dollars tonight. She'll work six days a week, easy. Total income for the week, let's be conservative and say an even thousand dollars. No taxes. They laugh in your face when you tell them to go work in an office for one fifty a week. They think they've got it good. Well, maybe they do. Maybe I'm the jerk!"

I asked him why they just didn't run the hookers and the Johns off the streets. Since I had been in Vancouver I had seen more hookers than I'd seen in ten Mexican border towns in the last five years. Kreuger snorted.

"The Charter . . . council used to have the right to control things under the general heading of loitering, vagrancies, soliciting. Not now. Under the new Charter, the courts decided that municipalities don't have the right. Too discretionary. Fascist. Subject to 'abuses' and that sort of thing. So pop goes *that* handle. According to the book, a hooker has to be 'insistent and obtrusive' in her trade. She has to practically grab the guy by his trouser snake and whistle. Anything less just won't stand up in court. Court, hell! It won't even *get* there. So what you have as a result is a lovely city like Vancouver and it's crawling with hookers. They're *everywhere*, like goddamned rats!" As he spoke, a white Corvette slipped by, top down, stereo pumping out *Abracadabra* by Steve Miller, loud enough to stop the conversation. Fifty feet further on, the older man driving it pulled over to the curb. A tall, lanky, unusual-looking black woman in a peach tank top and rose-coloured hot pants walked a stork-walk over to the door. Kreuger watched this happening with a mixture of anger and wry amusement.

"Now *there's* a guy who's in for a big surprise if he takes Lonnie home." He glanced over at me, waiting. "You don't see it? Well, she's paid enough for the tits alone to buy that 'Vette six times. Lonnie used to be a social worker, over at the Centre. One of the guys. Back then, Lonnie was a jock, a ball-player. A guy, is what I'm trying to get across here. He worked hard at straightening out the hookers, getting them to dump their pimps. All of a sudden, he turned. Started wearing skirts, halter tops. Got the medics to slip him hormones, worked on his voice. Slipped into the life in less than a year. Lost his beard. Lost his hair. Shaved his chest. A few months ago he got breast implants. Right now he's saving up for the big one. If that dork in the 'Vette wants more than just a blow job he's going to get a nasty shock. Lonnie will probably get the shit kicked out of her, too."

"Doesn't she know that?"

"Sure she does . . . that's what turns her on. She wants to get beaten up. That's just another one of the six thousand things I can't figure out about this street. We have girls who are trying to look like guys, guys who are trying to look like girls, girls who try to look like guys trying to look like girls. Beat me, whip me, kill me, but *pay* me. This is no place for a nice suburban kid like me."

"Hey, hey, *hey* Kreuger! Kreuger!" We turned at the call and saw a couple running up the street towards us, hand in hand, their faces bright and intense. I looked for Beauchamp. He was talking very intently to a tall Chinese girl in a Suzie Wong silk, one long willowy leg exposed by a slit that ran all the way to her waist and every inch of it unbroken by underclothing. She had her head bent forward, listening to Phil. A fall of glistening black hair bisected her oval face. She was heart-stoppingly beautiful. I was still watching her when the running pair reached us. The girl was young, too young, an ice-cream blonde with Linda Blair looks; soft ruby lips slightly puffed, baby cheeks covered with a fine golden down, an up-turned nose. She was wearing a black mini-dress and hot pink warm-ups, pink sandals, purple-painted toes. She had a scraped patch on her right thigh, roughly in the shape of five nails. Under the scarlet heart-shaped sunglasses a livid purple stain spread out across her cheekbone all the way to her hairline. Her companion was short, less than five five, in faded blue jeans, a vinyl leather jacket; under that an Ozzie Ozbourne tee-shirt ballooned over his sunken chest. His face had that thin patina of street-tough threat that breaks off like cheap shellac at the first punch. Right now, his face was all twisted up with something like outraged dignity. They both burst out at once. Kreuger put a hand up, stopped the rush, pointed to the male.

"Mike, you gotta *do* somethin' just look at Rita's face will ya? Fuckin' hamburger. I swear I'm gonna cut that fucker unless you stop it." He was angry, but not angry as a mate would be. His was a kind of injured trainer's outrage. He rolled on over any attempts to slow his monologue. "Just *look* at her! I got the guy's description, his licence plate; I got friends at Bell I can find out where he lives. Me and Billy and some guys we'll just ace on over there and cut the fuck out of his wife and babies if you don't *do* somethin', man, you're supposed to *protect* us we're *citizens* man just look at the poor kid – " here he broke off and took Rita's arm, pulling her closer to him, sliding his arm over her naked shoulders as if to protect her from the memory or the cold. It was hard to tell which. Mike Kreuger took the opportunity.

"Rita, let's see the face." Rita slid her glasses off over her long blonde perm, ruffling the careful curls. Her left eye was an unvarying patch of ruptured blood vessels and puffy purple flesh, a blood pudding from the eyebrow to the middle of her cheek. She ducked her face slightly, as if the light from the streetlamps hurt whatever was left of an eye in that puffy mess.

"Holy *shit!* Rita, why the hell aren't you at the hospital? You're in trouble with that eye, kid, it needs help! Tony, why the hell don't you have this kid at a hospital?"

"I will I will man we're goin' over there as soon as the, ah, the . . . as soon as things calm down, ah, on the street, man – "

"You mean as soon as the Johns go away! You've got this kid on the street working, don't you!" Although his words were angry, Kreuger's voice was soft and steady. I could see his hand resting on his garrison belt. Where his fingers hooked over the buckle they were ridged and white. Tony tried to change the subject.

"No no man we're just out *lookin'* you know, I mean I gotta find the fucker since you guys are too busy I mean she's my lady, you know, I gotta take *care* of her." He broke off again, as if overcome with the power of his love, and he looked at Rita, who returned the look with a maddening dependence. I could feel my own anger as a hot acid burn just under the heart. Kreuger grabbed Rita by the arm and stepped away a few feet, signalling Tony to stay where he was. Tony took my arm above the right elbow and clutched it, put his face up to mine so close I could smell his mint gum, whispering.

"I *know* you, man, you're drug squad. I can make a real big bust for you if you help me out with this thing. Kreuger's all fucked up about Rita and you know all he's gonna do is lecture me. All that happened was Rita was working off Denman, by the Sands Hotel. This fat dude in a Seville stops for her. I'm on the job, you know, I'm watching over her, so I see her get into the Seville, a big two-tone job pink on the top and black under. The guy's a regular, too, a lawyer from Burnaby. He's down here all the time. Likes the young ones is why he goes for Rita. She's got that special something. Anyway, she's supposed to take the guy up behind the Olympia for a fast deep-throat, which is her *specialitée*, but the guy can't get it up. He says he's nervous, so he gets her to take him further away. They go to the Park, down by the Fruit Loop. She has to get right out of her clothes, which is extra, before the guy gets anywhere. She deep-throats him right there. He wants some more. Now *that's* a half-and-half which is also extra. Rita ain't no asshole she tells him she'll need that in advance. What does this guy do? He grabs her by the neck and pulls her down on him again. He almost choked her, right? I mean, she was real frightened. So she bites him. The guy rips her off him and starts punching her and punching her. You seen what happened. Then he dumps her out, fucking naked, throws her clothes out after her. She has to walk all the way back to Davie Street. I can't let that kind of shit go down, not with Rita. I know somethin' real big is cookin' in Burnaby. There's maybe five thousand caps of heroin in the works coming right onto the street. You fix this guy for me, I'll turn the whole thing guaranteed." He was still holding my arm, talking fast and staring into my face, trying to read me. If he couldn't he was a fool.

"Why so concerned about just one of your whores?"

Tony jerked back, offended. "Shit man, I ain't no pimp. Rita's my wife, man, legal and everything. She's no whore! She's just helping me over a bad time, is all, I mean she and I we got a real thing going here. Soon as she heals up I'm taking her off the street for good. We're just saving up to buy a house." He could see how this was going over.

"Take her off the street now, go to a hospital. Promise me, and I'll see what I can do. But Rita's got to get some medical help within the hour. You can see that, can't you?"

Tony's tight face bobbed up and down several times. In the blue glow of Davie Street his skin looked luminous, as if lit from within by something rotting and phosphorescent. I pulled his hand off my arm and pushed him back a step.

"I'll get her off the street, man, right now right this minute. Hey, you know I will. She's my *wife* man, I don't know about *you* but that means something to me. She's as good as in the clinic right now. You got my *word* on it!" Tony said all this with a kind of freshman bounce, playing off his size and his boy's face, working his helpless street kid charm. He concluded by putting out a small wiry hand, as if we were accomplices sealing a deal. Kreuger came up very softly behind him; Tony's eyes were still on my face, just beginning to see what was in it, and he jumped when Kreuger tugged him over on his back and pulled him off the sidewalk. His sneakers made little black marks on a patch of fresh concrete. At the back of the Becker's store Kreuger lifted Tony up by the shirt. It ripped under the cop's fists but held long enough for Kreuger to bounce him off the air-conditioning exhaust fan housing three times. Tony was trying to say something but he kept losing his breath when his back hit the metal box. Kreuger stopped bouncing the little man. He stepped in close and pulled the man up to his chin.

"Just one thing you miserable little shit you get that little girl off the street right now right this goddamned second and into a clinic or Phil and I are going to come looking for you and you're not going to be a healthy little man when we get through with you. Do you understand what I'm saying? Do you?"

Tony's white face bobbed twice.

Kreuger dropped him into the mud and walked towards me.

"Another example of police brutality. I hope you took notes." He was smiling but he wasn't having a good time. Neither was I.

* * *

"3440 see the man 190 Chilco in the lobby a domestic disturbance log this eleven forty-six confirm?" Kreuger was driving so Beauchamp took the call.

"Yeah roger o div this is 3440 copy that car responding confirm at eleven forty-six." He put the receiver back on the rest and turned around to talk to me. "Chilco is right in the middle of faggot territory. Most of the homes in this area, Davie Street, Denman, Chilco, Gilford, along Beach Avenue by the Sylvia, a lot of the west end of Vancouver, are owned or rented by gays. Estimates vary. Maybe thirty thousand, but don't quote me. You can't really blame them, either. This city has it all. Great weather, when it's not raining. Mountains. Ocean. An off-the-wall population. Arts. Theatres. Film. People come here because it's wide open and not full of bullshit like most of the cities in the east. The gays come here for the same reason. They can meet, greet and screw here with no hassles. That was the plan anyway. Here we are – "

We pulled up in a matter of seconds in front of a tall white apartment building. A beefy man in a security guard uniform was waiting for us at the lobby desk.

"It's those guys in 455, they're at it again. Listen. . . ." The man, who looked more like a cop than either Beauchamp or Kreuger, walked us back out onto the lawn. From a balcony three floors up came the sounds of a fight, voices raised, bottles smashing, occasionally a solid thump of someone rebounding off a wall. As we stood there a telephone crashed through the plate glass window in the living-room and fell onto the grass about five feet from us. The noise got louder.

"I *hate* these goddamned calls!" Beauchamp whispered to me as we waited for the elevator. You could feel the fight going on through the floors. I asked him why.

He was quiet for a moment. "You probably know that Vancouver has the largest gay population in Canada?" I did. "Well, most people think that cops and gays are natural enemies, right, like cats and dogs. That's not really accurate, at least in this town. The gays live well, spend a lot of money. They're good for the economy. Most of the time, gay areas are not a big police problem. They run good neighbourhoods, keep things clean. Really, how much attention should anyone pay to anyone else's private sexual life? It's just not a factor in the day-to-day stuff off the street. But the gay life, from what I can see, is a major bitch in one area. Their relationships, you understand? They meet new people all the time. They depend on their looks and their money to attract new lovers. When the sex is fine, they seem to be pretty stable. But when that breaks down, when somebody gets jilted or cheated or when some younger guy rips off an older man – dynamite! There's a real desperation under all the cool manners, under the good life they put out front. Straight couples have a lot easier time of it. They have more going for them than just sex. But the gay life seems to run on strange sex and, I think, cocaine, speed. It's *in* to live the fast life. Very artsy, very wild scene, especially in Vancouver, which is a pretty wide-open town. What happens is, sometimes the life gets out of hand. Feelings get stepped on. Cruel things get said. Threats. A push. Another push – pow! You have something like *this* on your hands. But two guys fighting, especially over something like sex or love, man, it's awesome. They *hurt* each other. Badly. I know lots of policemen in this city who have stepped into a knife or caught a statue in the brain. We bust in and it's one of the most dangerous domestic calls you can make. Go through the door and *anything* can happen. If your luck is down, it will happen to you. As a class, gays are fine with me. As a call, I'd rather pass – " The doors slid open. The hall reverberated with bangs and a long high scream.

Beauchamp and Kreuger tightened their belts. Kreuger had his radio out and he called in to the dispatcher. "O div this is 3440 we are at 190 Chilco fight in progress request back-up please." The set hissed once. "Roger 3440." At that point, something hit the hall door hard enough to rattle it on its hinges. Plaster dust drifted down from the doorwell in a fine mist.

"Shit," said Mike, looking at his partner, "those guys are going to kill each other!" The two cops looked at each other for a second. Beauchamp was the senior. He would take responsibility for the decision.

"Okay, go!" Kreuger booted the bottom of the door twice. "Open up in there this is the police! Open up right now!" Nothing came back but more fight sounds. Kreuger went back along the hall to get the guard's key. He ran back and put the key in the lock. The two cops tensed, and Beauchamp slammed the door back against the inside wall of the apartment. Before it hit the wall he was running down the inner hall towards the sounds of battle. Kreuger and I were right behind him. The main room of the apartment looked as if something very big had picked it up and shaken it trying to get the pennies out. On the orange shag-rug in the middle of the room two young men were trying to kill each other. Both of them were hard-looking, lean and strong. The one on top was wearing nothing but a pair of lime-green briefs. He had his knees on either side of the man's ribcage and he was bouncing a fist off any section of the man's face that he could get at. He turned as we ran at them. The man under him pulled an arm free and clutched his opponent's face, sinking four white rigid fingers into the flesh around his eyes. The man in the green briefs screamed. Kreuger and Beauchamp landed on them, dragging them apart. As they separated, the man on the bottom arched his back and, straining, just managed to kick the other man once, very hard, in the groin. Beauchamp put a forearm under the man's chin and tightened it hard. The fight stopped suddenly.

"What the hell is *this* all about? Calm down calm down god-damnit!"

His eyes tearing up, from rage or pain I couldn't say, the man in the green briefs literally hissed at the policeman, "That bitch that fucking bitch I want him gone I want him *out* of here he's just a fucking *slut*!" and more along these lines. The other man, still locked in under Beauchamp's forearm, tried to spit at his opponent. The saliva just sputtered on his lips and then ran down over Phil Beauchamp's uniform.

"Fuck this fuck this. . . ." This was coming from Mike Kreuger, who was holding the first man off with one arm. He was looking at me. "I don't *need* this at *all*. This is no goddamned fun at all."

*   *   *

"*Wait wait wait oh man,* Phil it's the Nipple Lady he's gotta see the Nipple Lady come *on*!" Mike Kreuger's heavy body was jerked all the way around in the front seat of the car, his deep-set black eyes fixed on a young girl in tight blue jeans who was running after us, her hand up, calling something, a big smile on her face. Beauchamp grinned into his rearview at me, and lifted the red light off the dashboard. We pulled over in front of the Burrard Motor Inn and waited. When she reached us I could see that she was older, perhaps in her late twenties. She was pretty in a pre-raphaelite way, no make-up, no dye, healthy and straight in her approach to the officers. She glanced once into the back seat at me, and then at Mike Kreuger, who had rolled his window down. The rain had stopped and the night was soft. Spring had settled in early. On the lawn of the Burrard Inn three trees were heavy with cherry blossoms. The girl caught her breath, and said "You guys! I've been chasing you for blocks. Don't tease me, it drives me crazy. Hi Phil, how you doin', eh? You haven't been on nights for a while. I haven't seen you on Davie Street. All the whores are crying for you. Mike, lose some weight and I'll date you, all right? Who's this in the back seat? A new guy, a narc or something? He *looks* like a narc, I can tell you know, he's got that mean look in his eyes. Is this 3450? It's not your usual car, is it. I can always tell by the licence number. Were you in on that chase? Yeah? Wow, that was wild. I hear that Sherry was with the guy, y'know, I mean she was just tricking a little and the cops are all over the truck. I hear the truck was stolen and the guy, this pig from Quebec, he's trying to get her to give him head while the cruisers are chasing him. I mean, here's a guy whose Friday Night is *really* out of hand, in a stolen truck gettin' overhauled by a hooker with sixty-nine cop cars driving up his tail pipe. Wild! Right?" she ran down slowly while her eyes got a little brighter and her breathing got heavier.

"Do you want to have a little, Lucy?" said Phil, looking blank.

"Yes, yes – just for a bit, okay guys? I haven't had this one yet tonight was why I was trying to catch up just now." She stopped talking and waited while Mike picked up the red flasher unit from the tray between the seats. He handed it to her through the side window. She took it with a bright hot look in her eyes. *"Oh yes come to me little titty titty titty,"* she said, in a soft whisper, fondling it. She kissed the red dome several times, her lips open, her tongue flicking out across it. "It's still warm! You had it on in the chase, right? Oh I love this one, this is one of the Dominion Autolite ones, they have the best shape. They look just like nipples, don't you think, Mike?" She looked over the red flasher at me. "What do you think?" I didn't have a ready answer. She didn't wait for one.

"Oh my baby I love this colour of red, too. Some of the other cars, they have the cheap ones. Not so red. I don't get anywhere with them. These Autolite ones are the best. Perfect shape, nice deep colour. Look at how round they are, just like a breast. I love this kind." She kissed it again. Phil, his eyes on my face, said "Hey, Lucy, shall we turn the light on for you?" Kreuger shook his attention away from the spectacle taking place at his right shoulder.

"God no, Phil. For crying out loud! You remember what happened the last time?" Lucy wasn't really paying much attention to this debate. Her face was literally rapt, lost in a private dream connected in some indecipherable way with the red police flasher.

"Come on, Mike, loosen up. Lucy will behave, won't you Lucy?"

I had to put in a word here, before I got to see something I'd probably have to spend several nights trying to forget. "Excuse me, Mike, Phil, I don't think we want to intrude on the lady's secrets in such a public place. I'm perfectly happy to hear about this later."

Lucy looked up from her prize. There was genuine intelligence in her eyes, and she seemed to be perfectly aware of where she was and whom she was with. Her fascination with the light was a single anomalous ripple in an average psyche. Whenever she wasn't staring right into the light she was funny, clear, witty, and quite attractive. Neither Kreuger nor Beauchamp were being cruel with her. To them, she was just one of the regulars. I sensed that she was something of a mascot, theirs to tease lightly, but off-limits to any newcomer's facile dismissal. Lucy toyed with the flasher and gossiped with us for a few minutes, and then put the light back into Mike's hands. I never found out anything about her life.

* * *

Kreuger shut the lights off as the cruiser turned up into an alley behind a row of stores on Davie Street. Halfway up the laneway a new pearl grey Monte Carlo was parked beside a dumpster. From the lights overhead you could just make out the heads of four men sitting slumped inside it. Kreuger and Beauchamp stiffened a little in their seats. Mike put his uniform cap on straight. He continued on up the alley in the direction of the parked Monte Carlo. The two men in the front seat were watching us cruise up; you could see the headlights reflecting off their eyes. Their faces were broad and bony and expressionless. When Kreuger got the car alongside, Beauchamp rolled down his window. The men in the Monte Carlo, two in the front, two in the back, just sat there in the parked car and stared back at us. Nothing was said. Nothing was done. Phil said, after it became clear that Phil would have to say something, "Excuse us, guys. Can we talk? I mean, is anything going down here?"

The man in the passenger seat, a muscular blond with a face like Jimmy Cagney's, maybe Gaelic or Irish blood, and laugh lines around the eyes that he wasn't using right then, rolled down his window and said, "What . . . what is it?"

Beauchamp and Kreuger took this abrupt tone without a flicker.

"We have some information . . . a deal may be going on here. Is there some way my partner and I can check out this hooker? The Chinese number, in the Suzie Wong dress? She's onto something here, and we were thinking if it wasn't on your territory we might get some buy money and. . . ." Phil got cut off by a short movement of the blond man's left hand, a downward cutting chop, a clear dismissal.

"We're all over that bitch. Just keep your ass off her, okay?"

"Yeah, sure guys. Just wanted to check it out, all right?"

"Sure . . . no problem. Now clear off, okay, we got something happening here, you understand. I don't want any uniforms all over us. Goodnight, kids."

The blond man rolled his window back up and said something we couldn't hear to the other men in his car. We could hear their laughter, though, even through two sheets of glass. Phil's neck was red but he was still smiling as we drove off.

"Who the hell were they?" I asked, as we pulled back onto Davie Street.

"Drug Squad . . . major bastards, all of them. Stay away."

"What the hell is *this*?" Kreuger interrupted Beauchamp's warning. We all looked forward. A hooker in a lavender suede pantsuit was running at us, her wig in her hand, dirty and tousled, tears in her eyes.

"Phil, Mike – that fucking weirdo Captain Kraut the fat pig in the silver Volkswagen – he's running the girls down on Bidwell like it was bumper-car time." Kreuger opened up the door and the woman clambered in on top of him.

"Go go go I'll show you maybe this time you can catch the bastard!"

"You sure it's Captain Kraut?" Phil said as we accelerated up Davie Street, dodging a red Camaro filled with football jerseys.

"Is Christ Jewish? Come *on* move move move this pig!"

In an alley off Bidwell we came upon an interesting scene. Five angry hookers, their stockings torn, muddied up, dresses awry, shrieking with fear and anger, were gathered around a battered old Volkswagen Beetle, silver-coloured and rusted out. They were beating on it with their fists, with bottles and bricks and pieces of wood. The tall Chinese girl in the Suzie Wong dress, the one Beauchamp had spoken to earlier, was tugging on the driver's doorhandle with her left hand. In her right hand she was holding a broken Seagram's bottle. Her eyes were hot. Every time she jerked on the handle the whole car would rock on its springs. It occurred to me that she must be very strong.

Inside the disintegrating car we could see a pale pink face staring out at the hookers, the eyes full of tears, the mouth a slack terrified hole in pock-marked fat. The nose of the car was buried in the side of a dumpster. Pieces of trash and orange peel and bits of cardboard box were scattered all over the roof and hood of the car. When the cruiser slid to a halt alongside this scene not one of the hookers bothered to glance away, but the man inside started to scream at us, barely audible through the glass. We piled out of the car and pushed our way through the hookers while a sizeable audience of street kids, pimps, tourists, and assorted unidentifiables gathered in the lane. Mike Kreuger tried to push the big Chinese girl away from the car but she kept her hand gripped around the door. From where I was standing I could see big slow tears rolling out of the man's small eyes and trickling down his cheeks. He was obviously close to a faint. Kreuger had to put a muscular arm around the hooker's waist and drag her off before the others would calm down enough for someone's voice to make any sense. Beauchamp leaned down and rapped on the driver's window.

"Hey, buddy, it's okay. Open this up." The fat man just sat there, his breath misting up the inside of the glass, staring out at all of us as if he could make us disappear through an effort of will. The hookers began to scream threats at him again. That stopped when Beauchamp pounded on the roof. The car rang like a cheap Korean gong. The fat man jumped, and cried even louder. I looked in the back seat of the little car. There were at least a hundred pornographic magazines strewn all over the back of the car, bondage and sado-masochistic fetish books, rape fantasies with names like *Forced* and *Beaten*, gynaecological zoom shots as erotic as a coroner's 8 x 10 glossy, *Playboys, Penthouses, Hustlers, Video X, Adam*. I could see why the man was upset. He was well into a situation where the only part he would get to play was Horse's Ass of the Century.

"What the hell was going on here, anyway?" Beauchamp was getting weary. His voice was cracked a bit around the edges. All of the hookers began at once, like a conclave of harpies debating the boatman's bill. It slowly emerged that the fat man in the silver Volkswagen had made something of a name for himself during the last few weeks. He had gotten into the habit of cruising up and down the side-streets around Davie in his battered car, looking for hookers. Sometimes, he'd rent one for an hour, always in the car. Other times, he'd go berserk, roll up his windows, pull down his pants, take his genitals firmly in hand, and drive straight at any hookers who happened to be vulnerable. So far no one had been hurt, but Captain Kraut, as he'd been called, was getting on their nerves. The hookers claimed that they had made several complaints to the Vancouver Police Department but so far *nada* had been the consequences.

"Anyway," put in the big Chinese girl, her voice booming out over the shrill complaints of her colleagues, "*anyway* . . . just now he came belting up the lane near Bidwell and came straight for us here. Everybody ran everywhere but Eva threw a brick at his window and he freaked out and drove right into the dumpster. I laughed so hard I almost wet my pants. Then we figured we had him so why not kick his ass a few times, just to show him. But the big slimebag has himself all locked up in his krautmobile and now here you come to save his fat piggy bacon!" She huffed dramatically, swivelled neatly on her spiked heel, and stalked away. As exits go, it was a good one. The crowd began to drift. Kreuger went around to the passenger side of the car and tried that door. It was locked as well. Mike pounded on the window. "Come on, man, we're not going to hurt you. Just open up. We'll get you out of here, get you some help. Come *on* buddy. It's getting late. Don't be afraid – " Beauchamp cut him short with a wave and flicked his flashlight on. It lit up the interior of the fat man's car, sliding over an unbelievable detritus of wrappers, potato chip bags, kleenexes, nasty rubber novelties, more skin books. Looking into the man's Volkswagen was like peering into a garbage can full of snakes. Beauchamp started to laugh.

"What, what is it?" from Kreuger, looking up.

"Ah this is indeed a queer river said Bromosel, as the water lapped at his thighs. . . ." Beauchamp broke off into another low chuckle, "Captain Kraut can't come out. His goddamned pants are in the back seat. He's naked bare ass naked under that stupid bowling shirt." Kreuger looked in with his own flash, and then threw up his hands and walked away in my direction.

"Welcome to Vancouver, my friend," he said, and smiled.

*   *   *

Back at the station on Main Street, after Captain Kraut had been cleaned up and booked for Vehicular Assault and Indecent Assault, the duty sergeant called us over. He had a packet of papers in his hand, which he spread out on the desk front of him. In the pile were several photos of a man with his face badly bruised, and others, taken later, showing the scars of operations, reconstructive surgery of some kind.

Under the photos was a Warrant. Issued in North Vancouver, it was an RCMP Warrant for one Eugenio Mosca, a Chilean citizen living in Canada on a six-month visa. He was wanted for the Assault causing Grievous Bodily Harm of a Canadian citizen, an older man named Raphael Suni. According to the Warrant, there had been an unprovoked assault resulting in extensive damage to the victim, who had sustained, among other things, a shattered cheekbone and severe impairment of the vision in his left eye. In the photographs the left side of his face was a smooth arc of pulpy swollen flesh from his hairline to his jawbone. What was left of his face showed what had once been a very handsome man, Spanish in his eyes and the fine bones along his right cheek. His attacker, whose DOB made him at least ten years younger, had spared no effort in his attempt to kick Suni's face into raw meat. The duty sergeant tossed the papers to Beauchamp with a weary shrug of his sloping shoulders.

"I want you to meet this Suni guy on Burnaby Street." He gave them an address. "It seems that he thinks he knows where our mister Mosca can be picked up tonight. Check it out. If the guy is there, scoop him. RCMP wants this guy badly. It seems he's a Habitual who gets his jollies from thumping easy marks. He's got a sheet on him off the *ceepick* would put your nuts in cold storage." He nodded a curt dismissal. When we reached the door he called out to us.

"And guys, watch your asses with him. He's got all the makings of a real pain in the butt. If he gets all worked up, squash it fast. But bring him in. And, Beauchamp . . . don't let your observer get killed, okay? Bad for the force."

* * *

It was raining again when we passed by the Olympia Bar on Davie Street. At one-fifteen the cars were still thick in the streets. At the top of Davie Street a rockhouse was spilling its people out into the road, loose-kneed punkers in technicolour hair, mohawks, little girls in shredded tee-shirts and faces like five-day cadavers, everybody stepping and jumping and calling out to the passing cars; flaming youth in the grand old tradition, freaking out the straights, getting older every Friday night in syncopated time.

Along the rising hillside the dating crowds were drifting off to cars and buses. On the far side of Stanley Park you could see the long lines of red lights climbing Eleventh Street and the Capilano Road to their homes. The wet sidewalks outside the bars reflected neon and flickering street lamps, smearing the hot pinks and acid greens across the blacktop, the colours running down the gutters. Out in the street cars hissed over the water with a sound like ripping silk. Kreuger rolled down the window of the cruiser and the smells of fried food and gasoline, old smoke, the ozone reek off the wet wires, curled in over the ledge and filled up the car. I was trying to place the underlying scent. I had just realised it was the scent of apple blossoms from the park when Beauchamp braked suddenly in the middle of the street, threw the car into reverse. I slid forward and struck a knee on the door handle. Kreuger's coffee slopped over his lap. "God *damn* it!" was all Beauchamp said, then threw open his door and raced into the street. Mike reached over to the wheel to flick on the lights, we got out, locked the car and ran after Beauchamp, who was pelting up the sidewalk, hatless, his blue jacket slick with rain and his black hair hanging soaked down into his eyes. His boots made a spray of water bounce off the walk as they pounded along. He ran up to the Olympia and vaulted up the steps and into the bar without a backward look. We were right on his heels by the time he made it inside.

"What is it, Phil? What the hell are we after?" Kreuger was upset.

"Rita! I thought I saw Rita going into the back here! If that son of a bitch has her working I swear to christ I'll bust his fucking ass!" Beauchamp and Kreuger pushed through a crowd of teens milling around in the entrance way and walked quickly to the back of the bar down a fenced-off passage on the left. In the main room scattered tables of street kids in ragged jackets and black leather vests watched us go with sly and contemptuous grins. I couldn't see Tony anywhere.

At the back of the bar, off the kitchen, there were two plywood doors covered with spray-painted slogans and knife cuttings conveying the usual sentiments. One of the doors had a silhouette of a woman in black. Beauchamp hit this door with one hand, a solid booming smack. It jolted off the lock and struck the tiles behind it. Two young girls were standing in the filthy stall, facing each other. They jerked around when the door hit the wall, presenting four wide eyes ringed in sooty black shadows. The girl with white hair immediately dumped something that looked like a jelly bean into the toilet and pulled the flush. Phil just stared at them for a second, then stepped out and pushed open the door to the men's room. It was empty. He brushed by us and ran to the big steel door at the rear of the hall, kicked it open as he passed through it. We were in the lane behind the bar. The rain was coming down very hard now. Beauchamp looked right and left, his hair spinning out, wet spray flying off his white face. Kreuger, behind him, suddenly pointed off to the edge of the circle of light from the lamp above the door. A dark blue sedan was parked there. In the light it was just possible to see a patch of wool or tweed above the window. The two cops ran softly and rapidly over to it. Phil put a hand on the door, waited for Kreuger to get around the other side, and then wrenched the door open. A portly grey-haired man in a Harris Tweed sports coat fell out of the seat, tumbled out in a tangle of shirt-tails and flapping grey trousers. He hit the ground with a splash, sinking one elbow into the mud as far as his upper arm. The purple head of an erect penis rose up from the ruffle of shirt-tail like an obscene amaryllis. Inside the car the officer's flashlight picked out the twin red hearts of Rita's sunglasses floating over a wide red wet "O" of an open mouth, a caricature of shock and fear. Beauchamp stepped over to where the man lay in the mud, looking up at the cop, his face white and mottled. You could see the man calculate, working on a story, some way to explain all this in terms of his real-estate portfolio and the split-level on Marine Drive with the view of English Bay and his wife's charity work and the three kids one of whom is half-way through honours law at UBC and the stock options and the mortgage deferment codicil, but something in Beauchamp's face shut all that stuff up in the back of his throat. He just lay there in the mud in the back of the Olympia bar with his tailored slacks down around his flabby knees and his penis wilting in the cold wet rain, waiting for judgement. Kreuger pulled Rita out of the car. Her mini-dress was pulled down off her shoulders and her childish body was blue in the cold and rain. Mike took off his uniform jacket and put it around her shoulders. Rita had nothing to say. Her eye looked, if anything, worse than it had the last time I'd seen it. Phil Beauchamp got down on his knee beside the trick and put his whole body into everything he said.

"Listen to me, asshole, very carefully. How old are you?"

"How old? I . . . I'm fifty-two. What – "

Phil leaned a little closer. "I'm the one asking questions. You say you're fifty-two. Got a nice job? Just nod for yes. Yes? That's nice. Is it a nice job? Yes? That's nice too. We are *so* glad you have a nice job, aren't we guys? Yes, we sure are. Do you have a nice family? You do? I *thought* you would. Tell me where your nice family thinks you are now? What? Nothing to say? What about kids . . . you *do* have kids, right, I mean, even with your obvious sexual problems you *must* have managed to get off one or two kids right? You do? That's nice too. What are their names? Tiffany? Tiffany and what? Kerry? And how old are they? I said *how old* what's the matter is the rain getting in your ear do you think you could hear better at the station? Twelve? And? And fourteen. Twelve and fourteen. Tell me my friend how old do you think that little girl over there is? Rita! Tell the nice man how old you are. *Tell him*! Do you hear that, my friend? Little Rita is fourteen. Do you like them like that, young, fourteen? What did you think about while little fourteen-year-old Rita worked on you? Did you think about how she was old enough to be your daughter? Probably not . . . or maybe you *did*. Maybe you thought a whole lot about how Rita was old enough to be your daughter. Is that it? Is that the kick? How are you going to get Tiffany to understand all this? How are you going to get her *Mommy* to understand it? Maybe you could tell them that you were only helping little Rita to pay the rent and buy some horse to keep the chill off? Do you think that would be better? I'll tell you what happens now asshole. We have your licence number. We have you here on your ass in the cold wet mud. We have witnesses coming out of the drains. We *own* your butt you son of a bitch and if we ever see your car or your stupid businessman face down on Davie Street again we will personally bust your ass in technicolour and we'll see to it that everybody on your whole goddamned street finds out how you spend your off-hours!" Beauchamp dragged the man to his feet and pitched him in behind the wheel of his car. The man shook like a reed while he fumbled for his keys. Kreuger watched all this with a face set in deep lines. Rita stared stupidly at me. Phil kicked the door closed. "Now get *out* of here! Fast!" The man got his car started, ground the key once too often after the motor caught, and jolted his car out of the lane. Beauchamp and Kreuger and I stood in the mud and waited for his tail-lights to disappear around the corner. When they did, Beauchamp turned towards the three of us and said:

"God-*damnit* sometimes just sometimes this whole goddamned job is almost I said *almost* worth the aggravation!" Kreuger grinned back at his partner. Even Rita managed a smile. Kreuger put his arm around Rita and moved her to the door of the Olympia. Beauchamp looked over at me and said, "Come on, let's go get that ABH over on Burnaby and then *you* can buy *me* a shitload of cold beer! The way this night is going, we might even find that little bastard Tony and we can watch Mike eat him alive. Some days, I *love* this job."

* * *

We met Mister Raphael Suni on the street outside a toney Spanish steak house in the west end of the city. You could still make out the puffy area on his face where his cheekbone used to be. He was wearing thick tinted glasses, but even through the brown tint you could see that one eye wasn't tracking right. Suni was meticulously dressed in a tan Burberry, tie pinned in gold, a pair of what looked like Guccis on his feet, which were small and light and moved softly. He had a slight foreign accent, maybe Spanish. Mosca, the man on the RCMP Warrant, had singled him out at a wedding in North Vancouver, had ridden him like a picador, sticking him with insults, goading him in front of mutual relatives until even Suni's wife had had enough. Mosca was a classic *"maldito"*, a punk who always seemed to suffer unbearable insults from smaller and weaker and older men. The man was perhaps twenty-five, a weight-lifter. Suni had information that Mosca was at this moment attending a private party for members of a Spanish economic delegation and local city officials upstairs in this steak house. Would the officers care to go inside and verify this?

"Yes, Mister Suni, we will. But you will have to come up with us and point him out. Will you do that? We'll see that he doesn't hurt you."

"*Si*, it will be a distinct pleasure to accompany the officers." In the face of obvious fear, Suni was ready to make his point. I admired the man. Beauchamp, Kreuger, Suni, and I pushed in through the heavy wooden doors. Inside the air was rich with good cigar smoke, cooking odours of garlic and expensive beef on spits. The main room was still jammed with well-dressed celebrants, men and women in dinner jackets and black ties, odd sexual replicants mirroring each other in an eastern affectation, and others in silk dresses, off-the shoulder gowns, furs, lots of fast high talk and good cognac. A tango was in full cry upstairs. The steps were covered in thick red carpet. We made very little noise as we went up the dimly-lit passage, although the arrival of two men in police uniforms had caused a slight faltering of the pace downstairs. The elegant assembly regarded us with cool curious deadeyed stares until we passed out of sight. I could hear the talk ripple around the lower room when we were gone.

Upstairs the long narrow room was packed with people dancing and drinking. Off in the front, on an improvised stage, a five-piece band in frilled shirts was offering a reasonable facsimile of a *salsa* to a feverish knot of dancers. Heavy Spanish beams alternated with white stucco all down the room. It was smokier up here, and hotter. We waited in the entrance while our eyes adjusted. Suni, standing beside Beauchamp, saw his man at a table for four less than an arm-length away. The man had not noticed us arrive, but his three companions had. Beauchamp and Kreuger walked up to the young man, who was leaning back into his carved chair, one leg thrown over the arm, his sharp face back, raising a snifter of cognac and saying something loud in a fine Castilian manner. It occurred to me that this was perhaps an inopportune time to intrude, but I was tired and I wanted to go home. That's a luxury that Beauchamp and Kreuger weren't free to enjoy. They had a Warrant and they had to serve it and it didn't matter whether the occasion was a party or a funeral. We were noticed by almost everyone in the room before Mosca saw us. I think the gradual decline in noise was what alerted him. When Beauchamp, his cap in his hand, a polite tone in his voice, stopped in front of him, Mosca had some trouble keeping the anger out of his face. He saw Suni in the door, saw me next to Suni, and put it together.

"Excuse me sir. I'm officer Beauchamp of the Vancouver Police. We're investigating a Warrant here. I'll have to ask you for some ID, if you would sir." Kreuger stood off to one side. The room slowly stilled. Even the plate sounds from the kitchen in the back came to a sudden halt. Mosca looked at us for just a little too long, long enough for the insult to be clear. Beauchamp's face got less amiable. Kreuger put his feet apart a little more. Suni went downstairs, softly. I couldn't blame him. Mosca, stretching his arms in an elaborate mimicry of casual indifference, leaned forward again and said, "Pardon, mister officer, I could not hear you because of the noise. What did you want?" The look in his eyes was an intriguing amalgam of polite inquiry and sheer go-fuck-yourself as only the truly arrogant can achieve. Beauchamp, who ran into this look about as often as he shaved, sighed and repeated the question. Mosca drew back and began to address the issue to his table, his insolence now growing, taking some strength from the crowd of supporters and friends, but Beauchamp's harsh phrase cut that dead.

"Stop screwing around, sir. ID or outside." Beauchamp let this sink in. Mosca focussed on Beauchamp more closely, and then examined each of us in turn. When he got to me I realised how angry he was, and how close to violence. His deep brown eyes were smoky with threat and injured pride, little of it faked. I had seen enough of it during two years in Mexico and Central America. It was a holdover from the mythical days of the "bloods", the *hidalgo* boys who made it a matter of honour to fight at the slightest provocation. Mosca was aching for a chance to fight, but only if he was certain no one would see him lose. He had a good chance, too. Under the raw silk shirt his chest was bulky with muscle. Add the mood of the room, and odds were fifty-fifty we were about to get seriously thumped. Mosca put a hand into his jacket, everyone got tense, and he drew out a billfold. He flipped this at Beauchamp, who let it bounce off his jacket without blinking.

Beauchamp did nothing for about six heartbeats. Then he quite suddenly stepped up very close and leaned his bulk over the table at Mosca. Mosca jumped, spilling a glass of red wine over the pink linen tablecloth. He put a hand halfway to his face. You could see him regret it at once. It was a definite and unmistakable flinch. Phil smiled at him.

"Look buddy I need ID and not bullshit and you can show it to me now or you can show it to me later. You decide, but do it right away." He held the position, his big hands spread out over the table cloth, his weight on his feet, ready to drag Mosca out of the chair. Someone at the far end of the room called out in a shrill voice. I could make out a few words. Perhaps "fascist". Mosca picked up the billfold and extracted his Immigration Card. The name Eugenio Mosca was typed along the dotted line. Beauchamp nodded.

"Mister Mosca I have a Warrant here for your arrest on a charge of Assault Causing Bodily Harm. I'll have to ask you to come down to the station. I want you to know that you have a right to a lawyer. If you cannot afford one then one will be appointed for you. If you require an interpreter one will be supplied. I caution you that you are not required to say anything but should you speak anything you say can and will be taken down in evidence against you. Let's go, Mister Mosca." Beauchamp said all this calmly, clearly, with his eyes fixed on Mosca. Kreuger and I stood back a few feet. I had no intention whatsoever of laying violent hands on him or anyone else, but it never hurt to convey the impression that the three of us were a solid front. It had been made very clear to me that I was never to allow myself to become physically involved in any police action or risk facing charges under the Criminal Code. At times such as these, it was a hard law to obey. The room was vibrating with resentment as Mosca got up from behind the table and the four of us started down the stairwell.

Mike Kreuger was putting in a call for a transfer van from Main to take Mosca down to the station when a small figure brushed past him and ran down the stairs after Beauchamp and Mosca. It was a woman, a young one, in a grey silk suit with a charcoal blouse, grey stockings on under snakeskin pumps. Her hair was in a sculpted crest that bounced with the force of her descent on the stairwell. Her clutch bag was held high. I thought she was going to hit Phil but she only ran around in front of him and stood in his way, her breasts heaving with anger, her brittle good-looking face flushed and fierce under muted make-up.

"*If* you'll permit me officer I demand to know just *exactly* where and why you are taking this young man!" She said this in a high shrill voice that I recognized as the hidden source of the "fascist" charge a few minutes before. Kreuger and I were still halfway down the stairs. Behind us the room was buzzing with angry talk, getting louder. Below us the entrance hall was crowding with curious and unfriendly faces. People were saying things like "bloody cops" and "who do they think they are" and "jackboot bastards". The place was alive with the self-righteous anger of the privileged classes. They weren't used to cops breaking in on their festivities and they resented it. Beauchamp and Kreuger and I were clearly on the bottom of their calculations. Someone pushed me in the small of the back, but I ignored it. Right now, the room could have gone either way and there was no point in jump-starting it for a small push. At the bottom of the stairs the little woman was just getting warmed up. Her words were very polite. She enunciated them slowly and clearly, as if she were addressing a simple-minded goon. Beauchamp's neck was bright red, but he answered her as softly as he could manage.

"Ma'am I'm serving a legal Warrant on this man after properly identifying myself and my partners and after making sure that I had the right man. It's a Warrant for Assault Causing Bodily Harm and I'm a serving Police Officer in the lawful performance of my duty. Now I'll have to ask you to please step out of my way." At this, the lady stiffened. Her voice went up another octave.

"Is *that* all you're doing? Then why did you have to come charging into a private party and throw your weight around? Why have you brought two hulking men to help you?" I suppressed a smile. I had never thought of myself as hulking. "And why is *that* one laughing? You know we are getting *very very* tired of this kind of police harassment of private citizens for flimsy reasons. I demand to *see* that Warrant!" She put out a well-groomed hand, palm up, her pretty face set in stern lines. She looked very much like a third-grade school teacher disciplining a wayward boy. I got another shot in the back. It was stronger this time. A voice very close to my back said "who asked you in here you fascists?" in a cloud of good scotch. When he shoved me again, I bounced into Kreuger, who grinned back at me and said in a soft voice "Just let it pass, this room is getting out of hand." I couldn't have agreed more. Beauchamp sighed. Mosca was grinning but humble, a poor child assailed by brutes. Phil pulled out the Warrant. The woman read it over very carefully, going back over key phrases. The crowd upstairs watched all of this as if something very vital were about to be decided. I had no idea why Phil hadn't simply given the woman an Obstruct Warning. He had identified himself and his warrant clearly. If the woman persisted in her efforts to delay him, she was open to arrest. When it came down to it, she had shot her legal bolts. Then I realised the problem. Beauchamp had *The Press* on his back. He had *me*. This show of reasonableness was mostly for my benefit. I resisted the temptation to say that as far as I was concerned he could arrest the whole bloody lot and I'd cheer him on. Being prodded in the spine by a belligerent drunk plays havoc with journalistic detachment. For emphasis, someone tipped Kreuger's cap forward. Mike got a little room by spinning quickly on one heel and grabbing a man behind him by the shirt. The crowd backed off a bit. Downstairs the lady spoke up again.

"I see that the Warrant is legal but I seriously question your tactics and your good judgement. This young man certainly has an address. There is no acceptable reason why you could not simply let him go and ask him to appear in the Public Safety Building on Monday morning. But you had to burst in here and threaten him and frighten everybody and for what? Some minor legal technicality, a frivolous charge of absolutely no consequence at all. Just exactly the kind of quibbling harassment charge that has brought this force into such disrepute right across British Columbia – " Kreuger broke into what showed every sign of becoming a filibuster.

"Ma'am may I respectfully suggest that you don't know what the hell you're talking about here. I have seen the person this harmless boy assaulted and he has very little face left so I don't think it's accurate to call the charge frivolous – Phil, what the hell are you waiting for?"

"*Just* a minute, if you will. I heard you giving this young man his rights. You said he could have a lawyer present. Well," and she dug into her bag, her head down, hair bobbing, white fingers riffling through credit cards, make-up, hairbrush, a jewel case, a thick roll of twenties, finally emerging with a business card, which she stuck under Beauchamp's nose. "As you can see, if you read, I am a qualified lawyer licensed to practise in this province. Will you accept *me* as your lawyer, young man?" Mosca, startled, quickly agreed. From behind me another voice yelled out "Throw them out, *get out get out*" and some others took up the chant. Kreuger was speaking quietly into his radio. I was speaking quietly into my Saint Christopher's medal. Beauchamp shrugged his shoulders.

"Lady I don't give one sweet damn whether you're his lawyer or not. Before you can represent him I have to arrest him and right now you are within a very small step of Obstructing an Officer in the Performance of his Duty so I ask you to consider yourself warned and step out of the way. Now, Lady!" At this, Mosca jerked away. Beauchamp immediately trapped him against the stairwell. I felt someone again pushing at my back, so I turned and shoved hard at the press behind me. Kreuger moved to help Phil. The lady at the bottom of the stairs started to interfere with Beauchamp, tugging at his arm. Mosca twisted in the policeman's grip. The room came onto its feet with a low murmuring sound and somebody else struck me in the face. I thought here we go. Then five blue uniforms surged into the lower dining-room and the whole place cooled off faster than I would have expected given the tempers. In a matter of minutes we were outside on the sidewalk in a crowd of uniforms and people from the bar. Mosca was handcuffed and put into a police van. At the edge of the crowd I heard a familiar voice. The lady lawyer was still burning with a cause. Beauchamp, Kreuger, and a supervisor, were standing in an attentive circle, listening to her complain about the jackboot tactics of the force.

"And I *fully intend* to follow this van right to the station and to remain with my client until he's released – " the supervisor cut in: "Lady, he's being arrested on a lousy Assault charge. He'll be released on his Own Recognizance in a couple of hours." She shook her head firmly.

"I'm very aware of how prisoners, especially Third World prisoners, can expect to be treated in police stations in this province. I intend to be there and see that *no harm* comes to him. Do I make myself clear?" She had brass. That much I had to give her. Chief Stewart had ordered his men to make special efforts to create good feelings between the police and the public and they were certainly working hard at it tonight. Their persistence in this case bordered on the charmingly naive. Even Beauchamp, who had reason to charge the woman, was apparently trying to get her to see reason. He even listened to her last comment without choking in any visible way. She kept it up for a while, until the departure of the police van reminded her of where her true duty lay. She summed it up neatly in a few diplomatic and orotund phrases.

"Well, it *may* be that we have misunderstood one another here tonight but I deem it every responsible citizen's duty to concern himself with instances of abuse of power *wherever* they may occur. From where I sat it *appeared* as if these young officers, who may perhaps be less experienced and street-aware, it seemed that these young men were going out of their way to frighten all of us and particularly that young man from Chile, who, I venture to point out, is quite *probably* already too familiar with *oppression* and *police brutality* in his own country. God knows what *unfavourable* opinions he has arrived at about Canada thanks to these uniformed thugs you have working for you, Sergeant." She stepped back into the street where her friends had arrived with a car so that she could follow the van to the station. As she stepped back, she bumped into Mike Kreuger and I. Mike gave her as polite a smile as he could manage. She nodded, once, a slight dip of her patrician's face. I don't know what was on my face. On her way past me to the car she said, quite clearly and distinctly, in a fine well-modulated and carrying voice, for the pleasure of the crowds still watching, one word. The word was "Assholes."

* * *

After we got chewed out by the sergeant we headed back to the car. A soft rain was falling. It might have been getting lighter in the east. Everybody in Vancouver with any sense at all was asleep. Beauchamp stopped in the street, grinning. "If there is a God, boys . . . " and put the radio up to his mouth, "O div this is 3440 give me wants and warrants on one L as in Linda S P I N N E R DOB unknown member BC Bar Association. . . . " The little handset crackled and the rain got harder while the three of us waited.

CHAPTER TWO

Powder Blues

Policewomen, like most career women in this society, are on trial in their work. Police departments are a traditional male cadre, insular and tribal and hard to break into. In Canada, the official resistance to female police officers is still pervasive and deeply felt. Many older career officers, particularly those with a military background, remain firmly convinced that there is no place for women on the streets and in the trouble areas of the downtown core. They view the persistence of the femininist drive into these sectors as a breach of the most fundamental rules of life, an affront to natural order. Forced to bend under the social and political mandates so hard won by women's rights groups, they have attempted to divert the unwelcome female additions to the force into thinly disguised secretarial roles. The women have not accepted this. Recently, senior men in the departments have grudgingly permitted women to perform police roles identical to their male counterparts. Now there are PW's (Police Women) in Scout Cars and on Area Foot Patrol. They serve as undercover Operatives, perform risky surveillance work, act as decoys in high rape and assault areas. Male officers are frequently paired with a PW on regular zone patrols. The official line is one of equal opportunity. Unofficially, many senior, and many younger, officers hope that the PW's will fall flat on their collective faces. They hope the women will falter under stress, that they will make emotional decisions, that they will prove themselves unable to control and dominate violent offenders. In short, the secret hope is that PW's will show themselves to be biologically, psychologically, inadequate. This hope is not shared by all men in the forces. It is particularly not shared by men who have actually worked with, and worked for, PW's in demanding and dangerous assignments. There are many male officers on all the forces who sense that women police officers have singular and valuable contributions to make in daily police work. They recognise the importance, and the inevitability, of the female involvement in all aspects of their work. PW's have shown that they can perform as well as men in many positions, that what slight advantage they yield in physical strength is frequently offset by greater tact, by intelligence, and by the calming effects of a feminine presence in violent situations. And they have shown true courage when it was needed. In spite of this, the fact remains that PW's are still on tentative ground. Like all newcomers, they must do better than their male colleagues, they must excel and not merely succeed. They know that the brass is watching closely. For these reasons, the following conversations with PW's across Canada have been edited to allow the women to speak freely without fear of administrative prejudice or censure. The conversations were held as the opportunity arose, frequently in the field, sometimes during stressful encounters with offenders. The women interviewed were all serving PW's working out on the street. Most were Constables (First Class). Two were detectives. Their attitudes to their male colleagues varied according to their experience.

* * *

"They'll do this kind of thing to you — I'm in the division house less than seven weeks and there's going to be a demonstration, a sit-in thing, in front of the provincial parliament and the city hall. Abortion pro's and anti's are going to fight it out on the steps. The pro's are demonstrating without proper licencing and without filing bonds; they openly promise to commit civil breaches to protest the recent charges against Morgentaler's clinics. Controlling crowds is a police responsibility. I'm a policewoman. But I favour the pro's, and I think what they're doing is right. I make the mistake of saying something like this to the duty sergeant. Wacko! Guess who's assigned to crowd control on the pro-abortionist scene. If these ladies have to be arrested, I'm going to have to pick them up and drag them off to the wagons and I'm going to have to push the charges. What do you do in a situation like that, with your duty pulling you one way and your heart pulling you the other? I know what I did. I did my duty as a police officer. If you can't come down on the side of the law ten times out of ten, you shouldn't be wearing the uniform. God, listen to me! I'm the girl who joined the NDP in college. I'm the little girl in blue, now."

* * *

"You may have noticed that I have rather large breasts? Well, I do. Now between you and me I rather like my breasts. I've lived with them now for about twelve years, and we're used to each other. I look good in a bathing suit. I can't jog, but who cares. I'll tell you, the only time I've ever regretted having nice breasts was in police college. There was this big stupid farm kid, named Bjorn. Right out of the interior, Cache Creek or some place like that. The second day in the college this dork singled me out for special treatment. Hazing is something I knew I'd have to put up with in police college. They don't want you there and they don't care if you know it. You have to go in with the attitude that you can take it and that you can beat it. Sounds real tough, right? Well Bjorn made it as tough as it could be. And once one guy starts it up, everybody else takes their cue from him. You men are real pack animals, aren't you? Bjorn was funny enough to amuse the instructors so they let him haze me in classes. I guess they weren't all that upset about it anyway. Bjorn was a strong kid, too. Big loopy muscles on him from baling hay or toting that barge or whatever they do in farm country. I could stand the dozer-dyke nick-names. I could stand the melon jokes and the balloon jokes. What I couldn't stand was being groped in the self-defence courses. We all had to go through the basic jiu-jitsu and hap-kido moves, unarmed combat stuff. Naturally, Bjorn loved to take me on. He was much bigger than me, I'm only five five and one thirty. He was about six two and an easy two hundred. So of course I'd get pinned to the mat all the time. And while he had me pinned to the mat he'd grab my breasts and pinch and squeeze. You're a man, so it's not likely that you've ever had somebody hold you down and do something like that to you. The rage is almost unbearable. No matter how I fought, I couldn't get him off and I couldn't stop him. You can't go to the instructor with some candy-assed whining; the word would be all over the school and you'd be a joke. This went on for weeks. It got so bad I was dreaming about this shithead. I'd wake up with my hands around his neck. My boyfriend offered to thump him for me. As a matter of fact, my boyfriend offered to kill him for me, but I thought that might adversely affect my chances in the force, wouldn't you agree? Anyway, it wasn't my boyfriend's problem. It was mine. Finally, after one really gross incident I actually started to cry. I hate to say this, and if you use my name I'll kill you, but that's what I did. I sat there on that dumb hardwood floor in my dumb little grey sweatsuit and I cried. Not out of fear; out of rage. The instructor picked me up by the arm and walked me over to a corner. He wasn't upset or anything. He was mad. He asked me how long I was going to let that 'dumb goof' push me around. I think I just stared at him in shock. I mean, I thought he'd been enjoying it all along. He was an older guy, in his thirties. Mean eyes. Solid as a steel bar, too. Cold guy, I would have said. Now here he was telling me to get my ass in gear. I told him I'd been trying. He said 'bullshit', he said I was still stuck on being a woman. He said, and I think I remember it exactly, 'Until you stop thinking like a victim, that asshole will always beat you. You're beaten before you start. Just because he's big doesn't mean he's better.' Then he coached me on two moves, a foot kick and a pullover drop. And I mean coached. I missed dinner and I missed the late show. Six hours. Over and over until I couldn't stand. Then he drove me home and told me to kick ass in the next class. And I did. Bjorn zeroed in on me like a big dumb blond bomber. All I could feel was this cold anger, but for once, no fear. Not only did I know what to do, I *knew* I could do it! You understand? Bjorn came lumbering in and I gave him a little pivot kick on the inside of his left knee. It popped out like a Christmas cracker. While Bjorn was yelling about that, I stepped into his left side and pulled him over on a hip throw. He landed on his fat stupid head about two feet off the mat. Then I walked over real slow and shoved my hand down the front of his sweat pants and grabbed him by the cojones and when I had his attention I told him what I'd do if he ever groped me again. The whole room broke up. And that son of a bitch will hate me forever. So what? He'll never grope me again, either."

* * *

"I've been working in a car for about a year now; my partner is something special, too. He understands what it's like to break new ground, and he's done a lot to make it easier for me. A lot of our work is violent domestic stuff. We get the calls at one or two in the morning. Momma's getting beaten. Junior has set fire to the cat. Domestic calls can be very dangerous. Lots of good cops get stabbed or shot. The trouble with them is the context. You're in their house or on their lawn. You're mixing with forces you don't understand and a history you'll never know. You have to get a sense of the situation fast; who's crazy and who's sane. Who's most likely to come up with an axe. How to cool the thing out. It takes a lot of psychology. They teach as much of it as they can in the college, but nothing can replace the actual experience. We used to do psychodramas in the college. Get various students to act out parts. Pull surprises. It helps, but you have to have a . . . talent . . . for it. My partner says that working with a woman has made the job much easier. Somehow, when you come up the stairs and two people are at each other's throats, and they see that instead of two cops they have a man and a woman, it kind of shakes them. They get off balance. They don't feel as threatened or invaded. It becomes almost a social thing. I've seen men drop the hammer and offer you a chair. Chivalry lives! It's not something you can trust, but you use it to cool the scene out. You use anything you can. Sometimes my partner talks to the woman and I talk to the man. Sometimes it works better the other way around. Sometimes I have to hold the kid. It's hard to leave children in the middle of that kind of scene. But it's just as hard for my partner to leave the kids. He's married with two of his own. I see the difficulty he has as clearly as I see my own. But there are limits to the law, and we do what we can. If it gets rough, I can get rough. I had to use a baton once, on a man who came up behind my partner while he was calling an ambulance. I put it along the guy's ribs, just to take the wind out. My partner didn't even stop dialling. He knew I'd handle it. I'm not just a PW, you know. I'm a goddamned partner."

* * *

"I like just about everything on the job. I don't mind the kidding. I don't mind the nick-names, although Dickless Tracies gets on my nerves after the fiftieth time. You have to make allowances for the guys . . . they feel threatened. God knows why. If I were them I'd be relieved that some of those ugly copper faces were being replaced with a good-looking woman or two. I can even handle the boots, which I hate. But I wish they'd get the hats straight. I don't see why we can't wear decent billed caps, just like the men. But *ooohh no* . . . we have to wear these pollyanna caps with the little turned-up part and the cutesy-wootsie band; I swear they picked it out just to drive us crazy. It's just like the miserable bastards."

* * *

"If you want to know what I can't stand, and it's the only thing I can't stand, it's body searches. I get called in for body searches all the time. Now we don't get a good clientele around this part of town.

Rummies. Winos. Hookers from the Reserve. Bathing is a yearly ritual for most of them, and it depends on the monsoons, if you know what I mean. It's bad enough watching some floozie peel off a pair of panties that went on during the Diefenbaker government, but to have to check out what was under the panties for dope and guns . . . it's asking too much. I have perfected the art of doing body searches without ever actually making physical contact with the suspect. And I can now hold my breath for eleven minutes and thirty-eight seconds. Of course, I tend to faint a lot more than I'd like to, but I'm working on that part. I'm saving up for scuba gear, if the sergeant will go for it. I'll wear blue tanks with a red pin-stripe. Maybe a nice mask to go with it? What do you think?"

* * *

"You know what really kills me? A lot of the guys in this division get trouble from their girlfriends and wives if they get paired off with a PW. Now you have to know what life is like in a squad car to really appreciate the insanity of this particular beef. These women think that their husbands and boyfriends are going to go parking somewhere and neck with the PW. They think we'll check into the nearest Ramada Inn and spend the whole shift playing nude Russian Roulette. In the first place, anyone who would want to neck in a squad car is the kind of person who would like to make love in a trash can. They clean the damned things up as best they can, but mother, the things that happen to that poor back seat. People do terrible things in there. They throw up on it. They bleed on it. They piss on it. They stuff dead things under the seat. They cry on the glass. They leave their socks on the window ledge. And that's just the cops! No no no . . . only fooling. I mean the prisoners and that sort of thing. Be sure and say that, will you? So of course the squad car smells a lot like something with a terrible disease had crawled under it and died. You can hang as many little pine tree thingies from Canadian Tire as you want. We're talking gross here. Now, let's consider the logistics of necking in a squad car, even if you were degenerate enough to want to. Take a look at this uniform. More buttons than an F 18. Big silver buttons it takes two hands to undo. And the slacks. First more buttons and then zippers with teeth on them like a Komodo dragon. We won't even think about the combat bra and the Kevlar panties. The Sam Browne and the garrison belt. Feel that. Half-inch thick black leather and as flexible as a steel girder. Then there's the cuffs and the baton, unless you think that's something we should keep. Try to picture me with nothing on but my boots. How's that for sensuous? If I tried to kiss another cop who was also dressed in all this gear it'd take a blacksmith to get us separated. And the gun. It sticks into your kidneys every chance it gets, and it weighs about fifty pounds. So let's imagine that we somehow manage to divest ourselves of the gear. Presuming that what I see under all that blue tunic is still something attractive, which I strongly doubt, we lean passionately towards each other eyes ablaze in the romantic glow from the arc lamps over the Dumpster. Our bodies cry out to each other. Our lips tremble with lust. Our call sign comes up on the radio. There's a riot on Queen Street and an armed robbery on Dunn and all hell breaks loose everywhere. He fumbles for the set while I struggle back into my combat bra and just then the Supervisor rolls around to see how we're doing. I spend the rest of my career as a cell matron and he walks the beat in Go Home Bay. Let me simplify this for you. Are you having an affair with your editor? I don't think so. Why not? Because you are a professional. If those twits, those wives and girlfriends, think I'm going to blow my career for a kiss and a cuddle with a male cop then they're stupider than they look. Sorry to be so hard-nosed, but this 'sex on the job' rap really burns me up."

* * *

"When this division got their first PW I think they expected her to want to redecorate the place. You know, put little gingham curtains up in the booking room. A few hanging plants over the ceepick. A couple of angora throw rugs in the cells. Maybe a lava lamp in the Inspector's office. Really, the image you men have of women. It's absurd! You'd think we never had a serious thought in our lives that didn't revolve around men or clothing. The guys were really odd when she arrived. They'd open doors for her and help her on with her coat and go get her coffee, and then they'd bitch to the duty sergeant whenever she wasn't around. Gossip and plot, bitch and nag. Like a bunch of old ladies. She had to push and kow-tow to finally get them to put her out on the street. So they dumped her off on the meanest copper in the house. This guy couldn't keep a partner because he loved nothing more than busting heads and sooner or later the guys get tired of always getting into unnecessary fights. You can imagine how Mongo felt about this lady. He rode her hard, trying to get her to quit on him. He'd drag her into strip joints and sex shows and the worst bars in the division. All the time he's on her case, sniping at her, putting her down. One night he picked a fight with a real hardcase and it went badly for Mongo until the PW decked the guy with her baton. Conked him right out. In front of the whole damned bar, too. Mongo was sitting on his ass on the floor and she helped him up. He kept his mouth shut about that. So did she, until now. Don't use my name, okay? I owe it to Mongo."

* * *

"They paired me with a very nice boy. He was a kid from a cop family. His father and his grandfather were both cops. Had an uncle in the fire department. There are families like that all over the law enforcement business. They have it in the blood. My partner was a very fine policeman. I mean he still is. I use the past tense because he's not my partner any more. Let me explain. If I'm going to actually make it as a woman on the force, then I have to show all of them that I can really do all the jobs that they have to do. This policeman is an educated man. I guess I'd have to call him a gentleman, although he'd groan to hear me say it. When I first came to this division he sort of took me under his wing. I got ridden a lot by the guys in the college, and it was worse in the station. We weren't in a high-crime area. Suburbs and some light industry. Patrols were usually routine. We had B and E's, some rapes and assaults. Domestic troubles. Car theft, missing kids, cats in a tree. Eat No Pays. Standard suburban collars. But it was police work and the official policy was to put the PW's out there and see how they did. I sensed that I was on trial. Not only myself, but every other woman who wanted to work as a police-woman. Brad was genuinely interested in helping this process work. He had thought it out on his own and had come to the conclusion that women could make real changes in the way a police department works. We see things in different terms than men. We're not so burdened with the trial by combat ethic. We tend to favour compro-mise and reason. Urban life is much more complex now than it was when most of the senior officers were on the streets. The racial mix is much different. And people have different needs.

"There's a place for women in that new force. Brad could see this. He kept me from making too many mistakes while he showed me the unwritten rules. Like how to search a suspect without searching him. What sergeant to steer clear of. How to keep a crease in the pants. Where the best coffee was. What street kids to trust and what ones to come down hard on. How to bluff when you had to, and how to tell if someone was lying. Best of all, he taught me how to see the street, to pay attention, what to look for. Stuff you could never learn properly in school. They had us in cars doing patrols of the industrial areas.

"One night we got a call. A possible B and E, an alarm had gone off in a stereo warehouse. When we got there the doors were all locked. The place looked good but an alarm is an alarm and this alarm had never gone off without cause. The building was a single-storey blockhouse style surrounded by a Lundy fence. There was a loading dock on the side, down a laneway. A bank of lights was out down by the dock, and the lights had been on only an hour ago, because the warehouse was on our circuit and we'd checked it once already. So something was hinky here. We called in back-up and then we walked down towards the dock. At least, we started to. I got about half-way along when Brad stopped and told me to wait in the car. I asked him to repeat it. He said to wait in the car for the back-up. I was stunned but not angry. I told him that I was a cop and it wasn't my job to wait in the goddamned car. He got mad too. He said there was no way he was going down the lane with me. I asked him why. He said it was too dangerous. I said he was an idiot. I said I was going without him. I tried to walk past him and he grabbed me. I don't believe this, I'm saying to myself, even while I'm fighting with him. He wasn't kidding either. He did his damnedest to keep me from going. We were still struggling when the back-up car got there. He let me go then, and we all went down the lane. He never told me the true story, but I figured it out. It wasn't that he thought the lane was too dangerous for me. It was that he wasn't willing to go down the lane with only a woman at his back. He'd rather go alone. Then he'd have no one to worry about. In spite of all his good intentions, and they were sincere, he couldn't go the last step. He couldn't treat me like a partner when it was most important. I don't hold it against him. He's still a friend of mine. But he's not my partner any more. I found one who cared less about me but trusted me more."

* * *

"I sometimes think it's a mistake to put PW's out on hooker patrol. I think it's the one area where our judgement can get screwed up and a guy will do all right. I don't know why that is, or even if I'm right. I just know that whenever I see hookers out there under the marquee I get this tight hot burning feeling in my throat. I think about how hard any woman has to fight just to get even one man to see her as a friend and an equal. And there are the bimbos, selling their asses for fifty bucks and thinking they're the smartest things to hit town since white sidewalls. Every time a hooker drops her pants she sets the women's movement back ten years, at least in the mind of the jerk who bought her. The guys know how to handle them. They joke and curse and keep them moving. They bust them when they get the chance. I hate to say this, but I'd like to kick their brainless little hooker asses right out into English Bay. Not very ladylike, but there it is."

* * *

"PW's and hookers get along well because the hookers know that most PW's see right through them. There's this whole mystique about the hooker that the male world has dreamed up. Men love to see what they want to see. Policemen are no different. Even after five years up here they'll still get conned by some little tart young enough to be their daughter. Only a man would ever be dumb enough to imagine that a hooker was sexy and loving. Only a man would see nothing but the big eyes and the lips and the nice smooth bottom. Only a man would pay for the privilege of being screwed. Hookers are women too stupid to be actresses and too lazy to be wives. Most of them are brainless little assholes who hate every trick they lay. Their heads are stuffed full of *Tiger Beat* and *Screen Dream* drivel. They have the conversational skills of a mongoose. I could walk across this bar right now and pull the hair back off any one of those pretty little necks and show you eight days of greasy dirt. These girls don't wash. They make-up and powder. They cover themselves in Charlie instead of bathing. Their lives depend on the forty-watt bulb, preferably peach-tinted. And these hookers are considered better quality hookers, too. Not call girls. But good hookers. I've had to strip search some of them, and I know more about their standards of personal hygiene than their gynaecologists. Or their proctologists. Trust me . . . these little bitches are dirty and stupid and shallow. So look out on the street and tell me why I see so many Sevilles and Cadillac Fleetwoods and Porsches? And a fat rich eager old man in every one? All of them out to pick up one of these silly tarts and touch them all over. I wouldn't touch one of these girls without rubber gloves on. I fail to see the attraction. We once went along on a Drug Squad kick-in, up on the hill. The place was also a common bawdy house, we were counting on lots of found-ins and hypes and hookers. A real garbage day. I went up a set of stairs behind the detectives. They kicked in a room with two cots in it. On one cot this hooker was making love, let me rephrase that, was balling this John. On the cot against the wall, her child, a little girl perhaps seven or eight years old, was lying there in the dark watching her. I'm sorry but I don't see the attraction. I don't see the old mystique at work. I get along with the hookers because they know I see them for what they are. They can relax around me. They don't have to lie to me. They do, but at least they know they don't have to. Between ourselves, they make me sick."

* * *

"Men understand something that women often don't, and that is the need to act. In our world, the world most women grow up in, there is struggle, I agree. Women have confrontations and arguments and fights. But there is rarely anything at all physical about these struggles. The weapons are wit and logic and language. The confrontation is usually resolved without any physical contact at all. In sports, most feminine athletics call for endurance, agility, guile, speed. But never contact, violent direct opposition of power. Boys learn this stuff in grade school. They play hockey and football and tag and they wrestle and they box. They are allowed to extend their confrontations into violence. Sometimes they are encouraged to do so. Women rarely have this type of training, and there is never any social support for this trait in women. Now that's the kind of life I had. And here I am a policewoman. Unless I spend all my career in the division office, there will come a time, sooner or later, when I'm going to have to face a violent physical attack. I have the training now. I know what to do. I know how to sense its approach. I have been knocked around on the mat. I know how a blow feels. But there's always that missing element. No matter how fierce the trainer, you always know in your heart that there's no real anger here. No real danger. But out on the street it'll happen. I'm on zone patrol right now. So far nothing too crazy has happened. We've had to arrest a couple of drunks. We've had to struggle with a kid on dope. I got pushed in a bar but the guy backed off when I turned on him. Still, I know that someday soon we'll get into a situation where my partner won't be able to help me and I'll have to deal with a violent offender all on my own. I can't fall back on a gun without a good cause. No cop pulls his gun just because someone was getting rough with him. Every time you pull the gun, you have to file a report telling why. If you show some chicken-shit reason, you'll stand exposed as a gutless cop. So I'll have to toe-to-toe it with the guy. I know I won't back down or run. But how it'll turn out, I can't say. I admit it worries me. If a PW can't handle herself in a fight, then she's not a complete cop. And I want to be a complete cop. Otherwise, it's no good."

* * *

"In five years as a PW I've had my share of rough treatment. And you know what? It's no big deal. You men have made such a fuss about battle and courage and prowess and all that stuff. What great PR! You impressed the living daylights out of all us little girls. Only now the jig is up. There are women soldiers fighting combat patrols in Lebanon. There are PW's in the US doing street jumps and kick-ins. And here in Canada there are PW's in squad cars answering any and every call along with the men. Sure, the first couple of times, I admit I was frightened. You can't take that indoctrination all your life without buying at least some of it. The trouble was, I had six brothers. I was the second youngest. I *had* to learn to fight, or those buggers would have run me right out of the family. So now I'm on Davie Street and I say *big deal*. This bar is as bad as any in town. Look at the louts sprawled along the bar. They think they're the toughest bunch of bad-asses in the city. Of course, they're full of shit, but let them dream. On plain-clothes duty here you have to be as ready to get into it as your partner is, and the street people have to *know* that. How do they get to know it? They try you out. They want to see if you'll pull the rank or go crying to your male partner. But my partner may be on the other side of the room, talking to his own collection of bad-asses. If I take crap from some hood then I'll have to take crap from all the hoods, and I'll be run off the street like a fool. So I promised myself that the first time I got the chance, I'd make sure they knew where I was coming from. You never have to wait long for a chance, either. They get saucy, and if you take that, they get pushy. You have to jump on it right away.

"So I got some lip from this big doper from Burnaby, at the table, in front of everyone. I told him to shut up. He said something completely unacceptable. I kicked the chair out from under him. He started to get up off the floor so I kicked him right in the balls. Hard. My partner comes racing across the room to help. But it was over. If you've ever been kicked in the balls, you'll know why. It's only in the movies that fights go on for fifteen minutes. It's only in the movies that two guys will go toe-to-toe bare-knuckle for an hour. Try to think of your fist as a delicate bone cage. You don't want to use that bundle of nerves and bamboo for thumping people. You use your feet or your elbows or your knees. Or a chair. A lot of it depends on a combination of bluff, feint, and sheer nasty. I have the advantage because I have a badge and a gun. Even though I'm a woman, I have the power. Few guys will really want to go up against that. The ones that do take a second or two to make the decision. You never give them that second. If you see something developing, you jump on it. The surprise works in your favour. Most of them never really thought you'd hit them at all, let alone so hard and in such a spot. And if you catch one in the body or the face, it doesn't really hurt at all. I got slugged hard during a fight in a hotel. But you're all adrenalised. Your nerve endings haven't got any blood in them. It's all in your CNS and your large muscle groups. Autonomic response. It's not just the males who have fight responses built in. As far as I'm concerned, any trained woman will beat any untrained man no matter how much weight and muscle she has to counter. You men have been giving us nothing but PsyWar for centuries. You have us all thinking like losers, like victims. You have us convinced that we can't be feminine and fight well. My brothers taught me different. I'm not saying that all women everywhere can be good PW's. But not all men everywhere can be good policemen, can they? I'm not a dragon or a ballbreaker, either. I just can't be pushed around. That's all."

* * *

"In my first year as a policewoman I spent all my time filing reports and doing clerical stuff in the main building. Aside from the pay, I could have been working for an insurance firm. That was not why I had joined the force at all. It took me another year to get the head shed to transfer me to a street assignment, and another year after that to get into a position to work with victims of rape. I didn't set out to counsel rape victims. But PW's get drawn into that kind of thing because most rape victims don't want to have to tell it all to another man. It's kind of frightening to think that you get raped by a man and then you have to go tell it to another man. It makes some victims think that the world is run by men only. It increases their feelings of powerlessness and rage at a time when they least need it. So any sensible woman in the station will find herself trying to help out. You'd have to be a real iceberg not to want to help. Rape is a crime I think only a woman can truly understand. I found that I could help these victims and I could help the investigation as well. The sooner you can calm the lady down and get a decent description of her attacker, the better chance you have of finding the guy. It stands to reason. After a while I got sort of a reputation for this work. I met the Major Crimes detectives so much that we got to know one another. I liked them. They were good guys, men who really wanted to stop the rapists. They hated them as much as I did.

"Well, one night after we had gotten this poor young student through the hospital, through the rape-test kit thing, and after we had managed to get a good description of the guy, my sergeant suggested that I apply for transfer to Major Crimes for closer work with the detectives. The rapist who attacked this student was suspected of a number of crimes in the same area. His MO was to stalk women with a telescope in high rises. To single out a likely target. That kind of rapist is very vulnerable to a decoy operation. And I was going to get a chance to be the decoy. Now you get a lot of training for that kind of work, and it takes a few weeks. It was my first chance to get out and do some real police work, some detective work. It was a career chance. Of course, I took it. I learned all about surveillance procedures. I took advance courses in unarmed combat. I took more pistol courses. I even talked them into putting me through a combat pistol course. Turned in a pretty good mark, too. They showed me the wires and the patterns. How to call in help. How to avoid getting killed. They told me horror stories about snafu'ed ops. I wasn't the only decoy they had. And the duty wasn't full-time. There aren't that many rape MO's that allow you to use a decoy. A lot of decoy duty is just simple trolling in a high-risk area. Parks and beaches will always have some PW's on decoy work now and then, as part of a regular zone patrol during summer hours. Now *that's* strange duty. You go to work and get into your most outrageous bikini and you go lie in the sun on a hill. You have a wire in your purse, and your snubbie .38 and you pretend to read *Cosmo* while you watch every male within a hundred yards. It gets so you can sense when some man is getting ready to move in on you. Not for rape. I mean, just some creep trying to pick you up. They look at you and then they look away. Then they try not to look as if they're looking. Then they look in an obvious way, trying to get something going, trying to figure you. They'll move a little closer, they'll putz around. Next thing you know, they're sitting down on your towel saying something they memorised out of *Forum* or *Hustler*. Then you tell them to screw off. And in the bushes or in the van the guys are taking telephoto shots of everybody who acts hinky and listening to every conversation you have. The trick is to look vulnerable and easily frightened. That kind of decoy work is just fishing. No specific target.

"I never did get put on the student rapist; they got him through a composite. My big debut was the jogging rapist. His MO was to wear jogging clothes and dress up nicely. According to the victims, he'd jog along looking every inch the straight-up young professional type; neat mustache and good gear. He wore a Sony Walkman. He always raped in this certain park, always during daylight hours. He was supposed to be so good-looking that none of the women suspected him at all. He'd just go jogging past, give them a little jock-type smile, and then bang! He'd jump them so fast they couldn't scream. He used a knife. And he was sick. He did sick things. I don't want to get into that part . . . let's say that we all wanted him badly. There was a great deal of department pressure after the third rape. It looked like a good decoy operation. They assigned three of us on a rotating basis. We jogged through that park so often we got thigh muscles like marathon runners. Not often enough to look funny. But often enough to get seen. I wore blue-and-white striped shorts and a tank top. I look a little like Olivia Newton-John. It was a type we thought he might like. We laid out a sector in the park where we could cover all exits and where the three surveillance units could cover the whole sector. No real problems with arc lighting and neon and those bloody fluorescents. Fluorescents can really foul up your FM transmission. No big concentrations of iron or stone. Some stones have a radio-active half-life, did you know that? Some forms of granite and limestone. The trouble with my little tank top and short outfit was that it didn't hide the wire very well. I had to keep tugging it down. And it was hot that summer so the thing started to give me raw spots. I learned to hate that thing. One of the other women got a bad burn when it leaked from the battery pack. Naturally we jumped at every good-looking male who jogged by. I mean, we almost jumped. Gradually we got more and more convinced that the guy had changed his MO or made the operation in some way. A decision was made to put in an evening operation. At that stage some of us were sure that the guy had simply split. Nothing similar had happened in any other location. It looked as if he'd called it off. A lot of this work is like that . . . you stay on the case as long as you can, but sooner or later the operation has to be cancelled. Everybody hates that, but what can you do? The third evening I was just loping along in my route, running from one unit sector to another. I think I was just into the running at that time. Anyway I got jumped. Just like that. Bang! I never even saw him coming. He just came out of the trees as I went by. He got a hand on my mouth and I could see this big knife in front of my eyes. My snubbie was in my shoulder bag and that was caught in between his chest and my back. He ran a hand down my chest and ran right onto my wire. That shook him and his other hand came off. I kicked back at his instep and screamed. He dropped me and started to run. He made it about twenty feet before five men and two women had their guns on him and he just froze. They pushed him down and cuffed him. It's hard to describe how I felt. I felt as if my life had made a difference, finally. You know what I mean? Because of me, and the rest of the team, there was one less rapist on the loose. Only one. There never seems to be a shortage. But it's better than nothing. It counts. I don't do that kind of work any more. That bug was the only bona-fide rapist I ever caught. We nailed some flashers and sickies, but nothing like him. And he was back outside in three years. They decided he was 'cured'. As if rape and buggery were something like a head cold."

* * *

"I never was much of a joiner. In high school I joined the debating team, but we could never agree on something to debate. I liked being alone. I thought team sports were for weaklings. If you had asked me to pick out a career I would be least likely to follow, I would have chosen something like police work, the ultimate team tedium. I wanted to do something really important. I wanted to make the world better. That sounds silly, I know, but it's the way I felt. In college I started looking around for a career that would give me something real to do. But everything I looked at turned into bullshit. I thought of law until I realised that lawyers are nothing but games players and tacticians. They don't care much about goals, as far as I could see. I thought about medicine, but medicine looks like big business now. Social workers always seemed to have very good reasons for not helping anyone. Nurses seemed hardened and anyway it was too much a team thing. Motherhood still looks good, but I'm not ready for that. I saw a policewoman one day, in her uniform. She was talking to this lady from India. I think she was just giving her directions or something minor like that. But when she was finished she walked back to her cruiser and as she got in she saw me looking at her. She got back out and asked me if I needed help. I said no, thank you officer. She just gave a small smile and a wave and got back into her cruiser. I hate to sound so simple-minded, but I thought that she looked like a lady with some decent work to do. She looked like she had something solid to go up against. I joined later that year. I'm glad I did. It's no big thing. I don't do anything earth-shattering. I'm not a heroine. I haven't saved any babies from burning buildings. They haven't put me on the street yet. So far, I'm a kind of tour guide and receptionist. But I'm still young. And I think, in this job, I can go as far as I want. The bullshit level here is no higher than it is in any other job. Some of the guys are creeps. Most of them aren't. Some of the women are creeps. Most of them aren't. But their hearts are in it."

*　*　*

"Sure I'm on trial here. All PW's are on trial. But as the lady said,* 'Whatever women do they must do twice as well as men to be thought half as good. Luckily, this is not difficult.' We'll do all right. They can't get along without us. Sooner or later they'll figure it out. They're very bright boys."

(*Charlotte Whitton)

CHAPTER THREE

Scout Cars in Toronto

Like most things in life, Toronto looks better at night. The north shore of Lake Ontario looks like a black velvet table cloth covered with gemstones. The water is little more than an abstraction, a vast empty space curving away to the east and west, the little bays and inlets cutting into the field of lights. Toronto's downtown, not as large as it would like to be, is a minimalist triumph of luminous plinths, rising out of a flat glittering bed of lights that stretches north and east and west to the horizon and, presumably, beyond. Along the shoreline the lights are unbroken from Hamilton Harbour to Pickering. In the western part of the city an irregular oblong of blackness lies within a perimeter fence of dotted lights: High Park and the neighbourhoods. To the east a sickle of blue lights curves out into the lake where the Bluffs and the Beaches take the brunt of the fall storms, surrendering themselves particle by particle hour by hour to the water. Yonge Street runs north from the black waterline and the terraced lights of the Harbour Castle Hotel, through the dense canyons of bars and shops and cinemas, a scintillating fault-line that cuts the city in half, until it rises into the highlands and disappears northward into the cottage country around Lake Simcoe and Barrie. The CN Tower comes up out of the railroad rights-of-way like a spear head shoved through a curtain of silver wire. Over the vast arc of the night skyline there hangs a peculiar sulphurous suffusion of hazy light, an exhalation of vapour and exhaust and the aspiration of a million and a half people. The clouds glow, as if they were coals.

* * *

Police stations have a peculiar power to make people compelled to spend any time there acutely aware of relativity. In the waiting room you can sit on the hardwood benches and see that out in the street cars are flashing by, the neon flutters over Wo Fat's Chinese Hamburger Dragon in regular time, life continues at its breakneck speed. But inside, the minute hand on the big white Westclox is a painted illusion, stuck for eternity at a point halfway between the five and the six. Behind the desk the sergeant with the crew-cut and the red face holds up a kettle, tilted crazily, and watches as a thick stalactite of hot water oozes from the spout and falls slowly through the air over his cup. Two patrolmen take an hour to cross twenty feet of salt-and-pepper terrazzo floor. The room is still clanging with echoes of bars slammed shut fifteen minutes ago. You can hear voices but you can't tell where they're coming from. Somewhere to the right there's an argument going on behind a plasterboard wall. The tones are loud and aggressive but the words are indistinguishable. It's possible to light three cigarettes within thirty seconds of each other. I have a theory that this phenomenon is directly related to the use of overhead banks of fluorescent lights, in particular the six-foot lengths that produce a pale blue-green glow and under which there can be only two colours, a cadaverish green and a kind of bleached-out lavender. They use these lights in suburban schools and government offices and time exhibits an identical langour there. It's no wonder that even the policemen hate the division house.

Constable Philip Crittenden, a ten-year veteran with the bearing and the moustachios of a Guards officer, had perfected the policeman's art of bitching and complaining in a dignified and irreproachable way. We were leaning on the trunk of a bright yellow patrol car at the back of the 55 Division station. "Crit", as he was called by everyone but me, was enlarging on the subject of station-house life.

"Something the public does not generally understand is that policemen are possibly the least-free men and women in the country. I mean that we are subject to greater discipline, imposed from above, exposed to stronger criticism, usually from the public, and regulated all to hell by just about everybody. Kids see the uniform and the stick, even the blasted pistol, and think 'now there's a man with power to boot,' no pun intended. You saw the chap behind the desk, the one with the stripes and the frown? That man is known as a sergeant. Sergeants are men who hated being constables and now hate constables. I'm kidding, really, but the police *are* modelled on a military plan. Civilians work in factories, shops, offices, magazines. Take yourself . . . suppose an editor or somebody gets pushy with you. You can tell him to shove off. The argument may affect your work, of course, but you aren't required, as a part of your job, to tolerate a real dressing-down. You wouldn't allow any editor to stand you up with your back to a wall in front of a row of fellow writers and tell you that your clothes were a frigging disgrace, your shave is half-assed, your shoes are grubby. You wouldn't let him critique your moustache and you wouldn't let him check your fingernails for dirt. If he raised his voice you'd probably raise yours. How old are you, thirty-six? thirty-seven? You expect to be treated like a grown-up. That's more than a policeman can expect. Granted, we are on display, and sharpness is part of the job, something that commands respect from the public. We stand for law so we can't look like a bunch of bellhops in a cat-house. But it's hard to stand there and take a lecture from a man your own age as if you were a wayward child, and taking that lecture is something that *every* cop has to do some time or another. It doesn't happen often, and when you get it you usually deserve it, but when you get it, it burns. You feel completely taken down and embarrassed in front of your friends in a way that most people forget about after their sixteenth birthday. Oh, it won't happen in front of outsiders, and it won't happen in front of the other men unless the sergeant really blows his stack. But it'll happen. You pay for the power, you see?"

I asked him about the respect of the public.

"Respect? Is that the word? You watch, tonight, how much respect we get in the car. We're on the zone system tonight, around Gerrard and Broadview. Dense neighbourhoods, not much public area. Once a week we'll get a stone in the windshield, or a tomato. Kids on the street will call you names you can't even spell. The public thinks you're either a thug or a lazy incompetent half the time, except when they need you, and then you're a saviour. Forgive me for saying this, but you people, the press, the news guys, you're the worst. There are reporters in this city who are too lazy to go out and get real stories so they sit on their over-ripe duffs and write exposés on police brutality based on gossip and hearsay. We use our guns too much, or we're afraid to really crack down on criminals. We're lazy, or we're too ambitious, power-grabbing. It looks like glamorous work, so they know they can get the public to read outrageous stuff on cops. Everybody wants to hear it. And you can quote me on that, my friend."

Brotherhood of the badge, what about that? Crittenden stared at me for a long minute, trying to see if I was serious. Finally, he laughed.

"Regiments in the British Army have brotherhood. And policemen do too, but it's different, somehow. The lines aren't so clear-cut, for one thing. A soldier, he's usually in one of two places, at home or at war. When he's at war, it's usually someplace far from his own people. But a cop is at war and at home at the same time. Every day he gets up and walks around with the same people he has to be a cop with when he gets to work. A soldier is aimed away from the civilian. A cop is aimed right dead at his own people. Not that it's all confrontation, but civilians *think* about confrontations when they see us. Many people will feel guilty or nervous for no reason when they see a cop. And the cop is perfectly aware of that nervousness. Sometimes you just laugh. Sometimes you *use* it to do the job. But it always makes you feel *different*, outside, almost a freak. So cops stick together. There *is* a definite brotherhood. But a police force is not just a regiment, it's also a big corporation. Policemen are always thinking about promotion, more money, more responsibility, getting out of the uniform and into a special squad like Fraud or Homicide or just plainclothes work at the div. So you're in *competition* as well as co-operation. Some guys rocket up. Their buddies stay behind. A few guys play it dirty, back-bite, gossip around the sergeants. Character assassination. Innuendo, just the same as at Dominion Securities or Foster Advertising. Up the corporate ladder, fast-trackers, insiders . . . the whole bit. Cops aren't monks; they all want to get ahead in the corporation. The competition depends on things like good 159 sheets, the 28-day report that you get done on your performance. All the time you're on the job, somebody is watching you and taking notes. You get used to it, and you need the control because of the job, which is law enforcement, but it weighs on you. Freedom is *not* a big part of a cop's job. Most citizens are much more free than any cop. The only place where you can really feel in charge is out on the street. Out there, you are the boss, your decisions count. The public owns the city, but cops own the streets. But all of that is just part of the job, and we get paid pretty good. Why don't you ask me about off-hours?"

What about off-hours?

"Maximum good time *if* you work at it. My wife is the key to all of it. She puts up with the shift work. She'll listen when I get home, no matter *what* time that is. She'll stay quiet if I don't want to talk. God knows how she gets the patience. And her whole life is full of police talk because police don't go to civilian parties. Why not? As far as I'm concerned, because the civvies don't want you. Every time I go to a wedding or a mixed bash somewhere and somebody finds out I'm a policeman, it's a real pain in the neck. What's it like? Do you like shooting people? What made you be a cop? Can you fix this ticket? Why did this traffic cop do that? Why don't they put a crosswalk here? Why don't they take away that stop sign? I don't give a damn what other people do for a living, so why do they get so pushy about mine? I socialise with other cops because they don't want to talk about police work either. They don't make me feel like a monkey in a zoo. Basically, policemen are like soldiers in an army of occupation. The army has been there long enough to get friendly with the citizens, but the citizens can never forget that we're part of an army out there to control them. PR tried with that 'serve and protect' slogan, and the zone patrols and area patrols are aimed at getting cops back in the stream. Cars killed the rapport, I know; what's a cop in a car to a bunch of kids, and what are the kids to the cop? He's isolated from the turf, he moves through it but he's not part of it. Cars shunt from trouble to trouble. We never see anything in between. It's as if we were cut off from the people, and they're cut off from us, by this wall of uniforms. Citizens see that wall as something between them and us; I see the wall as something between the people and the criminals, the punks, the killers. But it's a wall, no mistake about that. We're just arguing about sides. Enough of this stuff. The tank's full. Let's go to work."

* * *

Crittenden's partner is a younger blond by the name of Fontana. He looks a little like John Voigt, only much more solid. Fontana and Crittenden have been partners on 55 Division Scout Cars for something in the area of two years. They work shifts, as all cops do; the shift system in Metro Toronto is complex, obscure, designed to keep men on the job during peak load periods like seven to midnight, or the rush hours, and to prevent the complete turnover of all division hands at predictable times in the day, which would be an invitation to criminals with wristwatches. Fontana and Crittenden are working the long night shift tonight; gas up and off the lot at six-thirty in the evening, and cruise the neighbourhoods in an area casually defined by Gerrard Street in the north, Pape in the west, the waterfront in the south, and Coxwell in the east. The area is predominantly residential, but there are some bars and restaurants down on Queen street, and more on the other main lines. Most of their work tonight will come up from the neighbourhoods.

"Violent Domestic, we call it. It's Saturday night, and the end of the month. Everybody has some money, everybody's going to party. We'll get some bar calls, maybe, and a break-in or two, but most of the work is making those old domestic calls. A lot of men hate them. You never know what's going to happen. On the street, the rules are pretty clear. But once you're inside, in close quarters, people at your back and all fired up, it can get dangerous. If you come up with us, you're just an observer, all right? You can't get involved, you shouldn't say anything other than 'hi how's it going,' otherwise things get too complicated. Can you keep out of it?"

I said yes, I thought that would be pretty simple. It wasn't.

I sat in the back seat of a uniform cruiser, yellow paintwork and thick black block lettering, the Toronto police crest on the sides of the front doors. Each car had a bar of emergency lights up top, and the motto "To Serve and Protect" decalled on the sides over the rear wheels. Fontana and Crittenden were both big men, in the crisp dark blue winter tunics and red-striped trousers of the Metro Police. A black leather Sam Browne Belt went from the right shoulder to the left side of the waist, and the holsters were black leather with a flip cover over the butt of their Smith and Wesson Model Ten revolvers. Both men also carried the new police baton with the added sidebar. Work goes on all the time in various commercial research centres in the US. Companies like Colt, Smith and Wesson, Fabrique Nationale, General Electric, and others, are constantly trying out and marketing new police equipment. In our car, 5509, there was only the standard police multi-band radio, an apparatus rather like a normal car phone. The department had recently commenced a trial-run of in-car computer terminals, complete with software packages like ANI ALI, which can match a phone number to its address in seconds, and photo retrieval codes, so any officer who needs to know if the man in the next car is Clifford Olson or just his look-alike can get a photo on the screen in seconds. Answering the needs, or anticipating them, is a very big business in the Canadian and US electronics world, and the labs are humming. Oddly, Crittenden and Fontana were part of a recent police development that was a step back in time, rather than forward.

In response to a major study into Metro Toronto Police operations, called the Hickling Johnson Report, Chief Jack Ackroyd had instituted a number of changes, including Zone Patrol. Ordinarily, 55 Division cars would cruise the division sector from end to end, overlapping and responding to calls as they came up. In the Zone system, 5509 had an area of special concentration, a Zone, and it took all calls that came up in that Zone. Crittenden and Fontana had picked their

Zone on the basis of familiarity. Knowing the Zone was critical in their line of work. 55 Division work was different from downtown stations such as 52 Division. 55 Division was mainly residential. That meant that trouble that started there was usually going to stay there.

Crittenden explained this in terms of successful collars: "In 52 they get a lot of action. Smash and Grabs, muggings, rapes, robberies . . . but the arrest rate is lower, not because they don't chase hard. It's just that downtown crime is always committed by people who don't live there, commuters, guys who drive or transit downtown for the purpose of pulling a robbery and who then fly off to their homes in wherever. So the detectives have an entire city to look at; the guy could have gone anywhere. Here, it's different. We don't get as many crimes like robbery or mugging, but we tend to solve a greater percentage of the ones we do get. That's because the people who *do* them tend to live in the area. Factors like that can make you look good or bad on your 159, depending on the insight of the man who's reading it. He can say, 'Look at Fontana here. Only eighteen collars all month; the guy's sleeping in the cruiser all night!' or he could say, 'Eighteen collars for Fontana, and sixteen charges laid, sixteen keepers. That man's on the job. I think I'll note his file for a good job well done.' The stats don't tell the whole story. They can be read a lot of different ways."

I asked them about the notorious "quota" systems that all policemen are supposed to have. Fontana, silent up until now, his attention all out on the street, spoke up.

"That 'quota' myth drives me wild. There's no such thing in any good station. If you had to work to a quota for collars each month, you could go out on your first night and make fifty collars, candy-ass collars like Jaywalking or Loitering or Spitting on the sidewalk. You'd make your quota in one night, although you'd be doing the paper work for the next week. But your 159 would read like Dick Tracy's hatband. Nobody in the station would talk to you. You'd be Dork of the Month, but you'd have those collars. That quota stuff is strictly off the tube. Sure, you have to perform according to division averages, provided something significant doesn't alter the game rules, like a new high-rise opening up or a bad bar burning down. All things being the same, you're judged on the basis of quality of arrests, not quantity." Crittenden broke in.

"Quality is everything. Supposing we were having a lot of trouble with Break and Enters, say it was in a residential area like the Danforth. One night the number of B and E's runs up to seven, and the overall monthly total doubles. It's a crime wave. This could go on for a while and people would be calling the Chief and screaming about inadequate police protection. 55 Division gets a reputation for B and E's. We all catch holy hell. Then one night Jack and I stumble on a parked van next to a house we know is on watch, the owners are on vacation. We go in and nail two kids with their arms full of stereo gear. They take a fall for B and E, but they don't turn any other charges and we can't prove they did all of them. Suddenly the number of B and E's drops back to normal. Did we catch the right guys, or did the right guys decide to go elsewhere? We might never know. Collar rates are deceptive, too. Supposing we get very stirred up about Break and Enters. We push Neighbourhood Watch programs. We step up the Zone patrols. We make it an issue. Then we start getting more B and E calls and we make twice the usual number of B and E arrests. But has the actual rate of B and E's gone up? The stats would say yes, but we know different. We just *arrested* more of the people who were doing that sort of crime. You can't judge the effectiveness of police work by statistics alone. If a neighbourhood has a high crime rate, remember that's *Reported Crime*, and maybe that's because the police are working very hard in the area, making lots of collars. On the other hand, if a neighbourhood has a low crime rate, is that because the crooks are staying away, or because the cops are lazy? It's too complex to dismiss on the numbers. That quota stuff is just more bullshit from civvie street."

A battered grey and maroon Toronado swerved out from a side street, narrowly missing the right fender of the cruiser. Crittenden, in the driver's seat, braked far enough back to pick up the licence plate in his headlights.

"That's Tango Victor King three niner zero a two-tone grey and maroon Toronado . . . got that, Jack? . . . I make four people. Look at him go . . . I want this guy, Jack, get the lights!"

The wrecker was pulling away fast. We were northbound on Coxwell, a wide street with a lot of private homes on it, but a dim street. Run down. There were potholes here and there, and the cruiser jolted through a row of them as we accelerated after the Toronado. It was now six cars ahead and drawing away.

"Is this guy running? Put him on the radio, Jack. Let's see what we've got." Fontana reached over and picked up the handset.

"Dispatch this is 5509 we are in pursuit of a grey and maroon '77 Toronado licence Tango Victor King three niner zero, that's Tango

Victor King three niner zero northbound on Coxwell at Fairford can you give me wants over?" The car set hummed for a span. "Roger 5509 will do. Do you want back up?"

Fontana shook his head. "Negative dispatch. This is no big deal yet."

Crittenden swerved to the left to avoid a new Seville that was blocking both lanes, idling up the street at twenty. The flashers were on, the frantic red spot was making a circuit around us, streaking over darkened store windows and the facades of old red brick housing jammed up tight to each other. It wasn't having any effect on the cars in our way.

Crittenden was resigned. "Look at this, will you. The law says to pull over to the right and stop whenever an emergency vehicle with its lights on comes up behind. Are they all blind?" He cursed once, softly. "Jack, give 'em a blip." Fontana flicked a toggle switch on the dashboard. The siren started to wail, a wild electronic whoop ascending through cycles. Five cars started to pull over almost at once. As Crittenden roared through, Fontana shut the siren off. We were closing fast on the Toronado, which was moving quickly but not evasively up Coxwell. I could see the reflection of the red light bouncing off his rear window. The driver was either stoned or blind. At that point, a white face popped up in the back seat, goggled at us for a second, and turned to the front. The brake lights came on immediately. At least, *a* brake light came on. The other tail-light was out, a shattered fragment of red plastic hung from the crushed chrome by a strip of cellophane tape. The driver came to a stop just south of a railroad underpass. Crittenden pulled in behind him, far enough back so that his headlights, on bright, were lighting up the interior of the car, and out a bit from the curb, overlapping the other car by about three feet, protecting the drivers from following traffic. They left the flasher on. As soon as both cars came to a stop, the driver's door opened and a young white male clambered out, his eyes squinting in our lights. He ran a hand through his shoulder-length brown hair, straightened his sports coat as he walked back to the cruiser. There were three other people in the car, two women and another male in the back seat; Saturday night and on the town. Three white faces stared back at us through the rear window.

"Dodging a seat-belt fine here," said Fontana, grinning at me. "They hop out looking puzzled and sincere before you can come up on them and see that they weren't belted in. We never clue in, do we Crit?"

Crittenden was already half out of the car, his cap on, tunic straightened, alert. Fontana got out on the far side and walked in a wide arc over to a point just off the rear window of the Toronado. He switched his big aluminum flashlight on and played it over the interior of the car. Crittenden meanwhile had intercepted the driver at his grill.

"Step over to the curb, please." The man looked nervous but controlled.

"What's the problem, officer?" he said, as Crittenden followed him to the edge of the roadway. Fontana stayed back far enough to see everything that every one was doing, resting a hand on his holster. Just a precaution, a habit.

"Sir, you entered a main street back there without signalling or stopping, and we've clocked you at sixty-three kilometres an hour in a forty kilometre zone. May I see your Driver's Licence, your Insurance, and your Ownership papers, please?" As the man pulled a billfold out of his coat, he seemed to get more nervous. Crittenden refused to take the billfold.

"Please take the licence out of the wallet, sir."

The man did so. As Crittenden looked it over, he looked back at the car, over to Fontana, around the perimeter, and into the cruiser at me. As he did so, he seemed to be wrestling with a question. Crittenden looked up from the papers.

"Sir, I'm going to cite you for making an Illegal Turn, Failure to Stop, but we'll leave the speeding to a warning. Didn't you see the flashers? We were right behind you for the last mile.

The boy looked sheepish. "Well, I don't have a rearview mirror, officer. It broke off just this morning and I was on my way to having it fixed." He managed a very sincere look. Fontana smiled at the words but kept his eyes on the car and the three people in it.

Crittenden said, "Let's take a look." The two men walked along the right side of the car. As Crittenden got near Fontana, Fontana moved to the far side, so that his partner wouldn't get in his line of sight, ending up standing off the left front fender. Crittenden leaned down into the car, said something polite to the people inside, and stood back up.

"Sir, it's a violation to drive without proper mirrors, and you also have a brake-light out, your muffler is loose, you have one bald tire, and no turn signals. I'm going to write you out warnings for all these things, and I want to see them fixed within forty-eight hours. Now if you'll please wait in the car, sir, I'll be with you in a few minutes." The boy looked even more nervous, but he got behind the wheel. Fontana moved back to the cruiser and got in next to Crittenden. Fontana pulled a black notebook out and began writing in it, while Crittenden spread the papers out on the attaché case beside him. Fontana asked, "Run him?"

"Definitely . . . he's uptight about something."

Fontana put the man's licence through the radio, his date of birth, his full name, spelling it out in the radio code that leaves no room for error. The dispatcher came back in a second with a roger, and cut off. In the few minutes it would take the dispatcher to punch in this information on the computer in front of her in the headquarters building on Jarvis, Crittenden and Fontana joked with one another about stationhouse gossip and wrote out the various warning slips and ticket forms.

"I've got court all day Monday. Supposed to be my day off." Fontana was resigned. Crittenden chuckled over his pad.

"What's the case? That kid with the typewriter?" Fontana shook his head.

"No, that's remanded. The kid's lawyer is trying to bore the witnesses off the case. He figures that if he gets the case put off a few more times then the evidence will get lost in the system or the witnesses will have heart attacks. He's still trying to get the store to drop the charges. The judge warned him that he had better have his case together soon or he'd go ahead in spite."

"Figure it'll stick?"

"As long as the witnesses hold up. Christ, we had him red-handed. I want this kid. He's been hitting the stores here for two years. I want him off the street. The judge is all right."

"Who've you got?"

Fontana named him. Crittenden grinned. "Old Thunder, eh? He'll come through. He hates B and E's with a passion. You're lucky you don't have the Angel of Mercy. He'd give a rapist twenty chances and then sentence him to ninety days community service. I had him once on – " he broke off as the Toronado's door flipped open and the kid got out. Fontana put a hand on the door lever. Crittenden watched the boy walk back toward the cruiser. His face was pale in the headlights.

"Excuse me, officers, I think you ought to know that I'm not living at that address right now. And also, I've got a couple of tickets outstanding, you know, and I think you're gonna get some – " the burst of static from the radio interrupted him.

"5509 I have a Lima Able Delta Delta first name Michael same address same DOB. He's wanted on a traffic warrant, tickets unpaid," she gave the numbers in a monotonal singsong voice, reeling off the details. The boy leaned on the window, his face paling, while Crittenden and Fontana put their papers down.

"Step back from the window, son," said Crittenden, pushing the door open. Fontana was already out on the curb. The boy stepped back and pulled out his wallet.

"You see, Officers, I don't have the fifty-six bucks with me right now, can I – "

"Sir, you'll have to pay those tickets in cash now or go in to the station and get someone to bring down the cash. There are warrants outstanding and we are obliged to follow them." Crittenden opened the back door, but the boy didn't move.

"Sir, I'm just on my way to my parent's house. I can pick the money up from them; I'll bring it into the station before eleven o'clock tonight. Can you give me a break on this? Please?"

Crittenden thought it over. "All right, son. But remember, I'm going to hold you to this. You bring the fines in, cash only, by eleven o'clock tonight or we'll come out and get you. You understand?"

The boy's face was glowing with thanks and relief. "You've got my word on it, Officer. We'll go there right now. Thanks, sir, thanks very much!" He was in his car and pulling away within ten seconds. Fontana sat and looked at the Toronado disappearing up Coxwell. "How much?" he said to Crittenden.

"A fiver . . . but I want odds," Crittenden was confident.

"Done!" Fontana shook his hand, "but no odds."

* * *

Most of the following four hours were spent answering minor calls for drunk removal or intercepting speeders for various infractions. Between calls the officers would station the car on a main street, near a major intersection, and write out the details of each call in their notebooks. Keeping a detailed and accurate record of names, times, complaints, licence numbers, vehicle descriptions, and events as they developed was a full-time occupation. If they hadn't finished it off by the time their shift was over, they made it a point to stay and complete the record before they went home. The policeman's notebook has to reflect every significant incident with which he has become involved while on duty. And they never get thrown out. If you wanted to write a detailed history of every police action in any city for any period of time, all you'd have to do is refer to their notebooks. Cops never know which detail might be needed five months down the road, as corroborative information or a clue or a proof of someone's innocence. Street time, action time, was a variable; every cop I spent any time with was occupied on a roughly equal basis with responding to calls, making routine checks on his tour, writing out a brief history of events in his notebook, and going to court. Of all these, court time was the most hated.

"Court is a bitch, no doubt about it." Fontana and I were having a cup of coffee in the cruiser while Crittenden talked with a plump grandmother in the donut shop. Fontana was no different from most policemen; he hated lawyers. From what I had seen across country, most lawyers hated cops, so his animosity wasn't being wasted. Fontana waved a cinnamon cruller in the general direction of the Old Court House on Queen Street.

"It seems to me that I spend all my time waiting in the witness rooms of that miserable building while some expensive defence lawyer bobs and weaves and manoeuvres his client out of trouble. It's the system, and I'm not trying to go against it. But defence lawyers, some times man, there isn't a rotten stunt in the book that they won't pull. As long as it's legal. They'll try fifty billion remands, hoping your case will dry up and blow away. They'll try to make you look like an ignorant fool in front of the judge. They'll imply bribery, they'll say you have a grudge, they'll dissect every decision you made on the spot, even if there was an emergency going on. It's easy to judge somebody else when you're sitting on your pin-stripes in a courtroom, but put them in the same place and they'll wet their panties. You scoop a kid, nineteen years old, he's stabbed an old woman in the chest while committing a purse-snatching, you chase him on foot for seventeen blocks, nail him on the fly with the purse and the knife in his hands, and you can find yourself sitting in court two years later being asked to justify your 'brutal attack' on a poor child who was neglected at home and who was only trying to give the old lady her purse back when she pulled a butcher knife on him. It's Looney Tunes all the time, and endless. Every charge you lay is going to be court time on your own hours, flack flack and more flack. Reality gets a mauling, you get pasted to the wall by a fat lawyer you can't even talk back to. Half the time, the kid walks. His family calls you a pig. Half the time, if you nail him and the case sticks, he gets a light slap and the victims hate you for not getting him the chair. No pleasing anybody. But they pay me a lot; I guess it's worth it."

I asked him the obvious question.

"It's like they say, I hate the job but I *love* the work. I could be sitting at a desk in an insurance firm. I'm out on the road, it's interesting. And I get $35,000 a year for my time. Where else could a guy my age pull down that kind of money without ten years of college? Anyway, I like to bitch. All cops love to bitch. Put any two cops together and you'll get a bitching party. It's therapy."

As Crittenden got into the car, the radio came up with a call. A fight in progress at an address in the neighbourhoods around Greenwood Park. Fontana picked up the set. "Roger dispatch 5509 responding." He belted in. Crittenden started the cruiser up and we backed quickly out onto Dundas Street. It was starting to snow. At the lights we waited for the green beside a long blue Cadillac Coupe de Ville. The driver had his window rolled down and a Christmas carol was coming from the radio. The driver, a venerable old Sikh in a white turban and a grey patriarch's beard, nodded imperially, looked into the back seat at me with a flash of curiosity, and then looked away again. Fontana sighed.

"Man, this city is changing so fast. It's a wonder that we're still speaking English. Look at the size of that car. Where *does* the money come from?"

Crittenden didn't approve of what he thought might be a racist comment. He was worried about the press.

"I don't know, Jack; I'm not getting any of it, that's for sure."

*   *   *

We rolled slowly up a dim tree-shaded street lined with two- and three-storey brick houses in the old Victorian style, narrow facades, one or two stained-glass windows, a big bay on the main floor, and a wooden porch stuck on like a circus wagon. Most of the homes were running down. They needed paint, or new woodwork. Few porch lights were on. The lawns, tiny worn-out patches of grass showing brown through a soft covering of new snow, were sometimes filled with junk or garbage. Half-way up the block on the right hand side an old woman was standing out on the snowy sidewalk in a yellow borg nightgown, her thin blue-veined legs projecting bonily from under the hem, two slender stalks ending in huge fuzzy slippers with a red tongue projecting from each toe, and tiny button eyes on the arches. Her hair was grey, stringy, and wild. She looked as if she had just gotten out of bed. As it turned out, she had. We heard about that at least ten times before she got around to the point.

"It's *them* again!" she extended one skeletal hand in the direction of a house across the street. There were no lights on at all, but as we got up to the porch you could hear a dull pounding coming from around the back. We went down the narrow walkway between the houses, a brick canyon no more than eighteen inches wide and littered with garbage. As we walked down it the sounds of a violent argument rose.

"We hear from these people about three, four times a month. They have a kid here, he's a handful. The old lady fights with her husband all the time. We do what we can. You can come up but keep your mouth shut, all right?" Crittenden went up the rotting wooden steps at the back and pounded on an aluminum door. The fight went on. Crittenden tried the door. It was unlocked, so he pulled it open and we went in. The porch smelled of aging cat litter.

"Christ I hate this place," said Fontana, stopping to scrape a piece of tomato off his heel. Crittenden went on into the kitchen area, which was a heaped waste-pile of dirty dishes and old pots full of unidentifiable material. On the cream-coloured kitchen table a large marmalade tabby was licking a pat of butter in a kitchen mug. There was a dirty knife sticking out of the middle of an open can of Spam. The overall effect was unpleasant to put it mildly.

Fontana spoke through a voice made hoarse by an effort to talk without breathing. I couldn't blame him; the house smelled like something very large and very old had crawled under it and died, possibly last summer. "Crit, give them a holler . . . we have to be invited."

Crittenden yelled up the staircase. "Hey, hey hello, we're police . . . can we talk to you!" The screams and the thumping stopped suddenly. One high shrill voice, slurred and angry, called down the stairs.

"Yeah, you come up here, I want this kid's ass out of here right now. She's trying to assault me . . . get *off* you god damned little bitch!" There was a sound like a slap, and somebody else screamed. We came up the dark staircase fast.

The only room with a light on was a low-ceilinged attic room at the rear of the house. It didn't actually have a light on; it was illuminated by the flickering blue glow of a huge colour television. The sound was off but Irv Weinstein, the Buffalo area newscaster with a memorable face, was speaking earnestly and intently out of the screen. As we reached the doorway the picture changed to a shaky, hand-held shot of a civilian being shot dead in a village street. It looked like Mexico.

Somebody cried out from around the door, and a bowl of chip dip hit the screen, stuck, and began to slide down over a picture of Mister Whipple taking the Charmin' away from yet another compulsive squeezer.

"God *damn* you shit look what you done now! Hey you cops, we're in here!" We walked into the room, trying to get our eyes adjusted to the light. I could make out an overturned chesterfield at the far end of a room full of potato chip bags, old beer bottles, empty chip dip cans, paper bags, milk cartons, shoes, socks, underwear, a Monopoly board, and other items I didn't care to catalogue. But there were no people in the room.

"Under this damned thing, *fer chrissake!*" The voice was coming from under the chesterfield. Fontana and Crittenden clumped over and tugged it back upright. A small wizened little gnome-like man in voluminous paisley-pocked boxer shorts was locked in an embrace with a very overweight woman in a yellow and black tiger-striped mu-mu. At least, it seemed to be an embrace. It wasn't. When Crittenden reached down and pulled the man's hand off the woman's mouth, she lunged forward and bit the little fellow in the cheek. He screamed, a shrill squeal I recognized from the stairs. The woman looked up at us while sinking her teeth into her husband's cheek and said something like *'gedda wee zee off a fuddinn wuzzer duh lidddo fitt trydda mudder meee!'* Crittenden had to pry her mouth away from the man's face. When she broke off, she literally growled at us, her powdered face layered in a week's supply of mascara and lipstick. She must have weighed at least three hundred pounds. Far more of her body than anyone would ever want to see was exposed by the position she was in, sprawled on top of the gnome-man, of whom little could be seen other than his shorts and his thin arms. When Crittenden dragged her to her feet she stood almost six feet tall, and every inch of it was mad.

"This son of a bitch has picked on my baby for the last goddamned time! I want him arrested for trying to murder me. Look, just look what he did to me leg!" She reached down to the hem of her tiger-striped mu-mu and tugged it up far enough to expose about an acre of pulpy flab, delineated, I was grateful, by large navy-blue gym bloomers, circa 1934. There were several marks on her thigh. Teeth marks. She dropped the hem and pointed imperiously down at the man in his nest of sofa cushions and shredded potato chips. He blinked up at us.

"He's a cannibal. He attacked me. I want him arrested and put in prison for a hundred years. I don't want him *ever* to come near me or my baby again. He's a *brute* and a monster!" Fontana stood at the doorway, making a valiant attempt to keep his face straight. Crittenden held up a large sinewy hand.

"Lady, where's your kid? What happened to him?"

The woman pushed by Crittenden and strode over to a cupboard door. She halted dramatically by the edge of the room, her hand on the knob. It took quite a while for all her body parts to come to rest. She jerked open the door. Inside the cupboard a teenage boy, equally fat, was crouching in a pile of coats and dresses, clutching a bowl of something to his chest. He was shaking badly. His eyes reflected the glitter off the TV set. There were tears in his eyes. The woman, his mother by the resemblance, leaned down and clutched him by the shirt. He came up at the end of her wrist as effortlessly as if he had been conjured. He was almost as tall as his mother, nearly equal in weight. They were quite a pair. I don't know how Daddy figured in the equation; he couldn't have offered a counterbalance to these human carbohydrate reservoirs if he brought along a Buick. The woman launched into a litany of woe.

As we pieced it together later, there was a running dispute in the house about diet; Daddy felt that an inordinate amount of the family income went out on potato chips and Moon Doggies and Twinkies. He personally loathed sweets and he wanted the policy changed. Junior had taken Mommy's side. Push had come to shove during the news. Junior had taken refuge in the clothes closet while Mommy and Daddy squared off in the TV room. Three falls later, the tremors of their disagreement had penetrated to the surrounding houses and the elderly lady had called in the cops. Crittenden listened to this story with an absolutely dead-pan face and not a flicker of emotion was present in his voice as he read them both the Riot Act and secured their promise to debate the matter in a more rational manner. Fontana helped the little man to his feet and set the room back in order as Crittenden spoke to the woman and her child. By the time Joel McRae was well into the first reel of *Foreign Correspondent*, we were on our way down the sticky front carpet and heading for the fresh air.

"Looney Tunes, Looney Tunes!" Fontana was laughing as he said it.

* * *

Most of the calls were like that: a ludicrous mixture of pathos and farce. People fought over trifles, while living in a state of permanent disaster. Money played a big part in these neighbourhoods; the recession was having its effect on the family. Men were out of work. Money was scarce, food was expensive. Beer wasn't. In a few hours it was as if there were only three tales of woe and misery on the whole planet and every house we went to was full of people who wanted us to hear them over and over again. In one house, towards the end of the shift at around three in the morning, I leaned against a greasy kitchen door and watched a year-old baby toddle around on the green tiles in a pair of mouldy Pampers. His mother was in the living room, holding a towel full of ice to her face, mopping the caked blood off her mouth where her husband's beer bottle had caught her as she walked by him to heat some Pablum for the kid. Hubby was on his back in the front hall, drooling and moaning incoherently, while Crittenden tried to get him to sit up. Fontana was on the phone calling for an ambulance. The child was overflowing around the edges of his diapers and he had stepped in it, so every time he put one of his pudgy little feet down he left a perfect imprint of it on the floor. His neck and shoulders were grey and streaked with perspiration. That was when I found out how hard it was to stay out of the conversation. In the end, they had to leave the child with them.

"What can we do . . . dirty is not a sufficient cause to call Children's Aid in the middle of the night. But I'll flag the case for their worker. They'll follow up; don't worry. You have to develop some distance or you'll burn up." Crittenden and Fontana seemed to have grown a curious kind of carapace on their souls; it was porous enough for them to do what was necessary but solid enough to keep the inexorable depression out. They made calls like this all the time. They tidied up the wives and straightened up the furniture. They talked and talked endlessly, trying to lessen the tension and introduce reason to situations where nothing was possible but a kind of viscous, bubbling animosity that stuck to every person in the house. You could develop a very dreary view of married life and the raising of children working Domestic calls in 55 Division. I said as much to Fontana while we were waiting to lock up a drunken teen who had punched his mother during an argument about his sexual preferences.

"What are we supposed to do? Leave them to kill each other. I like to think that when we show up, maybe something will get solved. Nothing major. But it's serious when the cops show up. Sometimes, people will stop and look at what they've been doing. Now and then, they'll change their pattern. Not often," he gave a weary shrug, grinning at me through a cloud of cigarette smoke, "but often enough, sir, often enough to count."

He pushed the hardwood chair he was sitting on back up into the wall of the interrogation room. Balancing, he folded his heavy hands in his lap. The leather of his harness creaked and groaned. He adjusted the holster so it wasn't sticking into his ribs, and propped his big black police boots up on the opposite wall. Closing his eyes, he drew a long time on his Rothman's, pulling the smoke down into his lungs. I could see he was close to sleeping. When his eyes were closed, all the control went out of his face and the lines around his jaw softened. He let the smoke out in a long sighing exhalation. It drifted up to the single hundred-watt bulb in the wire cage set in the middle of the ceiling. He was sound asleep before it stopped curling. I leaned forward quietly and took the burning cigarette out of his hand. In that hard-edged light there were deep shadows in his cheeks and around his eyes. He looked as tired as it's possible to get without being pensioned off. Crittenden came into the room a few minutes later. When he saw Fontana asleep, his craggy face broke up into a network of wrinkles and creases. He reached into his pocket and took out a five dollar bill. Folding it in three, he placed it between his partner's fingers.

"Let him sack out for a few minutes. He was in court all week and he still worked the night shift. He can use it."

I nodded towards the five dollar bill.

"Oh . . . that? Happens every time you give somebody a break. They stick you right in the ear. I'm up shit creek with my sergeant. That kid with the traffic warrants never showed up. I'll never learn, will I?"

As we walked through the stationhouse to the coffee room I glanced up at the big clock on the wall. The minute hand was stuck halfway between five and six. It seemed to take us an hour to cross twenty feet of salt-and-pepper terrazzo.

CHAPTER FOUR

Area Foot Patrol in Toronto

The dominant impression was stillness. Overhead six banks of fluo-rescent tubes were putting out a shimmering cold light and the large rectangular room with the ivory walls and the ivory tile floor was a shadowless blank. It would be impossible to sense the passage of time in this room. One of the fluorescent tubes was flickering erratically, and the air was alive with a thin metallic drone, like a dentist's drill heard through a heavy door.

Four tables with brown plywood tops and grey tubular legs had been pushed into a row in the centre of the room. Scattered around it were twelve grey metal chairs. They looked as if the people sitting in them had been called away quite suddenly, jumping up in a clatter and a rush, shoving the chairs back and away, pounding for the single open door set in the precise dead centre of the far wall. This call could have come minutes ago. Or years. There's no way to tell. One of the tables held a cheap foil ashtray with four crushed butts lying in it like bullet cases. The air was neither stale nor fresh. If it smelled of anything it was the atmosphere of routine, repetition, the tireless passage of days and nights and days, wearing the room down and polishing it smooth, an old ivory bone under the cold hard lights. This was at six forty-five. At six fifty, everything changed.

* * *

6:55 pm, 52 Division Parade Room.
"All right, all right, let's put a cork in it!" Sergeant Bleeker is losing his patience. He's standing in the Parade Room in his shirt sleeves, a clipboard under his arm, and he's not exactly yelling. Maybe bellowing softly would describe it. Around him there's pandemonium. Sixteen uniformed policemen, stocky, heavy-limbed men with flat, friendly,

raw-boned faces, some of them already wearing their massive blue reefer coats, are talking and laughing and stomping around the room like draught horses in a stable. The air is full of curses and good humour. Bleeker is trying to get them to line up so he can inspect them, but he's not having much effect. He walks over to the end of the row of plywood tables and pulls out someone's billy club, the new kind with the side-handle, and he brings it down onto the tabletop with a short, brutal stroke. The foil ashtray on it flies into the air and lands clattering and spinning on the floor. Before it stops spinning, he has silence. The men stand looking at him, fighting back smiles and nudging each other. "That's better. I've got some reports to pass round, read 'em and weep." Bleeker runs down the list of names and as each man hears his own he calls out "Yo" or "Here" or "Present". The others grin and watch Bleeker.

"We've got a new directive on the holsters coming up, so some of you will be in line for replacements. Donnelly, your B and E man, what's his name? Todd? He's back out, so watch for him." I look for Donnelly and see him at the far table, a bulky figure, not tall, slightly overweight, with a ruddy outdoor look, writing in a notebook, shaking his head. Without looking up, he says, "That sonovabitch Crown couldn't hold water," and the men laugh. I'm interested in Donnelly because Bleeker has assigned me to his patrol. Donnelly doesn't know this yet, and I'm wondering how he's going to take the news. Bleeker runs through a list of messages and announcements, most of them connected in some way with recent arrests made by officers of the 52 Division Area Foot Patrol. As the sergeant talks the men are taking notes or adjusting gear or, now and then, groaning at a particularly bad bit of news. A lot of Bleeker's announcements have to do with petty thieves or hoods who have been released on their own recognizance, which means they'll be back on Yonge Street tonight looking for trouble. Most of the men are in their late twenties and solidly-built. There are no new officers on Area Foot Patrol in this sector. Sergeant Bleeker has told me that the waiting list for Foot Patrol is almost two years, and few officers with less than five years of active duty stand any chance of being assigned to it. I'm about to find out why. He winds down a little, and the men who have been sneaking sidelong looks at me get their questions answered.

"We have a civilian observer along with us tonight," he gives them my name, "a writer who's trying to find out what it's like to do this job — " "Jesus, hide the drugs!" "Have you frisked him Sarge he's probably wired." The group starts to laugh, but something else is going on. I can't tell what it is. They're tense and resentful. "Wonderful!" "Great!" "Marvellous!" I stay where I am, leaning up against the wall and keeping my mouth shut. "Yeah yeah so pipe down for a minute. This is from upstairs and he's yours, Donnelly, so take good care of him. You and Hart are on Yonge Street tonight, the Pussy Patrol, so try not to lose him in the Charles!" Everybody chuckles but Donnelly and Hart who look at each other and then over at me. Four minutes after that we are on the street at University and Dundas. It's bitterly cold, and a razor-edged wind is sliding over the concrete walkway. Donnelly and his partner, Hart, a little taller and trimmer than Donnelly, with good lines around the eyes and a lop-sided grin, zip up their reefer coats and slip their batons into the rings. A brief silence follows while we stand around just beyond the entrance to the stationhouse. Hart becomes very interested in a group of teenagers chasing each other up an alley way. Donnelly steps up very close to me and says, very softly, so that only I could hear him, "Well my friend, you may have come down from upstairs but you're on my beat now and we ought to have some rules. We're glad to have you walk along with us, we're glad to have you write about all this, but if anything pops you're absolutely on your own. My concern is for the civvies and my partner and I'm not going to waste a lot of time nursemaiding you. This is a nasty strip. It has some genuine bugs. Try not to get in the way. Are we clear on this?"

We were.

* * *

8:05 pm, a sidestreet near Bay and Wellesley.
Hart and Donnelly spent the first part of their tour ambling up Bay Street, talking about their weekend in Buffalo, which they called "choir practice", and checking out back doors and delivery lanes. They always stayed about six feet apart, and they never spoke in the dark places. They seemed always to know where the other man was. Now and then the radio dispatcher would announce some barely decipherable report and the noise would come out of their "miters" (the walkie-talkies), crackling and full of static, and the pair would stop to listen hard, holding the speakers close and cursing quietly about the sets. When we reached Wellesley, they took me by the arm and stepped into the shadows at the rear of a locked-up and chained-off car dealership. "Ever been in a duck blind? You know, a place where you

hide out and wait for ducks to come along?" I had. "Okay, this is our duck blind. It's lesson time. We're going to stand in this alley way and look down this side-street and you tell us what's going on around us." Donnelly looked over at Hart who was grinning hugely. "The crash course, right?"

"Amen, Amen," said Hart.

We stood there in the chilly dead air at the corner of the alley and I tried to stop thinking and stay open to what was going on around me. The street was not well-lit. Half of the north side was a park, and then closed buildings and what looked like a warehouse. Down at the east end the traffic on Yonge Street honked and glittered. On the south side there was an apartment building closer to Yonge Street. Its foyer was locked tight, and a security guard was sitting reading behind a small desk. Closer to us, more locked-up buildings and then the back of the car dealership, and the three of us, standing in the shadows, freezing. I thought about lighting a cigarette. "No, don't smoke. No lights, no noise. Just watch!" This in a hoarse whisper, from Donnelly. Or maybe it was Hart.

So I watched, and time crawled by, and I began to feel like a fool. All I could see was an empty street and the occasional car cruising by. No strollers, no cats, no rats, no nothing. I said so.

"Look in the park. By the benches. Near the far edge." I looked. Nothing. Wait. Yes, a shadow. Two shadows. Three. And maybe another, further down. Just then a car pulled around the corner, and I realised that it was the same long black Lincoln Continental that had cruised down this street a few minutes before. The Lincoln had only reached mid-block when another car turned east onto the street. It was a dark Seville. As it rolled slowly past our "blind" the driver switched on his interior lights. He was well-dressed, an executive type, in a navy overcoat and a burgundy tie. I remember he had a wing collar on. The light stayed on for almost a hundred yards. Up ahead, the black Lincoln was pulling over to the curb. His interior light came on too. In my mind, the whole dimly lit street scene gave a kind of mental jerk, and it occurred to me that something very organised was going on here. I began to see other shapes. Men, singly, or in small clusters, were standing in shadows and dark corners all along the street. Down by the black Lincoln opposite the park, one of the shadows broke out of cover and strolled down to the side of the car. As it passed through the pool of a streetlight, I could see that the man was young, clean-shaven, handsome, in a starved, stretched way. Something about his clothes looked New Wave. Something about his carriage triggered the answer.

"This street is a cakewalk. We can make maybe twenty, twenty-five male hookers on this section alone. See the Caddy. That guy's cruising, he's a trick. Watch."

Back at the corner, another car, a Mercedes, and another lone male driver. It went by and I could see the driver watching the shadows. Another young man came down from the park, his hands in his pockets, his face a pouty mask, dark holes where his eyes should have been. "I love it!" Hart chuckled, "Half these tricks are lawyers or execs or politicos from Bay Street or Queen's Park. Down here with fifty bucks and a hard-on, looking for a thrill before they go back to wifey and the kiddies. Some of these guys make the rules they're busting right now. It's worth your pension to stop a car on this street. Heavy money on this block, every night of the week." Hart spoke out of the shadow. Light from the drug-store delivery door cast a hard yellow glare across his shoulder and his right side. His fist was clenched, but his face was still in darkness. When I turned to look back at the scene in the street, I saw something moving behind the glass window of the car dealership. At first, I couldn't make it out, and then something glittered in the light and I could see it was a Doberman guard dog, standing perfectly still, like a carving, in the empty showroom behind the dusty glass, his legs spread and his jaws slightly open, watching us as we stood in the alley. When I met his eyes, a tremor ran down the length of his muscular body, and he licked his teeth. Back on the street, the cakewalk continued. We watched for fifteen, twenty minutes, in the "duck blind", while massive luxury cars rolled down the dark street like floats at the Rose Bowl. The brake lights would come on, a boy would stroll down, a little talk, and then he'd get in and the car would speed away towards Yonge Street and Rosedale or Don Mills, or maybe just another dark alley a few blocks away. Donnelly shuffled, shivered, and said "Okay, let's break this up. I need a coffee." As soon as we stepped out into the street, the boys began to drift into the farthest corners and disappear, and the cars moved off.

Something must have been showing on my face, but Hart went on before I could speak. "Don't tell me, let me guess! Nasty old coppers punching out faggots and queers, right? They call faggots 'the gay community' now, don't they? Look, I'm not trying to stop people doing whatever turns them on, but I want them to do it at home. This is not 'victimless' crime. It's just crime. Half the kids on this street turning tricks are setting up their Johns a for a quick B and E later tonight. They get back to the guy's place and they get the job done and when the old fool is dozing off into dreamland they're getting a key waxed or simply calling up some buddies to meet him in the lobby. What's the poor sucker going to do? Call the cops? And tell them what? 'Gee, I was just getting my bell rope pulled by this under-age faggot and he let some friends in and they trashed my place. Can we keep this out of the Law Review?' The guy's going to look like a major dipstick, and he knows it!" Hart kicked out at a beer can lying in the gutter.

"And the drugs . . . tell him about the drugs." Donnelly was watching the corner, but I couldn't see what he was looking at because Hart pulled me around to face him. "Part of the reason the Johns are here is to score some drugs. PCP, blow, reds, even goddamn ludes, the world's most candyass drug, and what happens is the kid gets back to the John's place and they get wired and sometimes it's not strictly the usual stuff. I mean, these guys are into some bizarro stuff. And don't tell me otherwise, my friend, I've *seen* it, and I've seen the aftermath down at TGH Emergency or over at Wellesley. Pain, rough trade, getting hurt. Objects. Fists. It's tough stuff, and sometimes it gets out of hand. We've had guys set on fire over in Saint James Town, guys with Drano poured down their throats, one old dude with a blade shoved up him. There's no such thing as a victimless crime. There's just crime."

I ask him what they're doing down here if they can't stop it.

Donnelly walks back to us. "We've got some winos in back of the Parkside. How do you feel about puke?" Before Hart joins him, he looks back down the street. A large Caddy is turning into it from the Bay Street end, and the shadows are sliding back into the park.

"Why do we do it? To show the flag, my friend, to show the flag."

* * *

8:35 pm, upstairs in Cornelius' Bar, Yonge Street.
"You have some ID, son?" Donnelly was holding this pale skinny teenage boy up against the wall outside the men's washroom at the back of the bar. Heavy Metal rock pounded against the walls, and the main room was thick with smoke and noise and the smell of old beer and warm bodies. Although the bar was packed, no one was looking at us. Hart stood away, his hand on his billy, his back to us, watching the room. Donnelly asked the kid again. The kid looked as if he was about to faint. "Don't puke on my coat, son, it makes me crazy. Let's see

some ID." The boy pulled out a wallet and fumbled with the cards inside. If he was older than fifteen, I was Mazo de la Roche. Donnelly shook him by the lapels. I watched the boy swallow, fear coming off him like heat off a griddle, and it hit me suddenly that Donnelly was genuinely angry. He had on that open friendly smile that he specialised in, but there was nothing behind it that was kindly or gentle. His fingers were knotted into the boy's blue polyester bomber jacket so hard the skin over his knuckles was taut and the bones showed underneath. Hart kept his body turned slightly away, one eye on the crowd out in the main room. I looked down at the kid's feet and I saw that they were almost off the floor. Only his toes were touching, and they left little rubbery skid marks on the greasy tiles as he struggled to stay in balance.

We were "showing the flag", as Hart had called it, in a few of the nastier bars along the Yonge Street strip. It was a peachy area. Nothing to compare with Times Square in Manhattan or North Beach in San Francisco, but it had its own sticky little charms. Running north along Yonge from Dundas to Bloor Street was a sideshow straggle of all-night drug stores, record shops, army surplus warehouses, video game arcades, fading cinemas running five shows daily with titles like *Thousand Plane Raid* and *Killer Coeds From Neptune*, alternating with the occasional clothing shop and one or two respectable restaurants. And, of course, the bars. And sex, in all its splendid varieties, like an endless party seen through dirty glass and heard through third floor windows. On the jammed and crushing streets we had pushed our way north, the crowd of teens and sharpies and hookers breaking apart in front of Donnelly and Hart, no one meeting their eyes. The two policemen might have been invisible, but their authority was a palpable force, a membrane that we moved inside and that made us on the street, but not "in" the street; soldiers of an occupying army. Now and then in the middle of the continuous blare of rock and roll and engines growling up the street and the clattering honk-whistle-bleep of the arcades I could hear shreds and tatters of conversations, words striking and glancing away undeciphered, people laughing or cursing or making deals. Most of the crowd were young, kids from the suburbs and the neighbourhoods, wearing ski jackets and tight jeans, cougar boots, tee-shirts with the names of rock groups, with cigarettes in their mouths and tough faces pinned in place. They all had one face, a loose grinning hungry half-expectant predatory face with eyes that never stopped and that looked anywhere but into a cop's eyes.

Outside the Zanzibar three obvious hookers anywhere from sixteen to thirty turned into the door as we had passed. One of them dropped a small box of matches at her feet and covered it with her shoe, holding it there until we passed. Her stockings were the kind with the seam running up the back. I followed the seam until it disappeared under a ragged hem of dirty satin the colour of orange peel. When I looked past her I saw a man about forty watching me go by, waiting for me to stop, waiting for a customer. The door to the Zanzibar was open. Inside in the dark I could just make out the corner of a stage. A hot blue light was shining down on it, and a woman was lying on her back in the circle it made, rolling down a white net stocking and tossing her hair. In the darkness beyond the blue light a crowd of men huddled around, their hands clutching glasses of warm beer and tiny blue pinlights glinting in their eyes and on their lips.

We had wandered in and out of several bars before we reached Cornelius', and it was always the same thing. Donnelly would go in first, walking around the edges of the room, joking with regulars and shuffling the faces through his mental mug-file, looking for anyone with a warrant out, anyone whose face might have been on one of the wanted posters back in the division lunch room. Hart covered the front door and his partner, and kept an eye on the rear exits, waiting for someone in the room to lose his nerve and bolt for the doors. The patrons always did the same thing as well: tension when we first appeared, and then a calculated indifference supported by a furtive sideways look and a joke at our expense under the noise of the bar band. We checked out biker bars and gay bars and punker bars (The punkers were the best-behaved. Most of their arrogance was on their faces.), and cowboy bars and stripper bars, all of it surprisingly tame. There had been nothing openly dangerous, until we had reached the Gasworks and Cornelius' above it. The skinny kid that Donnelly had underneath his meaty hands up against the wall had panicked at the sight of the blue reefer coats and made a dash for the bathroom door, failing to reach it before Donnelly, in spite of a leap over two tables and a shoulder into a waitress in the serving door. I remember being surprised that Donnelly could move his short thick legs that fast. He had real speed, just snagging one outstretched hand in the shoulder of the boy's jacket, pulling him back and spinning him around and into the plywood wall so hard that the collision knocked a clock down and a hollow boom had rolled around the room as the kid's head rebounded off the wall.

Donnelly took the boy's licence, and handed it to me. I passed it over to Hart, who put the radio to his mouth and said, "Dispatch this is able delta fifty-two we have a male caucasian name christian delta able lulu echo given foxtrot roger echo delta dee oh bee July two six year one niner four niner address two niner one Broadview apartment one six zero one any wants or warrants." The miter crackled and sparked for an interval, then "Roger able delta fifty-two just a minute."

"I haven't done a thing so fuck off and leave me alone," said the kid, who looked scared and worried. Donnelly took no offence, his manner almost soothing. "Look, son, if you haven't done anything then why did you run?" The kid shrugged, and looked away. When he did, his glance crossed me and he seemed puzzled for a moment. Then he clouded over and spit a huge gout of saliva across the hall at me. "Fuckin' narc bastard having a good night you fuckin' asshole?" I said nothing, and Hart chuckled. I gave him some more room, and wiped his spit off my jacket. "Look, kid, getting ugly won't help," Donnelly said, nasty-sweet. "Just tell us why you ran and we'll let you go with a warning. This is no big bust. Let's not get all wired up here, okay son?"

"Don't call me son you cocksucker I ain't yer son!" Donnelly shook his head. Hart put an angry look on his face and said, "Hey, why don't we take this little fart around the back for a dance? Would you like that kid?" The kid said nothing, and my regard for his common sense began to revive. "Then watch your mouth, sonny, or we'll give you a lesson in manners!" At that point, the radio emitted a burst of static and "Able delta fifty-two we have a *Dale,* first name Fred same address same DOB licence reported stolen December one 1982 along with a quantity of cash." "Bingo!" said Donnelly – "and credit cards no arrests please hold subject." "Roger dispatch this is able delta 52 please send car to transport one Cornelius' Bar," and he gave the address while Donnelly turned the kid into the wall and pulled out his cuffs. The boy struggled, and I thought Hart would help his partner, but he didn't. After a moment, Donnelly had him controlled and was patting him down for weapons while informing him of his rights. The boy kept up a string of creative invective on the general theme of our probable sexual tastes and the virtue of our mothers. By the time we made the street, the cruiser was waiting. Donnelly got into the back with the prisoner, sliding hard up against him. The boy worked his mouth again and I thought *he's not that stupid is he* but he was and the wet stream caught Donnelly in the side of his fur hat. Donnelly brought his left arm up suddenly into the boy's chest. I could feel the blow out on the sidewalk. Hart and I stood on the sidewalk and watched the boy go very white and struggle for breath. Through it all, Hart never let that friendly lop-sided grin leave his face. At that point I didn't like any of this very much. Donnelly turned away from the prisoner and wiped his hat off on the kid's bomber jacket while he looked up at me. What I was thinking must have been all over my face, but all Donnelly said was, "I've seen more little bastards like this talk their way into the slammer. Let's go back to the station and see what he's been up to."

On the way back to the station I sat in the back with Donnelly and the kid. The kid was silent, and so was I, but no one was paying any attention to either of us.

* * *

2:30 am, the auto ramp, New City Hall.
We've been busy. In the last hour Donnelly and Hart have stopped and ticketed two under-age drunks, checked out several alleys and roof-tops, written out some parking tickets, and rousted out three winos from the Eaton Centre TTC Subway entrance. We're approaching the end of the shift, the three of us spread out and walking up the car ramp onto the New City Hall. The cold and the wind up here are brutal, and any exposed skin is burning and raw and numb all at once. Our breath jets out and floats away and the lights of the city are hard-edged and brilliant, like the eyes of cats. The city is slowing down, the steady dynamo whir of engines and crowds and traffic fading into a kind of suspended calm. Our feet scrape and echoes bounce off the deserted square below us. Donnelly looked at me with something approaching trust and chuckled.

"You dry yet?" In the dark up ahead I could hear Hart snickering. One of the winos had been too drunk to walk, so Hart had asked me to help him get the old fellow up the stairs and into a cruiser. Left on his own, the wino, who smelled like a dead yak and looked like three miles of corduroy road, would probably freeze to death in the street. It was customary for the policemen to roust them out of the air vents and stairways and send them over to various flophouses. But this one couldn't walk and couldn't talk and had to be carried. I had a tough time thinking of him as human, but the officers treated him with rough affection. "His name is Halloran. He's been living in this area for twenty years. Usually he's not this pissed. Somebody must have given him some money. Right Freddy? You in there, Freddy?" Halloran had looked up at the two of us carrying him. Something came into his cloudy wet eyes, and his mouth began to twist. Perhaps he was trying to speak. I wasn't listening. I had been watching three lice crawling out of his shirt collar and over my left hand. Hart had stopped in mid-stride. "You going to be sick, Freddy? You better not. We'll make you clean it up, won't we?" He looked over Freddy's ragged white hair and his eyes had a look in them as close to kindness as I'd seen there all evening. He made me feel ashamed. We had made it to the top of the stairs. Out on the sidewalk at Dundas and Yonge the cruisers were lined up like taxis. Several other cops from the Foot Patrol had customers for the Detox centre and the flophouses. Donnelly was holding a young mulatto girl at the end of an outstretched arm while she swung at him repeatedly. Drool ran down the side of her face, and her hair was matted with grease and dirt. Her eyes had nothing in them but a kind of animal fear. Donnelly had seen us walking towards him.

"Hey, writer! You want to see what it's like to be a cop. Take this little bitch over to Detox at 55. I've got a car right here." The cop at the wheel was leaning over and laughing. Hart grinned at me, so I had said yes I'd take her.

"Pretend you're plainclothes. You look more like a cop than I do anyway. Go on, the officer'll drive you back. It'll only take a minute." Donnelly had handed the child over to me by the collar of her coat. I took her arm and she hit me in the side of the face with her fist.

I rode over to the women's cells at 55 Division with the girl passed out in the seat beside me. I was worried that her breathing was ragged, but the cop at the wheel just looked back in his mirror and said, "Relax, she's just thinking about being sick," so I tried to think about something other than the way she smelled. All there was to think about was how this little girl had gotten into such a state and I knew that if I had the answer it wouldn't change a thing so finally I just sat in the back with her and watched the street lights flicker past the window. In the back of the cruiser the windows were covered with greasy finger-prints, so every time the car passed a streetlight the glow would show up all the grubby streaked marks of hands and tears and dribble and sweat. It was a kind of record of events. They sell used police cars as traders. People buy them and use them as family cars. I recall wonder-ing if the children in the back seats who fall asleep on the slick beige vinyl on the way home from their Aunt Frannie's place or Canada's Wonderland or the Zoo or McDonald's ever dream of dark alleys and heating vents. Do they ever have nightmares? Is a police car anything like a haunted house, a psychic dry cell, holding a charge, the extract of endless nights transporting drunks and thugs to holding cells, seeping into the struts and metalwork like rust?

Lost in this reverie, it had taken me some time to realise that the girl had wet herself and the warmth I was feeling in my legs was her urine running out over the vinyl. That was why my pants were still wet when Donnelly looked over at me on the way up the City Hall auto ramp and asked me if I was dry yet.

I said no.

*   *   *

2:45 am, a hot air vent in a deserted alley in downtown Toronto.
What I had taken to be a pile of dirty rags thrown into a corner next to a wall turned out to be a young drifter, huddled up against the warm air vents jetting out from the heating system. Donnelly walked over to him and poked him with his club. It took several pokes to wake him, and the first thing he said was, "Holy shit mom I already took it out leemeealone willya?" in a bleating adolescent whine so I tagged him mentally as a runaway and relaxed. Hart stood to the right of the boy as Donnelly pulled him to his feet.

"Why are you sleeping out here, son? Don't you have a home?" Donnelly had the same gentle tone for every drifter and street punk we'd stopped all night and I didn't trust it any more now than I had when I'd heard it in the back hall at Cornelius' bar when he was shaking down The Kid Who Loved To Spit, but I had my mind on a scotch and bed so this was just more of the same. The kid staggered slightly. Donnelly let him slump backwards into the slots of the heating vents. The boy was blond, and his jeans were new. He had a leather jacket on that must have rung in at $250 and his hands, bare, had three gold rings on his left index finger. His eyes looked clear and alert, but he was mumbling and seemed not to know where he was. There was about five days growth of pale blond beard on his white skin. He was older than I had first thought. I put him at around twenty. Donnelly repeated his question, but louder.

"Yeah, I godda home. Who're you guys?" Donnelly grinned. Hart said, "Cops, son, don't you recognise the blue uniforms? Let's see some ID." The boy looked at Hart and then at me, his face a dull mask. "'N who's this guy?" he slurred, looking over at me, "'n'other fuggin copper?" I stepped back to avoid the spit but he only worked his lips and staggered. Donnelly asked him if he was drunk or stoned. "What are you on, son? Have you taken anything? Uppers, Downers. You look pretty stoned. Show me some ID or you're going in for the night on a charge." Donnelly was a little tense, but I couldn't see why. I wished he'd skip it and we could all go home. The kid reached into his jacket and tugged out a billfold. He held it out to Donnelly and swayed slightly.

"No – just hand me the licence. Keep the wallet." Donnelly was getting tighter. I looked over at Hart, who was standing easily, his weight on his left leg, his eyes on the boy's hands. The boy staggered again, fumbled stupidly with the billfold, tugged at his papers inside, then dropped the whole thing in a flutter at Donnelly's feet. Donnelly stepped back, and said, "Pick that up, son," in a hard flat voice. Hart shifted his weight softly. Something was happening here. I thought these two policemen were zeroing in on this poor bloody drunk and we were all alone in this deserted alley at damn near three in the morning. I suddenly felt sick and tired and angry and I thought *what will I do if they start in on him? Call a cop?* and I started to laugh, but no one was listening to me.

The boy stared dully at the three of us for a moment, and then shifted his eyes down to the billfold at his feet. He licked his lips, swayed again, as if he were going to fall, and bent over to pick up his papers.

I was watching him and I still can't say for certain where the knife came from. There was a blurred motion when the boy reached the ground, and then he was coming up and out with his arm stiffening, a thin blue glitter caught the light, tracing an arc from the ground to the point where it connected with the downstroke of Hart's baton. I recall hearing a dull thump. The blade whirled up into the air, strobing in the city lights, glittering blue and cold like a helicopter's blades. The kid cursed and hit the ground, a high-pitched thin sound coming from him like the sound you get when you strike a taut cable. Donnelly moved over him and put a hand on his back. I stood there in stupid surprise. Hart stepped in with a set of cuffs. From behind me I heard a ringing clang as the knife struck the concrete several feet away.

"Silly little bugger," Hart chuckled, as they slipped the cuffs on him. "You'd think we'd never seen that stunt before." Donnelly looked up at me. "He was faking the whole thing. Didn't you see it?" I shook my head, seeing nothing in my mind but the terribly small piece of night air between the tip of the kid's knife and the shiny blue fabric of Donnelly's reefer coat.

"How could you miss it?" Hart asked amiably. "You smell any

booze? You saw his eyes? Perfectly clear. No drugs, no booze. We had no grounds for a charge. We just suspected he might have some surprises for us. Got to take your time, right? Let him make the move. We *said* it was tricky out here. Weren't you listening?"

Hart stepped away from the now-quiet boy and picked up his miter.

"Dispatch this is able delta fifty-two we've got a customer here for you let's have a car," and he gave the address.

"Roger able delta fifty-two any injuries?"

Hart looked down at the boy, who was still cursing softly.

"Negative dispatch this is able delta fifty-two nothing serious just a little tussle everybody fine out." Hart and Donnelly were relaxed, amused. I was not. I felt a sudden and almost uncontrollable urge to step softly over and kick the boy, once, in the side of his head. I did nothing. Hart stepped in between the boy and me. He laughed once, not bitterly.

"Look, don't take it all so personally. You can't always tell what's coming up, you have to be ready, but you can't take liberties. I figure the kid's got Wants and Warrants on him like the Magna Carta. There's only one really important thing to remember on this street and that is to always know precisely what the hell is going on. Think you can remember that?"

I could hear him talking but all I could think about was how loose and gullible I had been and how easy it would have been for that kid to take me. I could feel a hot place in my stomach where the knife would have cut through the belly muscles and on into my body and I knew what it would have been like to lie there in that cold deserted alley in the middle of the city at three in the morning and feel my blood freezing into a sticky mass and all of it just because some miserable little psychopath thought it would be a neat way to round off his evening. The urge to strike out at the kid, to hurt him, was sliding over me in coils.

I focussed on Hart finally. He was smiling at me, the same lop-sided friendly grin I'd been watching all night long, the question still in his eyes. Was I all right?

I said, "Yes."

CHAPTER FIVE

The Piece

The .32 calibre Colt Semi-Automatic bearing serial number 333 - 738 came into being on the forge floor of the Colt firearms plant in Hartford, Connecticut sometime during the month of March in 1924. A forgeman in a scarred leather apron selected a length of cold-rolled bar stock and thrust it into a shimmering haze of light in the interior of an acetylene furnace. When he could feel the heat in his tongs and when the end of the bar stock was glowing white hot for a distance of twelve inches, he withdrew it, stepped across the stone floor and placed the glowing ingot beneath a drop-forge. Holding the bar with one black and corded arm, he triggered the hammer. A hydraulic valve hissed once. A massive oiled steel block dropped down along two greased channels. Twenty tons of cold steel struck the glowing ingot at roughly forty miles an hour. Under the rolling clang a deep booming wave shuddered through the old red brick building with a sound like distant artillery. When the hammer withdrew, the ingot was a thin pie plate of cooling metal. Buried in the pie plate was the angular steel frame of a semi-automatic pistol. The forgeman pried it off the forge receiver with a practised torque and threw the pie plate onto a milling table. The metal was now a dull grey but the wooden table-top charred under it. The forgeman turned back to the pile of bar stock while all around him other forges dropped and the factory floor drummed with the same sounds it had felt since Samuel Colt built it on the edge of the Connecticut River after the Civil War. The cooling pie plate with the gun buried in it ticked softly, waiting on the mill table. It had to undergo some twenty-four hundred separate operations before it was complete. The man who would die by this gun would not be born for another twenty-five years.

*   *   *

Craig Alfred Munro was in his early twenties when his dying father, twisting in the coils of yet another drunken rage, hit him, backhanded, above the left eye. The nerve was damaged. Craig began to wear wire-framed aviator glasses with one tinted lens to disguise the injury. He also took up weight-lifting. As he worked his way through his twenties Craig could see that his father's road was leading nowhere but to a bitter grave in the wet grey clay of North York. Ever since his leukemia had flowered in the old man's marrow, Craig's father had passed the time sitting in the overstuffed armchair in the basement swilling cheap whisky and brutalising his twelve children. To Craig it followed as a bruise follows a blow that the straight life was for suckers. Craig Alfred Munro had brought himself to the attention of police in the Borough of North York for an assortment of derivative crimes and misdemeanours falling generally under the heading of Juvenile Delinquency. Records on his early career are closed, by official fiat, to journalists, but unofficially Craig got caught up in the street life in suburban Toronto during the Sixties. If there was any clue there to the direction Craig's criminal career was ultimately going to take it lay in the file marked Weapons Offences. Homicide officers later concerned with Craig Alfred Munro, refusing to elaborate for reasons connected with an impending appeal, will only say that Craig "liked guns" and that shotguns and rifles made up part of his *modus operandi.*

Unwittingly adhering to the classic pattern of beaten sons, Craig made it a point of honour to develop a reputation for fighting in west-end bars and out on the baking tarmac flatlands of shopping malls like Yorkdale and Crang Plaza. Sometime during this period he may have developed a taste for heroin, it's not clear how or when. It would be easy to say that heroin was the fulcrum in Craig's life, but his part in the events to follow is too complex for that kind of excuse.

Objects and people that seemed completely disconnected, separated by hundreds of miles and walled off by divergent experiences, were thoughtlessly and relentlessly converging to a single fatal point, the night of March 14, 1980. Those of you who wonder about predestination may put the question to the mystics. If there was anything that any of the players could have done to alter the outcome, it will never be known. What happened is chiselled in stone.

*   *   *

In 1973, while Craig and his eleven brothers and sisters were coping with a dying father, Michael Sweet finally got out of the police college at Aylmer and fitted the red band to his officer's cap. Sweet was twenty-three at the time, a strong, amiable young man with brown hair and an easy grin. He liked police work, and he was proud to be a member of what he felt was the sharpest and best police force in Canada. The Toronto Police Force assigned him to 52 Division, then in its old redstone building at College just west of University, in an area most of the officers in the force thought of as a prime assignment. He and his wife Karen set about making a family and working on their house in Ajax. All in all, barring accidents or a malevolent *deus ex machina*, life was shaping up just fine for Sweet and his nascent family.

* * *

When the action that later became known as the Mexican-American War heated up in 1848, General Sam Houston sent a young cavalry captain named Samuel Walker up north to find a better and more efficient small arm. Walker met with Samuel Colt. The result of that conference was a gun that would hold the world record for weight and power in handguns until the late 1950's and the appearance of the new Smith and Wesson .44 Magnum. Colt named it the Walker Colt. It was a cap and ball pistol, which meant that it was loaded in each of six revolving chambers with a charge of black powder, a patch, and a conical or round ball weighing almost half an ounce. The Walker Colt was a huge gun, featuring a rifled nine-inch barrel and an overall weight of four pounds nine ounces. Captain Walker commissioned a thousand of these guns. Colt got together enough money to set himself up in Hartford, Connecticut, turning out Walker and Dragoon pistols for the US Army, which, if you note the year, 1851, was a boom time for wars and territorial disputes. Colt and his firearms prospered as America prospered. And it's not too long a reach to say that much of the strength and power of the present-day United States can be directly attributed to the reliability and power of the handguns Colt and his heirs designed and manufactured in the two plants Colt built in Hartford. Colt himself died, in bed, on January 10, 1862, having made certain that Colt Firearms had aligned itself with the Union Army in the Civil War. As an indication of the continuity of this link between Colt and the United States government, the chief lawman's gun of the 1860's, and on, was the massive Colt Peacemaker, a .45 calibre cap-and-ball revolver that was adopted by the Union Army and commissioned by the thousands from the Colt factory. So many of the men of the Union Army who went out into the Territories after the war took along this weapon that the Colt .45 Peacemaker became inextricably linked with the myth and legend of the American West. By 1865 the new plant at Hartford was running out of production space and it was clear to the owners, at that point headed up by a man named Elisha Root, that a new plant was needed, a requirement made even more pressing when the old one burnt down in 1866. Colt had already designed a new handgun factory, and the heirs adopted the design completely. The grim peak-roof structure in red brick with deep-set windows and heavy beamed ceilings was a perfect mirror of almost every factory being built all over England and the Americas as the Industrial Revolution gained momentum. Root and his men built the new factory in a flooded meadow on the outskirts of Hartford. They put up a dike to keep the Connecticut out of the forges, and set about the business of mass-producing weapons.

By 1875, the booming Colt plant had been joined on the Connecticut River by Smith and Wesson and an off-shoot of the Henry Arms company known as Winchester. Other plants followed as gunmakers realised that the one hundred miles of the Connecticut River from Vermont and Springfield, Massachusetts down past Hartford and into the Atlantic at New Haven, Connecticut had everything that modern industry needed. The river was broad and strong, a steady source of power for mills and lathes, and the growing numbers of immigrants being processed through Ellis Island in New York offered a talent pool on which fortunes could, and would, be made.

Hartford has grown out and around the plant today, although the factory itself is much the same. The copper roof has been replaced. The ancient red brick structure is black with over a hundred years of fire and smoke from the forges. A clutter of modern commercial buildings crowds right up to the perimeter fence, which is well-maintained, topped with barbed wire, and fully electrified. Security is pervasive and enforced. The process of gaining clearance for a very restricted tour of the Colt plant involved an FBI certification and clearance report, which took several months to obtain, and the application of whatever pull I could muster in the Canadian Military establishment. The reason for this level of security is not difficult to infer, since Colt, still tightly linked with the Federal government, makes many of the military small arms now in use by the US Army, the Marine Corps, as well as various "advisor-aided forces" in such places as Japan, Israel, El Salvador, Honduras, and the Far East. The famous M 16 is made here, first tested in the Vietnam War, now turned out in classified numbers, probably over a hundred thousand a year. Other classified projects include the new M 16 A2 program, which will update the M 16 and give it added stopping power with a heavier barrel and a bigger bullet.

The grimy smoke-shrouded red brick plant at the edge of the Connecticut sits at the beating heart of whatever constitutes the "military-industrial complex" in North America, so you can bet your passport, as I did, that it was going go be hard to get into, or out of. A sullen-faced guard in a glass gatehouse slipped the blued Colt Police Match .38 calibre revolver out of the worn holster on his Sam Browne as we passed into the compound. He checked out the clearances with as much humour as a Zomo in a Gdansk shipyard. In the entrance room, more security. Metal detectors, pat-downs, and a phone-check of all papers. Tape recorders are "checked with the security desk" and no manner of electronic gear is permitted inside the plant. Cameras are out of the question. We are taken onto the forge floor, a huge high-ceilinged hall with stone floors and rough-cut beams for pillars. Close at hand a milling section generates intermittent banshee wails as the rough castings from the drop-forges are put to the grindstones for initial shaping. Far in the distance a row of drop-forges, large as elephants even at this distance, pound slowly and repeatedly into the forge-plates, every stroke a thunder-clap followed by a clear hard tone of metal on metal, like a sabre cut being parried. We are not allowed to speak to the men, and the guide is a paragon of obliquity, saying nothing while speaking endlessly. We were all glad to reach a sound-proofed coffee room on the fourth floor. Seated at a rosewood table in a stucco room surrounded with pictures of Colt-bearing plainsmen such as John Wesley Hardin, Judge Roy Bean, Buckskin Frank Leslie of Tombstone, Wyatt Earp, the Clantons, Jesse James, William Bonnie, aka Billy The Kid, and Joaquin Murieta, we are burdened with a corporate indoctrination film designed to crush any further interest we may have had in Colt. In the blue flickering light from the projector I sit and watch my coffee in its cup. The black surface is pulsing with tiny concentric rings. They start at the edge of the cup and ripple inwards, as uniform as a file of guardsmen. Nothing in the room could be causing this. It takes me several minutes to realise that each pulse is the visible shock wave of the drop-forges three floors below. The pounding is steady, smooth, and endless, like the beating of a huge drum. When the ripples meet in the centre of the cup, they rebound and churn outwards.

* * *

After lying in Cosmolene for thirty-six years, the .32 Colt Auto left the Colt Factory in Hartford sometime during the spring of 1955, part of a shipment of guns consigned to a Canadian Wholesaler, probably, but not certainly, Peterborough Guns. The records are unavailable. It left the Colt compound in Custom Bond, sealed by a Canadian Customs wire. It would stay in bond all the way through the green mountains of Vermont, across Lake Champlain, over the New York State Thru-way, as it's called, and into Canada at the Peace Bridge. The consignment for Peterborough Guns was organised in the usual way. Demand, even in the 1950's, for Colt weaponry was so high that the manufacturer "piggie-backed" orders for the popular guns, such as the Colt Python and the Colt .45 Auto, with a selection of less popular guns, such as the small calibre plinking guns like the Junior Colt .25 Auto and the Colt single-shot Woodsman. The dealers and the whole-salers in Canada, like their colleagues in the United States, took what they had to take in order to secure sufficient numbers of the high-demand guns. In 1955, the Colt .32 Automatic was considered a high-demand gun. The particular Colt .32 with which we are concerned sat in the bonded warehouse of Peterborough Guns compound for some time. Dealers in Toronto would call up or mail in order sheets for guns in two categories. Guns that were kept as stock items were usually the high-turnover guns such as the .45 Auto, the .38 Police Special, the Colt Trooper Mark III, and the top-of-the-line Colt revolver, the .357 calibre Colt Python, a big-bore weapon with a ventilated rib along the top of its six-inch barrel, checkered walnut grips over a blued-steel frame, and an overall weight of forty-one ounces. The second category was special-order guns. According to the police, the .32 Auto was a special-order gun. That means that some-time in the early part of 1956, probably in January, someone came into a dealer in Toronto and ordered a .32 Auto from Colt. The dealer who sold this Colt Auto was Lion's Sporting Goods, on Bayview Avenue. The man who ordered it was, as it turned out, the third most fatal link in the chain of events to follow.

* * *

In 1977, Craig Munro's father died of leukemia. Craig had been running in and out of trouble all through the 1970's, and he had lately persuaded his younger brother, Jamie, only eighteen in that year, to help him out in some of his "projects". Jamie was smaller and weaker than Craig, but he had a better instinct about the direction Craig had chosen for his life. Jamie married, the year his brutish father was buried, a girl named Rose, and tried to pull out of his brother's vortex. Craig took this badly. According to police in North York, Craig and Jamie fought about Jamie's unwillingness to "stand by" his brother in small-time thefts and drug dealings. Craig was as violent as his father, and stronger than Jamie. It seemed to be important to Craig that his brother take part in "the life". He may have introduced Jamie to heroin as part of this campaign; this cannot be confirmed, and may be nothing but self-serving extenuations put out by Jamie's section of the now-warring Munro family. Testimony during the trial given by Jamie's wife Rose suggested that Jamie had only come along on the fatal night at George's "to help Craig score a thousand dollars he needed for a fine." Craig also took a lady named Connie DiChristofero, and started a family, but she seems to have been unable to keep her husband off the streets.

Nothing about these two men allows you to side-step the inference that they were fast becoming another pair of low-grade hoods adrift in Toronto during the late Seventies. In the end, the distinctions put forward by various wives and relatives at the trial seemed pale and pointless in the face of the killing on the night of March 14, 1980. It's fair to say that, for whatever reasons, the two men had allowed themselves to become part of a horde of stateless young men with the ethics of lizards, their eyes firmly fixed on the delusion of main chance. Despite his pronouncements about reform in 1977, Jamie is on record as having purchased a Cooey Model 840 twelve-gauge single shotgun in Fenelon Falls less than a year later, in November of 1978. According to the records, and trial testimony, he bought the gun at a Canadian Tire Store "for hunting", an argument that lost a great deal of its credibility when it was revealed that he had shortly afterwards cut twenty inches off the barrel with a hacksaw and made a half-hearted attempt to obliterate the serial numbers with a file.

Barrel length in a shotgun is the chief determinant of a quality known as "spread". Spread is the pattern of tiny holes the pellets of a shotgun shell will make when they are fired out of the smooth-bore barrel. As the distance from the barrel increases, the small swarm of lead balls will spread out more and more. They may emerge from the muzzle, in a cloud of superheated gas and flame, in a pattern no wider than a half-inch in diameter. At ten yards from the barrel, they may be as wide as six inches, due to the various effects of air resistance, wind, original charge, recoil of the weapon. At thirty yards, the pattern may be a foot wide. At a hundred yards, the pattern of lead balls may occupy a space as wide as ten feet. Clearly, the density of this cloud will decrease as a factor of the distance from the muzzle. That's not a problem when you are trying to bring down a duck for the family dinner; a hit with only three or four of the original mass of twenty or thirty pellets will still kill. As a matter of fact, if you want to find enough of the duck to eat, anything more than three or four pellets is too much. So to suggest that the field applications of a shotgun for hunting are in any way improved by hacking twenty inches off the barrel is arrant stupidity. The younger Munro boy had cut the excess length off the barrel for two reasons; a cut-down shotgun will deliver a pellet spread of four feet ten yards from the muzzle, and a shotgun twenty inches shorter than usual will just fit under a trench coat. Jamie's little "hunting piece", so amended, would blow an oak door off its hinges from six feet away. It was small and easy to bring to bear in a closed room, and its stopping power was nothing short of awesome. Guns such as this have only one purpose. Jamie Munro knew this as well as any hood in town.

* * *

Twenty-two years earlier another man had bought another gun for an entirely different purpose. Out of consideration for the man himself, and at the request of the Homicide officers investigating the case, we cannot name this man. We can say that he was in his early middle age when he went into Lion's Sporting Goods and placed an order for a Colt .32 Automatic. He gave as his reason for purchase his interest in "collecting". He had, at that time, what I am told was a very extensive collection of handguns and rifles. The Colt .32 Auto was described in the Colt catalogue of that year as Model Number 1903, complete with an eight-shot clip and a three and three quarter-inch barrel. It was proposed as an excellent home defence gun, and highly recommended for women, since it was easy to conceal and simple to operate. The man ordering the gun was no different from most of the people who bought legitimate handguns over the counter in that year. Colt's records are inaccessible, but unofficial estimates of all handgun sales for the year 1956 run to a quarter million. This sounds high, but there were over fifty million legally-registered handguns in North America in 1978, and an innumerable amount of rifles and other weapons. Canada had three million handguns registered in 1978, and police admit that there may be thousands of unregistered guns.

The man standing at the counter of Lion's Sporting Goods in 1956 ordering the .32 Colt Auto felt in no way furtive or shameful. Owning a handgun in 1956 carried no more stigma than owning a car; buying one was a similar process. The businessman paid his money, and the dealer ordered the Colt from Peterborough Guns. In due course, the new Colt arrived, and the businessman dropped in to pick up his weapon. On the 25th of October, 1956, the RCMP Firearms registry in Ottawa received a registration notification of a .32 Colt Automatic Pistol Serial Number 333-738. On the form the reason for purchase read "home defence". The new owner, a sportsman and an ex-athlete, may have felt the gun would serve as some security around the home, something to make intruders worry. Perhaps he felt a little safer with the .32 around. What was in his mind at the time isn't really important. He took the gun home and put it in his collection. Aside from the odd cleaning, and some intermittent target practice, the .32 Auto stayed in this man's collection for nineteen years, all through Constable Michael Sweet's childhood and teenage years, through Craig Munro's hard times with a hard father, through the conception and birth of his younger brother Jamie, through Sweet's passage into the Police College and his assignment to the 52 Division branch – a gun innocently purchased, duly registered in accordance with the law, filed and legal, stabilised, no threat to anyone.

*   *   *

The world changed. While the .32 sat on the businessman's wall, crime in America and Canada swept through the naive post-war society, leaving a fractured age and a seriously strained judicial and enforcement system in its train. In the major cities of the American northeast, entire boroughs and sectors became free-fire zones. Montreal developed into a Mafia stronghold, a training ground for armed robbers and murderers. Toronto went through convulsions of drug wars, biker clashes, petty assaults, firearm offences, although the murder rate rose very slowly. Winnipeg found itself a battle ground in the bars off Main Street, as four to five thousand disenfranchised and hopeless native Indians settled into the area, warring with each other and the police. Vancouver changed from a congenial extension of the

Pax Britannica into the heroin and homosexual capital of Canada. Windsor border crossings from Detroit became the single most active entry point for illegal weapons, most of them high-grade handguns from the Colt and Smith and Wesson plants along the Connecticut, all of them brought in on the body by day workers and "tourists" who sold them in the bars all along the Golden Horseshoe. Biker gangs such as the Satan's Choice, the Pair O' Dice Riders, the Vagabonds, the Lancers, and the Black Diamond Riders made literal fortunes out of drug and weapons wars during the Sixties and the Seventies, until most of the gangs disappeared into the economic mainstream, having achieved a metamorphosis wrought by wealth and corporate ambition.

Crimes that would have brought enraged citizens out into the streets during the Fifties passed into dreary commonplaces. A whole civilisation protected its complacency with a shroud of leathery detachment. The Me Generation reared sons and daughters seraphically free from moral or ethical compunction, flat-eyed street kids who could see no barrier between the desire and the deed. Gratification delayed became a *casus belli*. The handgun became a symbol of adolescent virility. Finally perceiving the threat we began to change the Gun Laws.

* * *

The Liberal Government passed sweeping alterations in Canada's firearms laws in 1978. Handgun purchases ceased to be as simple as buying a new car. Any citizen wishing to purchase *any* firearm now had first to apply for a Firearms Acquisition Certificate. This legal-size form calls for full details of your age, residence, and an extended investigation of your character, to be carried out by the local police department in your province. Searches are conducted for any criminal record, any history of mental instability, any reports of domestic difficulty, any history of violence or aggression. Your personal references are verified. Any symptom of erratic behaviour is grounds for refusal. The investigation may take up to three weeks, and the decision of the Firearms Officer is virtually final, subject to a re-application requesting special circumstances, which is usually unsuccessful. Many sporting gunmen in Canada have raised objections to this FAC requirement, citing infringement of personal liberties and a dangerous concentration of discriminatory powers in the police. They may be right, but no one has come up with a better idea and so far the system seems to be working fairly and well.

Having been granted an FAC, you are then free to go to any store dealing in firearms and select your weapon. If you want a rifle or a shotgun, all you do is present your FAC and your Driver's Licence, pay your money, and take the weapon home.

Buying a handgun is a much different story. If you qualify for an FAC, a vetting process similar to applying for a job with a defence firm, you then go to a sporting goods store or any place which deals in handguns and make your selection. No money changes hands, unless you wish the dealer to place a special order for a particular gun. If you find a gun you like, you then go to the nearest police station and fill out a request for a Restricted Weapon Permit. This request is actually a questionnaire, and on it you'll have to explain how and where you'll store it, who you are, what if any character witnesses can you supply, and why you want to buy the gun. According to the Criminal Code, citizens of Canada are permitted to buy handguns for personal and home defence, but in practice no Restricted Weapon Certificates are ever issued for this reason. In the opinion of most Firearms Officers and Attorneys General, buying a gun for home defence is not a sufficient justification. The argument, which seems to stand up, is that the combat uses of a handgun are very difficult to master, and that few private citizens have either the inclination or the time to master them. Therefore, a handgun in the home poses more of a threat to the owner and his family, in the event of accidents or domestic rage, than it ever will to any intruder, and might possibly end up as stolen in any case. Hitting anything with a handgun is not as easy as it seems; a waver of a millimetre off target will mean a clean miss at fifteen feet. It takes a steady hand, which few of us could show in a life-threatening situation. So, the police don't like to issue permits on that basis. There is only one usually accepted reason, and that is a purchase for sporting use at a registered gun club. Membership in one, verified by a letter which also states that you have completed a Basic Handgun Training course at the club is a condition of the issuance of a permit.

That means that you then go off to a qualified handgun club and apply for membership. They *don't* have to accept you. If a member will vouch for you, or if you can persuade them of your reliability, they will issue you with a provisional membership and enroll you in a Basic Handgun Training course. You'll use a club gun. You'll be taught how to load, unload, and clean the gun. You'll be drilled in the etiquette of the firing range, in the proper positions, in the correct grip, how to cope with recoil, how to return to target, how not to kill yourself or your family through carelessness or stupidity. In the meantime, the members will watch you closely for any indication of something odd, some trick of the mind or a way of acting that might suggest a faulty or suspect personality. This is hard to define, but the judgements get made one way or another. If you pass several weeks of testing and training, they will give you a full membership and a letter to take back to the Firearms Officer that states that you have passed a written and practical Handgun Safety Test and that you're a member in good standing.

The police will send you back to the dealer, who will then accept a fifty or a hundred per cent deposit on the gun of your choice. He'll give you a paper describing the gun, showing make, type, and serial numbers, say a Colt .32 Auto Model Number 1903, serial number 333-738. The police will, if they are satisfied that all is in order, issue you a detailed Permit To Convey your Colt Auto from the store directly to the police station. You go back, pay the man in full, and collect your gun. You then take the most direct route to the station with that gun. If you're found off that route for *any* reason, you are open to a charge of Illegal Conveyance of a Restricted Weapon. At the station, the police will compare the actual numbers with the bill of sale and the registry forms. You will then be given a Permit To Convey the gun directly to your residence, and a Permit to Own a Restricted Weapon. If you want to shoot the weapon, you must apply for a Permit to Carry the gun to and from your club on a regular basis. You will only be allowed to carry this handgun on the way to your club and back. No deviation from this route is allowed under any circumstances. You can't leave the gun in your trunk. You can't carry the gun on your person. It must be transported in a locked case, unloaded, and the ammunition carried separately. It must be accompanied with your green Permit To Convey, current and unaltered. You will not be able to take the gun to quarries or fields for casual practice. You will not be considered for a Permit To Carry. Any violation of any aspect of these restrictions is chargeable under various sections of the Criminal Code. While at home, the gun must be kept under lock and key or you're in violation of the Safe Storage Laws. If the gun is stolen and later used in a crime, and it can be established that you did not have the gun under lock, you may be charged.

The new Gun Laws have caused some intriguing side-effects. Handgun purchases, according to a local dealer, are increasing slowly and steadily. It has become very difficult to "surface" any unregistered gun, since what was once a mere formality is now a potential criminal charge for possession of an unregistered gun. Anyone discovered carrying an illegal weapon, particularly a handgun, can expect to be arrested on the spot, searched, handcuffed, taken to the stationhouse, questioned closely by detectives, jailed for some time while a decision is made to release on recognizance or to hold without bail. Charges will certainly be laid under the Code, and a jail sentence of at least one year is a good possibility. The gun will be confiscated and ultimately destroyed. If you were arrested while in the commission of a crime, the handgun will add up to fourteen years to your sentence. Tragically, increased restrictions of handguns even before 1978 may have been a factor in the decision of the businessman to sell his .32 Colt, and in the manner he ultimately chose.

* * *

It's not hard to picture the expression on the businessman's face in March of 1980 when Homicide Detectives of the Metropolitan Toronto Police Homicide Squad showed up at his door asking about a .32 Colt that he had registered in October of 1956. Full details of the case cannot be released since the whole matter is currently under a pending appeal by the Munro family, but the essentials can be sketched out.

The man had kept the gun in his collection for nineteen years. He was known in his circle as a gun man, and many of his friends admired his guns as much as he did. Early in 1975, a friend of his had approached him about the Colt .32 Auto. This man, let's call him the Second Man, since we've been asked not to name him either, wanted the little Colt to give as a gift to another man, for defence purposes. The Third Man was a travelling agent, he spent a lot of time on the road in bad places, he wanted a gun for protection. The Second Man knew about the little Colt. It seemed the perfect defensive gun; easy to conceal, and reliable. The Second Man came to the businessman with his request. For reasons no one will ever understand, this honest, responsible, respected, and intelligent man, a man who had dealt with firearms all his life, a man who had owned guns for thirty years without a single mishap, this paragon made one stupid and fatal error. He accepted the man's offer and he sold the Colt for fifty dollars. Unregistered. No paper. No FAC. No Permits To Convey. No Gun Club training. In one transaction a duly registered and legal gun became an illegal and unregistered gun. If there was any moment in this quickening vortex of circumstance at which Constable Michael Sweet's death became immanent, fated by God, that was the moment.

* * *

Craig Alfred Munro had a new piece. As handguns went, it was a status piece. Most of the weaponry Craig was used to fell into three categories; first, the standard semi-automatic or bolt-action .22 calibre rifle, just like the one most of us grew up with; next, the twelve- or twenty-gauge shotgun, usually a single-shot weapon that broke at the rear. Both these weapons were usually cut down and shortened by various means, the stock sawn off and the rest of the gun wrapped in masking tape in the mistaken belief that masking tape won't show prints. This was the kind of gun Jamie Munro had bought. The third type of gun that the Munro boys would have seen would be something we've come to call the Saturday Night Special. The original Saturday Night Specials were generally small-calibre revolvers from factories in Belgium, Spain, Germany, or Italy. These guns were copies of Colt or Smith and Wesson originals, made without permit in European plants. On the whole, they weren't as bad as their reputation; they'd hit what they were aimed at. They broke down after heavy usage because of inferior steel and milling, but usually they were only needed once or twice. They carried names like Astra, Rossi, Star, Llama, and they were generally .32 or .25 calibre. The Munros would have thought themselves lucky to score one.

Most of the hoods in Canada make small arms out of starter pistols. They drill out the barrel to take a .22 calibre slug, and grind out the chambers to accept the cartridge. In a sense, this gun most perfectly suits the context we're looking at. The gun is made of white metal, painted dark blue. The action is similar to a child's cap pistol. It can be had for thirty dollars over any counter. Since the barrel is blocked, it requires no permit. It is a noisemaker, a toy. Only someone with a child's mind would think of it any other way. The bored-out starter pistol is the kind of form-and-function match-up that would delight Arts Majors and Sociologists, a fool's gun, wildly inaccurate, as reliable as a hooker's pledge. With luck, you could squeeze ten or fifteen rounds through it, and perhaps hit within three feet of your target at a range of fifteen yards. On the last round, and there would be no way of telling which one this would be, the slug would turn in the bored-out barrel, jamming, trapping the explosive gasses that are pushing the lead slug out at a speed of 1800 feet per second, and the barrel would blow up in your face, sending bits of hot metal flying in every direction. A fool's gun.

Well, tonight things were going to be different. Craig and Jamie sat in their borrowed car on the street outside George's Bourbon Street Bar on Dundas Street in downtown Toronto, wired on the adrenalin and fear, and feeling the almost sensual power emanating from the new Colt .32 Auto that was burning a hole in Craig's ribcage. A gun like this was as hard to find as a Porsche Turbo Carrera. It made Craig feel raw, twitchy, dangerous. He hadn't been able to bring himself to mark it up at all. It was so good-looking, so goddamned efficient, so lethal! He loved to pop the magazine out of the grip and run his thumb over the brass cartridge cases with their flat conical lead slugs lined up like pearls on a string. He'd slide it into and out of the slack along his waist inside his belt, feeling the reassuring weight and the slick hot steel hard up against his body. He was always working the action, pulling back the trigger and forcing the slide in towards his wrist. As the top slide moved backwards a sear would scoop out one of the small .32 calibre cartridges and lift it up into the barrel. Craig would let the slide run back over the interior barrel and the action would drive the cartridge home in the breech. Loaded, and at full cock, the gun was ready to fire. If he pulled the trigger, the hammer would strike the sliding pin in the breech block, which would hit the tiny button of fulminate of mercury in the bottom of the cartridge. This would explode, igniting the main charge, which would force the lead slug out of the brass case and into the barrel in a violent burst of hot gasses and superheated metal. The slug would engage the rifling lans in the entrance to the barrel, which would impart a lateral stabilising spin to it. The slug would emerge from the barrel three and a half inches further down, spinning left to right, at a forward velocity of roughly 800 feet per second. The excess exhaust gasses would drive the breech block back into the slide spring, extracting another cartridge from the magazine as it slipped over it, cocking the hammer back, then go forward again until it reached the end of the slide channel. The little gun would jump in the hand with the same kind of sensation you would get from catching a fastball, and the barrel would tend to rise up from the target. There would be little smoke. A spent brass casing would fly out of the breech as a secondary action of the blow-back. The Colt .32 Auto would now be ready to fire again. All that would be required is slight pressure with the second joint of the index finger against the trigger. The Colt would fire one shot each time the trigger was squeezed, until the magazine was empty or until someone had shot the user dead.

Craig liked the way the gun jumped, and the sharp coughing sound it made. He cleaned it repeatedly, its rifling was as spotless as bank brass. There was a thin sheen of gun oil on the outer casing. When Craig ran his thumb over the slide it left a greasy trail, like a snail's track. The gun did something to Craig, he wasn't sure what. Jamie jerked around to watch him and swallowed hard. Jamie grinned back in the sick yellow light from the street lamp, broke the Cooey open for the nineteenth time and rubbed the brass cap of the twelve-gauge shell in the breech. Craig drew in a ragged breath, and reached down into the murky recesses of his imagination for some intonation, some power words, to signal the start of his fantasy, to mark the moment, but nothing came. They got out into the street.

* * *

Following a reference from the businessman, the Homicide Detectives found the Second Man at his office. Yes, he had bought a small automatic from the man they named. Well, as a matter of fact, he laughed nervously, no, he hadn't bothered to register it, *ah*, himself, *ah* that is, well, you see he was only going to give it as a gift to the Third Man. Yes, he figured that the Third Man would certainly register it then. That was all right, wasn't it? I mean, nothing will happen to me, will it? Are you going to charge me? What was going on in the minds of the two detectives on this case is hard to imagine, and they're not saying, but anger must surely have been buried in the chemistry somewhere. A policeman was dead, and these honest citizens were worried about charges. The cops let them worry. Where is the Third Man?

* * *

March 14 was a cold clear night. Constable Sweet and his partner Constable Doug Ramsey were in a cruiser, doing the usual Saturday Night duty in 52 Division, ferrying drunks and winos to assorted DeTox centres, picking up punks from the beat cops, stopping cars for moving violations. Most police work is composed of long hours of routine punctuated by short intervals of panic or rage. Sweet took some kidding about his family, all girls, Jennifer, who was six, Kimberley, who was four, and the latest, a baby named Nicole, born only six months past. The guys were kidding Sweet about boy babies and his chances of getting one before he had enough girls for a field hockey team. Sweet hadn't given up, and he took the kidding well. The night had been slow, so far, and the officers were looking forward to a Code Seven and some hot coffee. The cruiser still stank courtesy of their last customer. Ramsey opened the window. A cold wind slid along the dashboard. The night rolled on towards two o'clock.

* * *

The Third Man showed up at the Homicide Offices at 590 Jarvis Street. He was short and out of shape, breathless from fear and nerves, anxious to please, anxious to show that he too had meant no harm. Yes, he'd kept the gun for two years, until the new gun laws in 1978. Well the laws were quite strong, you know, and here he was with an unregistered gun. No, as a matter of fact, he hadn't registered it at all. Could he be frank. The officers didn't smile. Be anyone you want, they said. Just tell us why you didn't register the gun. I was afraid I'd be, you know, charged, or something. Anyway, it was just a little gun. Where is it now? Well, like I said, the laws made me nervous about an unregistered gun, so I sold it. For fifty dollars. I had a friend, a business associate, he wanted the gun for personal protection. He bossed a construction crew. He had to spend a lot of time in the sheds at night, on a deserted lot. It made him nervous. We talked about my piece, and he said he'd take it off my hands, you know, for only fifty dollars. I had it in my car, parked out behind the hotel. We went out there at night, he stood by the trunk while I got it out. I threw in some ammo. The piece was wrapped in a dishtowel. It needed some cleaning, you know, I'd never fired it. He gave me the money. I gave him the gun. You want to know where he is? When? When did this happen. God, maybe March, 1976. I can't recall it exactly. Why don't you ask him?

* * *

Craig hit the front door first, with Jamie right behind him. They had on their stocking masks. Craig's face felt hot and wet under it. He could feel his breath puffing over his cheeks and eyes. Jamie had the Cooey out and Craig jerked the Colt out from his belt. The time was ten minutes after two in the morning, the fourteenth of March, 1980. The circle was closing.

* * *

The Fourth Man came in fast. The Homicide Detectives figured that the Third Man had called him. He was a beefy older man, his skin roughened from working out of doors. He was stiff, truculent, with a look on his face such as Jesuits wear, his mouth a bloodless crease in a cloud of puffy flesh. Yeah, he'd bought the piece from the Third Man. So what? No, no paper. Why? Well, it was already illegal. Anyway, I never figured to use it. Just keep it around for luck, or in case some dipshit gets his shorts in a knot over the cashbox. It was dirty when I got it. I cleaned it up a little. Fired it a few times. No use in having a gun if you can't hit what you shoot at, right? It was a nice little piece. Got it for forty bucks. Did he say fifty? Yeah, okay, fifty it was. Sure, some of the guys on the crew, they knew about it. Hard to keep something like that secret, right? Nice little piece, too. I had it right through, say 1976 – I got it in March, I think – and it was in my tool box for 1977, right up to March, April, May of 1979. Yeah, I think that's right. No maybe, maybe it was July! No, I got promoted up to foreman in the head office. No way I could keep the piece. Anyway, the guys were always asking to use it or borrow it or screw around with it. Pain in the butt, right? This German guy, he was really hot for it. Loved guns. It turned him on that the piece had no paper. I mean, you guys made it really hard to get one of these things. I mean, it was really dicey trying to keep it quiet and I was looking at the slammer if I slipped up and you guys got onto me. So I dumped it off on the kraut. Got my fifty, too. No, no idea where he is . . . so, what's the story? Am I in the slammer, or what?

*　*　*

George's Bourbon Street Bar was winding down when Craig and Jamie went in through the front doors. Groups of people were scattered around the bar in the middle of the room, flirting, talking quietly. Craig was on the customers in three steps, his right arm rigid, thrusting the Colt out from his crouched body, hissing with a rage he told himself was only something he put on to scare the straights. Jamie went wide, covering the crowds, shouting, all over the room, kicking over tables and poking the sawed-off Cooey under counters, always moving, dancing, jumping, talking fast and crazy with excitement and fear. Craig said, "The money assholes where's the fuckin' money?" over and over in that lizard hiss voice he'd practised in front of the mirror in his bathroom. Everyone froze. Craig stepped over to a waitress called Cindy Shanks and knocked her to the floor. He stuck the Colt up against her temple and said, "Tell us where the money is little girl this gun is big enough to blow your fuckin' head clean off!" Craig liked that line. He'd liked it ever since he heard Clint Eastwood use it in the movie *Dirty Harry*. Cindy Shanks, not having seen *Dirty Harry* and therefore ignorant of the apposite nuances implicit in Craig's act, took him at his word. In tears, she pointed out the office safe. Jamie and Craig started to herd the terrified people into the office. One of the staff did not move quickly enough, so Craig struck him in the kidney with the barrel of his Colt. The man screamed and Craig hit him again. The Munro brothers had told their wives they were at an all-night card game.

*   *   *

The German was a worried man when the Homicide Detectives reached him at his home. His wife and kids stayed in the basement in front of the TV while the man downed schnapps in a water glass in the kitchen with the detectives. The detectives laid their notebooks down on the MacTac cover of the table and looked at the German, who looked at his schnapps. He had a way of clenching his hands around the glass when answering a difficult question. He had no thought to lie. Yes yes he had the gun from this man in the list. This man he was working with at the site, yes? He has a gun which he is not wanting to keep because of the new laws yes. This gun is a very nice gun which it would be a waste to throw away as the owner was threatening to do. Guns are craftwork, yes? Not something to be afraid of or to hide away. Anyway, the gun is only for collection and for around the house. The neighbourhood gets worse and worse, yes, and the lady would perhaps use it for herself. But no, the gun is not to her liking. She says to get rid of it, to throw it away or give it back to the police. So maybe this I should have done but the gun is costing me fifty dollars, yes, and this money you are not finding anywhere. No no it had no papers and I was not wanting to attract the police, yes? This boy at my work he knows all about guns. He says to me "give me the gun" he will take it away and keep it safe. No trouble. I think about this for a while. How long? Some time I am thinking. I don't think the boy is a good one. The gun is something he wants too much, I think. But my wife is angry with me all the time and the police are everywhere. Anyway, I sell it to him. So you see I have done nothing wrong, yes, since I have not kept an illegal gun. He gave me fifty dollars for it which was very fair. His name. It was Carlo. Carlo Sipione. I took it to his house. He did not want me to come inside, so we talked in his car garage, yes. I had the

Colt in a brown bag with paper towels so it looked like just my lunch. He did not look at it, just gave me my money. He was very excited about the gun. The month. It was September. I remember because the rains flooded the yard. September 1979. Carlo still has the gun. He promised me he'd keep it safe. You go see him, yes?

*   *   *

A waiter was sitting upstairs in George's Bourbon Street taking it easy when the Munros burst in. He heard the shouting and Cindy's frightened voice as Craig had jammed the Colt in her temple and hissed at her. At first it seemed like a stunt, a joke. He came down the stairs at the back of the restaurant to look. Everyone was on the floor except the manager, who was working at the dial of the office safe. A short broad man in a plaid jacket was standing over him. There was something in the man's hand that looked like a gun. He had a mask on. Another man stood a little away from the group on the floor and he was holding a short gun, a sawed-off shotgun on the people on the floor. They were lying face down with their hands on their heads and they were silent. This was no stunt. He slipped off his shoes and eased his way back upstairs. There was a window on the back, looking out into the parking lot. He ran to it as noiselessly as he could.

*   *   *

Carlo Sipione was known to the police in Toronto. He had a record of petty theft, B and E's, some small-time gambling and assault charges. He was hardly a crime kingpin, although he liked to think of himself as "connected". When the detectives saw his sheet come up on the computer they groaned. The trail of the Colt .32 had finally led to the street life in Toronto. So far, they had been confronting honest citizens, stupid, careless, even small and greedy, but clearly not criminal. Privately, the detectives doubted that charges would be laid against any of the men through whom the Colt had passed on its way to Carlo Sipione. But now they had encountered the first level of the underclass, and they knew that there was nothing up ahead but self-serving bragadocio, lies, and plea bargaining. It was a game the detectives played well, but it would be very hard from this point on to say with certainty exactly how the gun had moved through the backstreets. The interviews would become interrogations. The information would be guarded, shaded, often totally false. Carlo didn't disappoint them.

* * *

The waiter forced the upper window open and stuck out his head. His manager was just climbing into his car in the rear of George's. There's a robbery going on, said the waiter, in a voice thrumming with fear, like a guy-wire struck with a pipe. A fucking robbery! There's two guys in the front with guns. Go get the cops, for chrissakes! The cops. The man stood, hesitant, and then he drove off.

* * *

After a while, Carlo Sipione told the truth. It's not easy to lie well hour after hour, under pressure. Carlo tried to make himself look as good as possible, which wasn't very good. Yes, he bought the piece from the German. But he'd only kept it a few days. It was a hot item, that Colt. A gun like that is very much in demand. A smart operator could make a few bucks on the deal, play it off to somebody with a use for it. He never kept them, guns, they were too crazy. Easy to move, for a guy with his contacts. He kept it in the trunk. Do the bars, make a few calls. Shouldn't take long, the word gets out that Carlo has a piece. A buddy tells him to call Jeff. Jeff who? Jeff Kramer, says Carlo's buddy. Bingo! says Carlo. Kramer is a heavy dude, you know. Done some time, right guys. He needs a clean piece, no paper. Carlo sets up a meeting at a downtown bar off Yonge Street. Kramer is there, drinking as usual. Kramer is a tough boy, not an actor. Carlo is polite. The piece isn't here, of course, but I can get it, he tells Kramer. Kramer says "how long?" Gimme an hour. But I got to see some bread. Kramer says no piece no bread. The classic dealer's dilemma; how to exchange drugs for cash and still have the cash and your liver. Kramer doesn't care how, he just wants the piece. Finally, they go out together, a situation Carlo does not appreciate. If Kramer wants the piece for free then Carlo is SOL, as they say, right. Sipione's car is up an alley way. They make the trade in silence. Carlo gets an unverifiable amount of money, probably no more than two hundred dollars. A hardcase B and E man named Jeff Kramer gets a Colt .32 Automatic, serial number 333-738, no paper. This is in October, 1979.

* * *

The manager circled on Simcoe Street a couple of times and then headed for the 52 Division station. On Duncan he passed a police cruiser headed in the other direction. He flashed his lights and honked his horn. The cruiser stopped. Doug Ramsey rolled down the window to hear the man's beef. Fifteen seconds later the yellow cruiser was accelerating up the street, no lights, no siren. Sweet got on the radio. "Dispatch this is 5209 we have a possible armed robbery one eight zero Queen Street West request assistance confirm please." Sweet and Ramsey were not overly excited. They were experienced men, and part of that experience had been gained responding to any number of phony armed robbery reports. They had followed the book and were responding to the call, but they weren't going to go flying off like a pair of rookies. Still, Ramsey kept his polished black boot right to the floorboards all the way to Queen and they stopped with a side-drift half up on the curb outside George's Bourbon Street. Before the car stopped rocking on its springs, they were out of it and approaching the front door. Across the street a couple of people stopped to watch. Inside, Craig was screaming at the manager to get the safe open, so neither he nor Jamie heard the cruiser pull up outside. Sweet and Ramsey stopped at the double oak doors with the brass handles and drew their service revolvers.

* * *

Kramer was hard to find. When they did find him, he said little. Yeah, he had picked up a piece from that wop. Yeah, it was a little automatic. No, he didn't have it any more. He'd sold it. No, he couldn't remember his name. What about charges? What if I co-operate? Okay, okay, his name was Mooney. Mike Mooney. Kramer could see by their faces that they knew the name.

* * *

Police procedure is explicit in matters such as Armed Robbery. Any officer or officers responding must wait for at least one back-up team before attempting an entry. But every situation has its own parameters, and only the men on the spot can see clearly what they are. Ramsey and Sweet decided that this was the real thing, and that there was a distinct possibility of innocent citizens coming under fire if they held off and waited for back-up. It's likely that one of the officers pushed the door open quietly to see what was going on. They made a judgement under stress, probably the correct one, and the two men went in after Craig and Jamie Munro.

* * *

With Mike Mooney the Colt passes into limbo for a period of

months. Mooney was an Armed Robbery specialist with a lengthy record. He had no reason to help the investigation, and little interest. The detectives spoke with him for a long and tedious time. Mooney lied a great deal, and the police aren't saying how the investigation proceeded past him. He admitted, so I am told, that he had given (or sold) the .32 Colt to another man, a biker named Phantom Phil. This was a problem. Phantom Phil was a member of the Satan's Choice motorcycle club, an all round hardcase who'd picked up spare cash for the Mafia in Hamilton and Wentworth by smashing knee and elbow joints with a balpeen hammer, as part of their "debt enforcement branch". But Phantom Phil had bungled a job, by the most reliable reports, an assassination order. Knowing that failure was its own reward in Mafia circles, Phil volunteered to become a witness for the Crown against all of his Mafia contacts. He was a sensation in Ontario law enforcement circles. As a consequence, Phantom Phil, also known as Cecil Kirby, was as easy to get to as Mohammar Quadaffi. The Ontario Provincial Police had him hidden away in a safe house, and no one, not even other policemen, were going to get near him. The trail lost itself in red tape.

* * *

At George's Bourbon Street it was coming down to firepower, as these things usually do. Sweet and Ramsey carried the standard Canadian police force issue revolver, a Smith and Wesson .38 Calibre Military and Police Model 10. The blued-steel revolver with walnut grips uses a .38 special, or high-powered, round that fires out of the five-inch barrel at roughly 900 feet per second with a 158-grain load. The slug itself is called a semi-wadcutter. It's a lead slug shaped like a cone with the top sheared off to make a flat surface. The shoulder of the slug may have a copper sheathe to help it engage the rifling in the barrel, since lead tends to shear away. The police departments settled on this type of gun because any smaller load was unlikely to stop a man, and any larger load was too likely to pass right through a target and injure innocent civilians. That was the theory. But most policemen who have to use the gun know that, in a fight, adrenalin will keep an opponent moving far past what we normally think of as the mortal wound. The .38 special slug will ricochet off a car windshield. It takes four or five solid hits "in the centre of the visible mass" to knock down and disable an opponent. Smaller guns, such as the Colt .32, are even less effective, since they present even less striking surface at the point of impact, which means that Craig Munro's treasured little Colt was even less of a killing machine than he hoped. Small bullets tend to nip right through muscle and tissue, unless they strike bone, in which case they tumble, surrender all their kinetic energy to the target mass, and do all sorts of internal damage. Since the stopping power of the .38 special is so notoriously poor, policemen are trained to empty their guns into their targets as fast and as accurately as they can. But they carry a built-in disadvantage when shooting against a semi-automatic. The Smith and Wesson Model 10 .38 Special is a double-action revolver. That means that, as the trigger is squeezed, the internal levers force the hammer all the way back to full cock and, at the same time, rotate the cylinder until a chamber with an unfired cartridge is brought into line with the barrel. As the trigger squeeze is completed, the hammer is released to plunge down and strike the rear of the cartridge, igniting the fulminate and exploding the main charge of powder in the brass case, and driving the semi-wadcutter slug into the barrel. That dual purpose served by the full trigger squeeze is known as double-action, and in combat terms it means that the gun must be subjected to greater muscle movement in order to fire repeated rounds. In the Colt .32 Auto, as in all Autos, the slide is blown back by the force of the explosion, which clears the breech and a spent casing, recocks the hammer automatically, and loads another round in the barrel as the slide hits home again. Thus, an automatic pistol may be fired with much less effort and very little waver due to muscle movement while triggering. The Colt in Craig's hand had very little stopping power, but it was an automatic, and therefore could deliver a much higher rate of fire. Craig could get eight rounds off in the time it might take Michael Sweet to fire six rounds. Add the officer's training, subtract the double-action handicap, compute the plusses or minuses, factor in fear, rage, the quality of light, stopping power of the .38 special compared to the smaller .32 auto. Try not to think about the real threat in the confrontation, which was Jamie's twelve-gauge shotgun with the mutilated barrel. Thank your several gods you didn't have to be there. Mike Sweet and Doug Ramsey had to be there.

At this point the area dispatcher was issuing a special alert coded armed robbery. The duty officer at 52 Division was taking a practical look at the disposition of his officers and men around the Yonge and Queen Street sectors. He had only seconds to decide which men could safely be diverted to respond to the back-up request unit 5209 had called in. Dispatch was given authorisation to put this code on to another frequency, in order that the general mobile channel not be tied up with radio cross-talk concerning the George's Bourbon Street call. A call went out for Constable John Latto, who would be assigned to handle the situation at the scene. Latto was a veteran of the force, and had considerable experience in tactical and strategic decisions on the street. The roving Emergency Task Force Unit was also flagged and put onto the special channel reserved for this call. All of this would have been accomplished in seconds. No duty officer would allow any single situation to draw all operational units away from other patrol assignments, and the 52 Division sectors included many of the worst bars and roughest streets in Toronto. But he also knew that every man in 52 Division would be aware of the trouble at George's, and would be listening carefully to any open-channel calls. The back-up car called in on the tactical channel. They were at the scene. Unit 5209 was out in front, empty. The officers were inside. As they made the report, a knot of white-faced people burst out of the front doors of the bar.

* * *

Jamie Munro almost shot his leg off when he saw the two cops hit the doors. It never occurred to him to stay and shoot it out. He cleared the crowd on the floor in one startled leap, his jacket flaring, the cut-down Cooey clutched in his right hand. Craig missed them, but the bone-white stretched look on his brother's face, and his miraculous leap, told him that something was wrong. He hit the floor and rolled, snarling, half-crying with fear and rage, got some chairs tangled up, scrambled to his feet, the Colt forgotten, a cold weight in his hand. The crowds saw a chance and took it, bolting. Sweet and Ramsey dodged the crush, trying to keep the gunmen under sights, cold things rolling in their bellies, perhaps even some grim excitement. For once, the call was real. The dimly-lit bar boiled and churned, people screamed or swore, tables and chairs struck walls and clattered away. Angry voices said "shoot shoot the fuckers" from out of the dark; all of this roared around the heads of the two policemen, who knew only that the crisis was real and that there was no clear shot, no way to get off three or four killing rounds into the two rolling, dodging, panicked men on the far side of the room. Sweet said again, in a hardening voice, "Police officers drop the guns now!" but things were moving too fast for that. Craig, on his belly again, saw three people in a frantic tangle near a back door. No blue uniforms yet in that direction. He slithered along the ground, rising up before the mindless cluster in what must have been a fearful sight, his hair wild around a slick wet balding crown, eyes red and hot, his clothes dirty and disarrayed, and that Colt in his shaking hand, the round black hole in it's muzzle dancing and jumping, full of lethal promise. Craig shoved the Colt in their faces, searching for Jamie, who was already streaking towards him with his hair flying, and drove the people through the door into the kitchen, falling over them and springing up, cursing again, and flinging it shut seconds after Jamie made it through. Jamie hit the stove on the far side with his hip and cried out, a short sharp yelp. Craig shouted through the door, "Back off you fuckers we've got people in here and we'll kill them all," and the knot of people immediately charged back into the brothers, screaming, panicked, eyes wide and wild, shrieking, running blindly into and over and past the brothers, whose sidearms were useless in the press. In a matter of seconds, the kitchen was empty. Craig and Jamie leaned against the counters, throats blocked with panic and a kind of animal bile. "Jamie," Craig hissed, "Jamie watch those doors and kill anything that comes through them – those bastards they'll come up the back way – I'm gonna shut the basement door!" He scuffed to his feet and pounded out of the kitchen, his breath whistling in his throat, fear coming off him like steam off a new-cut furrow. Jamie could hear him going down the stairs, a syncopated tumble, the Colt scraping along the walls.

Turning the corner by the back door, Craig heard a sound at the lock. He pivoted off one shot with the Colt. He heard a hoarse cry, and jumped the last five feet into the darkened basement. Out in the rear yard, a Metro policeman named Lee Train clutched his pounding forearm and stared at the shattered tangle of gears and crystal that was all that remained of his watch after Craig Munro's wild shot through the closed wooden door.

*　*　*

Phantom Phil was a dead end. Phil, who cannot be described, admitted that he knew Mike Mooney. No, he didn't know anything about how Mooney worked. No, he didn't know where Mooney got the Colt. Mooney always had some kind of piece or another. Mooney was always waving one around at parties. Mooney was a jerk. Phil would no more front a piece for Mooney than he'd gargle with Sterno. Anything else? What happened to the piece? What piece are we talking about?

* * *

The book has something to say about room-to-room searches, too. In the first place, you don't undertake them without body armour. Officers get some combat training in this art. The theory is that you keep your off-side, the side without a gun in it, flat against a wall. You step very lightly. You keep the piece cocked, so that it only takes a slight pull to fire. You keep your piece muzzle up, so you don't shoot yourself in the foot. Approach an open door the way you'd approach a cobra. If the door is closed, detail one man to go up and listen through it. Tell him not to put his head up too high. Few doors can stop a bullet. Stay to the side. If you have to go in, kick the door right beside the knob, and kick it right off the wall. Better yet, blow the hinges off with your shotgun, if you have one. If you don't have one, go back and get it. If you go in, go in very low, gun up and braced, and move to the side of the room right away, so you don't block your back-up, and so that if you catch one, they can fire back.

For Sweet and Ramsey, the blood was up. The call was real, and the gunmen had bolted into a back room with some citizens. This had all happened in seconds. There was as yet no sign of back-up. Once again, the men were faced with a field decision, unaided, under pressure. The rules were clear about that next closed door. Now that the robbers had been warned, bursting through that kitchen door was a rookie's ticket to oblivion. But there might be other citizens loose in the place. There had been a lot of shouting, a lot of panic. If anyone ran down the stairs, they might still be around, they might still run into a panicked gunman or a cop who didn't have time to think about who they were. One of the bugs had already made hostage noises through the door, so let that situation cool out. Priority One: find and clear out any innocent bystanders. Sweet and Ramsey reached this conclusion as their back-up team came in, cautiously, through the front doors. They conferred, out of the line of fire in front of the closed kitchen door, behind which Jamie Munro was crouched, his Cooey in his hands, his cheeks the colour of wet grey clay. In the street outside, more cruisers were arriving. The situation was developing fast, as they say in the book. Mike Sweet expressed some concern for innocent people who might be downstairs, in the warren of rooms under George's Bourbon Street Bar, with no idea of what was going on or how to get out alive. Someone would have to go down there and check it out. In situations such as these, "someone" is always a cop. There was a dispute, amiable

but real, about who would go, each of the men unwilling to leave the
chore to someone else, each of them reluctant to go themselves. In the
end, since it was Sweet's idea, he persuaded them to let him go. The
time was approximately two twenty a.m. Ten minutes had elapsed
since Craig and Jamie Munro crashed into the bar. Sweet started
down the front stairs leading to the restrooms underneath the bar.
Doug Ramsey followed behind, his revolver at half-cock. Give or take
a week or two, it was fifty-six years ago that month that twenty tons of
forge head had dropped onto a white-hot ingot of steel and pounded it
into the frame of a Colt .32 Auto. That gun was now in the hands of a
young man named Craig Alfred Munro, 28, a small-time punk about
to step into the major leagues.

*   *   *

Phantom Phil was asked to think harder. Mooney may have had
several guns. The gun the homicide detectives were after was a .32 Colt
Auto pistol, it had an eight-inch shot clip, serial numbers still intact,
good condition, sort of like a small .45 Colt Commander. Phil ought to
know what a forty-five looked like. So, had he seen Mooney with a
gun like that? Yeah, said Phil, sure, I know that gun. It was a nice piece,
well-made. But nothing to write home about. More of a purse gun,
something to keep with your car keys and your mad money. No
stopping power. No real . . . authority, you understand? Mooney was
worried about it, because he thought it might be warm, you know.

*   *   *

The basement was a rat's nest of corridors and storerooms. Sweet
and Ramsey drifted further and further apart, trying to check them all.
They went as softly as they could through the rooms, opening cup-
boards, stepping over boxes, letting their breath out through their
mouths, slowly, so it would make no noise. The movements would be
familiar to anyone with a taste for video cop shows. To actually walk
into a darkened room, hunting for someone with a gun, someone who
can and perhaps will shoot you with it, is a feeling difficult to imagine.
It calls up memories from your childhood, the pictures you had of the
thing that lived under your basement stairs, the shadow that glided
along your ceiling at night, the rustle at your window. Your skin will
shrink in odd places, muscles under it tensing to take the shock. You
must not think about this or the fear will overwhelm you. You have to
keep it jammed down tight into a cold place in your chest. Someone

once said that a coward was just a hero with a good imagination. Seconds spent thinking are seconds spent not listening, not looking.

Craig Alfred Munro was poised at the bottom of the back stairwell. Had he heard a footstep? It was hard to hear over the sea-shell roaring in his ears. Sweat was running in a channel down the middle of his chest. He wanted to scratch it but it would have been too loud down there in the ponderous quiet. His heart was acting funny. He was trying to remember where he'd felt something like that. When he was a kid he'd had a bike, just a hand-me-down, but he had put some streamers on it, and one of those toy fans made of curved plastic sections. If you held your hand just close enough, you could feel it spinning on your skin. You could cup both hands over it, if you were careful, and it would flutter in your hands. Not too close, though, or it would stop. The figure just rose up out of the dark at the far end of the hall. Craig jerked up the Colt.

* * *

You do not prompt a subject during an interrogation. You do not coerce him. You do not threaten him. You do not touch him. If you can't live by those rules, you should get out of homicide work. They had a slogan in the department, something the guys in Homicide used to quote to one another. If you can't get them with your brains, you can't get them at all. The trail of the .32 Colt faded away into the faceless dancing dissolving underworld of dealers and hoods and hardcases. The last transfer, the final link, could not be found.

* * *

The interval between life and death can be as short as a synapse. Craig Munro had spent most of his life passing on his pain to other people. His life so far had been rotten. No one had spared him. He would spare no one. His father had been hard. He would be hard. It was all their fault, anyway, all of them, all of those suckers. There were no innocent people. Innocence was someone else's problem. That night, it was Michael Sweet's problem. He was down in that basement looking for innocent people. When the two guns came up together, Michael Sweet had to think about his target for one brief interval, long enough to decide guilt or innocence, long enough to be certain before he fired. Craig Munro had made his choice a long time ago. The Colt jumped in his hand seven times, seven sharp little cracks, not very loud in the basement, no louder than the sound of a hand striking. Five of the shots missed. Two did not. One slug cut a furrow on Michael Sweet's chin, glancing off the cheekbone and finally coming to rest in his right shoulder. At this moment, he was angled slightly to the right, his left arm back, hand down, jerking away from the hot fire of the bullet trace in his cheek, his eye burning from the shock. His right arm was extended, pistol up and cocked, the barrel wavering as the first little slug struck home. Sweet began to come back up, his finger tightened on the trigger of his .38. Craig kept on pumping out the slugs, the little gun bucking in his sweating hand, his mouth a wide wet hole in his dripping face, the brass cases jettisoning, ringing tinnily off the ceiling, the tiny barrel trained on the dim blue shape at the far end of the hall. Sweet jerked back, and a small hole appeared in his right arm. It punched into his uniform shirt, his tee-shirt, into his skin and through the trapezius under the skin, slowing in the thick muscle fibre, tumbling, until it struck a rib, and then it burst through, rolling, slowing, still tumbling, into the lung sack and through that on into the peritoneum, ripping and tearing, breaking up. Sweet went down as Munro flicked out the magazine and slammed another one home in the butt. There was a smell of something burning in the close air. Brass cases rolled out of his way as he rushed forward towards Sweet. He could hear heavy feet racing down the hall. Someone shouted "Mike! Mike!" Craig shrieked at the voice, "Get out of here I've got your man I've got a gun!" The footsteps halted. Munro grabbed the wounded, dying man, by the tunic and began to drag him up the back stairs.

* * *

Craig and Jamie Munro held the dying policeman hostage in the kitchen of George's Bourbon Street for a little more than an hour. Several times during that hour, Michael Sweet asked the two gunmen to give up, to let the police come in with a doctor. He was lying on the kitchen floor, on his back, his blood seeping out. He could feel something hot inside. Perhaps he could feel the weakness in his fingers and legs. He may have known how badly hit he was, that he was bleeding internally. His mind was on his family. What would happen to them? He tried to talk Craig into giving up. Craig came over to Sweet and pulled him up by the tunic, pulled his back off the wet floor, away from the puddle of bright new blood.

"I've been in 'Nam, pig, I've seen men die. Put your hand over the holes and you won't bleed to death. Take it better, will you, you're getting on my nerves!" Then he dropped him back onto the tiles. Sweet hit with a moist sound, and went taut with a deep pain. Jamie looked at his brother and at the policeman on the floor and did nothing. Craig slapped him and said: "We're gonna stand the fuckers off we're gonna get us a car and get the fuck out of here don't you sweat it kid they'll never fuck with us! We've got one of them in here with us. You think they're going to come in here blasting away if there's a chance that the cop'll buy it?"

Out on Queen Street the three big men from the Emergency Task Force stalked restlessly up and down, shotguns loaded and braced against their chests, talking softly to each other and shooting murderous looks over at the Mobile Unit where the negotiating team was dialling the kitchen phone of the bar. They wanted to go in at once. Their team leader, Sergeant Ed Adamson, the son of Police Chief Harold Adamson, had said so several times, in a progressively more forceful tone, and each time he'd been told to wait. He was angrier than he'd ever been in his whole life. The other uniformed men gave him a wide berth. The street was full of red flashing lights and men in dark blue jackets. The Press was busy.

The talk went on for half an hour. Sometime around three in the morning, Craig Munro appeared at the front door of the main entrance. Every gun was on him as he walked with a policeman over to the parked car at the side of the road. Craig fumbled around in the back seat for a while, retrieved something small, and walked back to the doors of George's with it. The fact that it was probably heroin did little to calm Adamson and his partners.

For reasons that are hard to understand from this distance, the talk between the negotiators and Craig and Jamie Munro went on to little purpose for another half hour. It was 3:34 when Sergeant Ed Adamson and his two partners issued an ultimatum. A cop was on the floor in there, dying slowly. They had heard Craig striking him, they had heard Jamie and Craig taunting him about his wound and his wife and his daughters and his chances of seeing them again. The three ETF men gave the negotiators a choice. Give us permission or get the hell out of the way.

At 3:35, Sergeant Adamson fired two tear gas rounds into the kitchen and they went in after Craig and Jamie. There were three of them, big men in flack jackets and peaked caps, holding riot shotguns crossed in front. They were angry men. Through the smoke and confusion, they could see well enough to deliver a hot burst of number six shot into Craig Munro's left side. Jamie got seventy-five percent of his stomach blown away. They came with ambulances and took all three men to the Emergency Ward at Toronto General Hospital. Mike Sweet was taken into the operating room at once. Jamie and Craig were treated in another room. Craig's wounds were not considered serious.

When Karen Sweet got to the hospital, one of her husband's partners took her aside and told her that Michael had died on the table. He had just lost too much blood. If he'd been brought in sooner, he might have lived.

Craig Alfred Munro was sentenced by Justice Frank Callahan of the Supreme Court of Ontario on February 8, 1981. He was given a life sentence for the first degree murder of Constable Michael Sweet. His brother Jamie was given a life sentence for second degree murder. Craig Munro's parole was set at no less than twenty-five years. Jamie's was set at ten. Jamie is currently imprisoned at Millhaven. Craig Munro is serving his time in maximum security at Kingston, Ontario. No one else was ever charged in connection with this killing.

The Colt .32 Auto is now in the Police Museum at 590 Jarvis Street in Toronto.

Karen Sweet has re-married just recently.

Mike Sweet's partner Doug Ramsey, still serving at Toronto's 52 Division, is unable to talk about the night of March 14, 1980 and the death of his friend.

Colt still keeps the mould for the .32 model 1903. It's fallen out of favour, superseded by heavier calibre guns, guns with a better kill-to-stop ratio. But they're ready to put it back into production if the market changes. As guns go, it wasn't a bad design. It got the job done.

CHAPTER SIX

Hold-Up Squad in Montreal

At Sainte Anne de Bellevue the Saint Lawrence River breaks out of the hundred-and-fifty mile corridor imposed upon it by the north slope of the Adirondack Mountains and rushes out into a silted delta. Here the river cuts three channels through the soft fertile country. The northernmost branch, a river called Mille Isles, defined the edges of Ile Jêsus, flowing out of the broad flat bay called Lac des Deux Montagnes. At Ile Bizard a central stream cut straight through this mass, separating Ile Jêsus from the main island of Montreal. The Saint Lawrence itself establishes the southernmost edge of this brief archipelago, running strong and dark through the built-up city relatively tinted by the passage. Ile Jêsus is now Laval, and what was once a dreamy flat swamp is now a crowded platter of duplexes and apartment blocks and suburban clutter. Across the narrow Rivière Prairies, north Montreal pushes right up to the water's edge. Mônt-Royal climbs up out of the dense streets, covered with maples and pines, a citadel for the English families overlooking the warrens of French-Canadian housing stretching far off into the west and the east and the south. Montrealers don't think of a narrow, formal downtown; you bring your own boundaries here. If you're an anglo you settle in the west, in Dorval or Pointe-Claire or Lachine. If you're French, then you go to North Montreal, Laval, or the rougher streets in Saint Jean or Saint Leonard. If it's anywhere, downtown Montreal descends from the grey rocks and terraces of the mountain, down the slopes at Des Pins, Sherbrooke, de Maisonneuve, Dorchester, and Sainte Catherine, streets as final in their own way, as categorical as Second and Fifth and Seventh and Tenth Avenues are in Manhattan. These famous streets run west to east, more or less, and it's in the short surprising connecting blocks between them that most of the fascination of Montreal lies. It's dense in here, and not always clean, but it's rich and edgy and vital. Streets like Crescent, Drummond, Stanley, Metcalfe, and Saint Urbain, lined with shops and clubs and bistros, give the city a scintillation, and a touch of threat. Where so much is given, much will be taken. It's not surprising that the bishops and bankers of Canada found Montreal so worrisome; the French nourished a civilisation here while the English built a business. Montreal looks a little worn. The pull-out of English money has hurt. So has the PQ and their rabid anglophobic legislation. On the broad streets the people of Montreal are direct, self-absorbed, striking. Most of the life is on the streets. Montreal feels like New York or London. It's no more purely French than New York is purely Dutch. The women are devastating. The men don't give a damn what you think of their clothes. The winters are long and deep. Spring comes suddenly; one month it's a grey frozen island, and the next the river is rolling by and the days are full of scents. The city has the same light that you can find in the Low Countries, Holland and Belgium. It was a wide-open town when Duplessis ran the cabinet and the cops; organized crime flourished here until just a few years ago, when it split into two factions, the organised faction ascending into legitimacy and the criminal faction becoming disorganised. It has always been a city that needed a strong hand, and it usually got one. It's a restless city. You have the feeling that great events are imminent, that something outrageous is about to happen, that you can have anything you want if you have the heart to work for it. Or the nerve to take it.

* * *

The Armed Robbery division of the Police de la Communauté Urbaine de Montréal is on an upper floor of the municipal offices on the edges of Old Montreal. The offices are classic Fifties cop decor; cream-painted walls with old blinds, heavy metal desks, rows of small glassed-in offices partitioned off along the walls. Posters of wanted men are stuck up randomly, rough men with truculent or beaten expressions staring out at the police photographer or turned full-profile with deadened eyes looking downwards at their cuffs. Some of the faces have black-marker crosses drawn on them. Either the men have been caught or they're dead.

The big room has the same feeling that all squad rooms have in any police station in the world. Business gets done here in an exclusively masculine environment. There's no attempt to lighten the look with greenery or colourful posters. No one has created an individual look for his desk. In one or two of the corner offices senior men have pinned photos of their children to the corkboard right beside mug shots of killers and bank-robbers. Big men in shirt sieeves and wrinkled suit pants slouch over old Remington typewriters and punch out reports in triplicate with two fingers of each hand, cigarettes burning down forgotten in tin ashtrays. Over in a corner a grey metal wastebasket is surrounded with crumpled-up pieces of carbon paper. There are one or two crushed cigarette butts on the floor. The air in the long room is heavy with the stale ozone scent of routines endlessly observed. Outside in the blank concrete streets of the Court House blocks a slow cold rain is falling. The Sergent de Détectives who finally comes into the cubicle with two hot cups of black coffee in his thick hands has drops of rain on his trench coat. It takes him a long time to relax, and even longer to get to the point. Not only am I Press, I'm Anglo Press. There has been a recent scandâle, a senior inspector of their Drug Squad has been charged with trafficking in narcotics, apparently stolen from their Evidence Room. The whole force has tightened its ranks. Under this man's broad Irish looks and his easy smile I recognise the impenetrable stonewall of the harassed cop. When he takes off his windowpane check topcoat he has a .357 Magnum with Pachmyr grips stuffed into a well-worn shoulder holster. Raymond Chandler would have felt right at home with the Armed Robbery Squad in Montreal. They were old-fashioned cops, completely unburdened with the newly-fashionable liberalism of the forces in other cities. When the street changed, they would change. Otherwise, get out of the way. He had a strong grip and calloused hands. His accent was pure Québécois.

"What do you want us to do? Stage a robbery for you?" DuRoche was smiling but wary. Montreal was growing tired of its reputation for spectacular bank robberies. Yet you could see that DuRoche felt he was part of an elite unit, working a dangerous trade.

In Vancouver or Halifax or Toronto bank-robbers are fairly predictable. The robberies are usually confined to suburban banks. One man would come in with his hands in his pockets and line up for a teller. When he got to the wicket he'd hand her a note. The note advised the teller that the man had a gun somewhere and that he'd be rather piqued if the teller didn't immediately fill up his paper lunch bag with small bills. The robber would be counting to himself . . . twenty-nine . . . thirty . . . thirty-one . . . when he got to sixty he'd grab whatever was in the bag and run. Sometimes an assistant manager would run after him and bring him down on the sidewalk with a flying tackle. The tellers would be excited but not afraid. The police would arrive minutes later in a squeal of tires and the pounding of heavy feet. The manager would put a hand-lettered sign in the window: sorry due to a robbery this branch will be closed for two hours. The tellers get a bonus cheque for a hundred dollars every time they are robbed. The head office is strict about co-operation and not confrontations. The robbers are usually loners, single men or boys, often out of work and desperate. They'd have a brief career, which would end in one of three ways: they'd lose their nerve or regain their senses and quit; they'd graduate to something more dramatic; or they'd get caught. Firearms are rarely used and, when used, used to little effect. The standard weapon is a cut-down .22 rifle or a shotgun, or the starter pistol. The MO strictly flash and grab. But here in Montreal, well, things were a little different.

"We 'ave the syndicates 'ere," DuRoche was saying, in a voice that rumbled under his paisley tie. "They made a kind of tradition for the *voleurs* to live up to. Back in the Thirties and the Forties, Montréal was controlled by several families. The Du Bois people were very active, and it is claimed that the Bonnanno family of New York had a lot of influence here. I've heard that said by people who should know. Anyway, for some of these reasons, we developed a wide-open style of bank robber here. A soldier of these families was expected to make pocket money by hitting a few banks. He gained respect by hitting the banks hard. Also, they had good information. They penetrated the systems and they knew what they were doing. They relied on fire-power.

"In the Fifties you'd 'ave a robbery, it would go like this . . . a stolen car would pull up outside a bank in downtown, say on de Maison-neuve or Sherbrooke, in the middle of the morning. The streets are crowded, it's a Friday and the paycheck accounts are full. Five men in stocking masks would run into the bank. They'd have a man at the door, another man to take out the guard, a third man who would cover the house and count out loud. The other two would clear out the cages and persuade the manager to open the vaults. If anyone in the place hesitated for even a moment, a guy would knock him to the ground. Or shoot him dead right on the spot. And they had the guns. Forty-five autos and Winchester Pumps and Smith and Wesson .38 Specials. Sometimes a man would just blow off a light fixture to get everybody's attention! As I say, it was wide-open. No one would interfere. It was all up to the police, to us, right?

"Then, later, we have the Front de Libération du Québec. They study the old masters. They were very dedicated men and women and they needed money. There was a feeling on the streets that the banks were only Anglo fortresses. 'Les maudits anglais' and 'les autres!' You remember all this? So then the FLQ started to hit some banks as well. Sometimes there would be open gun-battles on the street here in downtown. Citizens would get hit in the cross-fire. I know one time they tried to scoop a man from a café on Metcalfe. He saw them coming and ducked down behind the customers. Bullets flew every-where. Ice cream dishes burst apart. The Cinzano awnings got all cut up. The customers were on their bellies in the sidewalk. Miraculous that no one was hurt at all. The man, finally he ran out of ammunition and he just stands up and surrenders. Everyone was cursing us. But that was how it went in those days. If you couldn't out-gun them you were useless. On the squad we had very little of the movie detective stuff. We got our information and we laid our traps. It got rough sometimes. But we took the streets back."

The nostalgia was deliberate and intentional. DuRoche got up to greet an older man, a huge tanned man in a beige three-piece suit with a large and badly-knotted tie. The new arrival lowered himself into an oak office chair, leaned it back against a worn patch on the wall, and threw a heavy canvas bag on the desk. It hit with a metallic clunk.

"I thought you'd like to see what we use out on the street. You know something about guns, eh?" DuRoche said nothing, although the new man was a stranger to me. He didn't wait for me to answer.

"I have been with this force thirty years now. Gone through two wives. It's not the fashion now to have tough cops. Now we have college graduates with degrees. Little boys who think you can talk your way out of anything. Kindness will tame the criminals. They are only misunderstood. I tell you, and you can tell the papers, that no college boy will ever learn how to be a cop in a classroom. I learned on the street!" Here, he struck himself in the middle of his vest with a large clenched fist. The impact was like pounding a tree. He pushed the chair off the wall and leaned forward very close to me. He had thick black hairs on the backs of his hands and his face was pouchy and bitter. "We let the soft cops run the department and pretty soon the crooks will have the city back again. Then, we have another war. But not me! I'm retiring next year. You want to know about how we work. I brought the tools along for you to see. Look at this! These are what keeps Montréal safe!" He stood up and jerked the zipper back on the canvas bag. It fell open and the big man reached into it. He pulled out a machine gun and two thirty-shot clips. Each clip was fully-loaded. He cleared the action on the machine gun to make sure it was unloaded and handed it to me. As I took it from him he reached into his suit jacket and pulled out a Colt Python and laid it down on the table. He smacked the desk top beside the gun.

"Firepower. Guns and a street cop with sense. That's what keeps the city in line. You tell them that in your paper. Maudit étudiants!" Saying this, he scooped up the weaponry and put the Python back into his shoulder holster, zipped up the bag, and clumped heavily from the office. I watched him go with what had to be a particularly inane look on my face, because DuRoche started to laugh, a broad full-chested sound in the tiny cubicle.

"Quite the one, eh? Don't you pay Roger too much mind. He's pissed because he thinks the babies are taking over the police force. That man has been on the detective force here for almost twenty years, and before that ten years in uniform. He's one of the old-style cops. All blood and guts. But his bite is worse than his bark, eh?"

I corrected the useage, thinking he had reversed the metaphor.

"No no no," he interrupted me, "I meant that. He's killed a few men who thought otherwise. When Roger says to the crook 'drop your gun' the crook has only one second to decide. If not, Roger decides for him. On the street, when a crook sees Roger, he goes the other way. Around here, he's someone the younger guys look up to. Maybe his views are old-fashioned. But in his time he has done more good police work than ten other guys. Now he's old and angry. Like an old bear. No patience. I think we'll all get that way, in time. The work does it."

I asked him why that was.

DuRoche was silent for a full minute. His open fair-skinned face was quiet. I noticed a laceration around the left ear. A row of freckles dotted the bridge of his nose. He was either thirty-five or ten; the combination of boyishness and experience gave him a memorable face. One eyebrow went up in a very Gallic way, startling in that Irish face.

"Change," he said. "Everything is changing on the street. The old faces are gone. The hoods are younger every year. But not only that. Everyone is . . . worse. Crazy. Unpredictable. Roger thinks everything now is crazier than when he was starting. And I think everyone is crazier now than when I started. Something is happening to the streets."

I asked him to explain. He told me a story.

* * *

"There was this kid, let's call him Noel Croxon. That's close enough to his real name so that if he reads this he can figure out what I think of him. He was in Montréal from out of town, an Anglais, not one of our kids. Now there is a difference between the Anglo kids and the French kids. The Anglos love to fight. They'll stand up and brawl in the bars in the west end. Those are bad places, but not dangerous places. Fights all the time, but not a lot of weapons. For weapons, you have to go to east Montréal, to the French streets. For some reason, it's always the French kids who love to shoot each other up. I was in uniform patrolling those streets and it was crazy even fifteen years ago. Guns and knives everywhere. Noel was Anglais but he also loved the guns. Now this part I can't tell exactly like it happened because I had finks involved, and other people. But the centre of it is true, the part about the streets and how they changed. Anyway . . . Croxon finds himself a flat up in Laval. At this time he's not yet twenty-five. I'm talking about a period less than two years ago. This isn't ancient history. Croxon does not go looking for work. He's a dealer, into drugs and that kind of thing. A little part-time fencing. I heard also some minor theft, stuff under two hundred dollars. He had a record for petty crime going back to his eleventh birthday, or damn near it. I still maintain that some kids are born criminal. I hear a lot of bullshit about how society has failed this poor child and how we are all to blame whenever a punk rapes his mother or shoots up a schoolyard. If you want to know what most cops think about that, they think it's a defence lawyer's wet dream. The worse the crime, the more deprived the criminal. He killed so we stink. Anytime that idea gets real acceptance in the courts and you can say goodbye to civilisation. If nobody is responsible, if nobody has to say 'look, I know I got rough treatment but I'm not going to pass it on' then we'll have anarchy. Society has to have the will to protect itself. You have to think that you have something worth protecting, even if you feel the guy attacking you got a raw deal. And Croxon, from what I can figure out, never had a raw deal.

"It doesn't take him long to make his connections. He came into town with references. The drug people are pretty tight; they know who to call to get information. They're careful. Croxon got some deals, made some money in Laval and Saint Leonard. The Drug Squad began to see him around in the bars. The finks got onto him.

"Finks . . . you know what a fink is? The definition of a good detective is a cop with good finks. You acquire finks like you build up stocks. A guy gets busted for something, you do a deal for information on someone bigger. After a while, it becomes a financial agreement. There's a set rate for finks in this office, and every fink has a registration number. We actually have a file on each fink. He has to give that number whenever he phones in a tip. No number, no cheque. That's another thing that drives the old guard wild. It used to be that a man had his finks, they were *his*, like a man runs horses. He took care of them. It was a matter of trust. But now they want to have finks registered so that the cop doesn't have control of them, so that he can't pull them off when he goes, like a salesman will take his best clients. The brass wants to control the force. No individuals. Anyway, a fink is your best way to get information off the street. Our finks talked to us about the new kid in town. We got ID from ceepick. He was just a small-time punk. Drug Squad was on him. We left him alone. But Croxon had a dream. He wanted to get into the big time.

"Croxon started going through his friends, talking about needing a driver. He was setting up a big score, and he wanted a car and a good driver to take care of things. Croxon was just a little guy, jeans and long hair, the usual street punk. Maybe the reputation Montréal had for bank jobs was what got into him. When he started casting around for a driver, the finks got wind of it and put it on the wire. But there was so much talk and so little action from most of them that it got lost in the crowd.

"There used to be a professional cadre of bank-robbers in Montréal, as I said. These were men who had decided to rob banks for a living. It was what they did, like somebody works in a bank or drives a cab. These guys were what I call professional criminals. They took precautions and they were dangerous, but they never killed for fun. For kicks. Croxon was not like that.

"Croxon had a piece. He'd picked it up from the druggies. They always have a piece around somewhere, to protect themselves from rip-offs and to enforce collections. Croxon got a revolver from some friends in the crowd. An illegal piece will run fifty to two hundred cash. It gets sold in a brown paper bag in the parking lot of a bar, just the same as heroin or grass or speed. Now after a few weeks of setting it up, Croxon has a piece and a driver and he has a car picked out. He settled on a bank in west Montréal, with good entrances and wide streets. He spent the night before at a friend's house, drinking, and they both went out to meet his driver in the middle of the night. The driver had already stolen a car. The driver did not know Croxon, and Croxon didn't really know the driver. That is how it is these days, a casual meeting of strangers for a one-time only hit on a bank. Divide the money in the car, drop the car, change to other vehicles, and everybody goes in different directions. No professionalism. No experience. And lots of drugs to give them courage.

"In the bank, Croxon was jumpy and tense. He had the gun in his pants, a revolver. When his turn comes up he steps forward and sticks the gun in this teller's face and screams that he wants all the cash. She froze in the spot. You can imagine why. Everybody talks about facing a gun. It's in all the movies. But you don't know what it's like until you face it. This young woman froze. Now a pro, he would have recognized this. He would have gone to another place. He would have had the whole bank controlled. Or he might have decided that the job was blown and he'd get the hell out of there.

"Croxon shot the woman in the face. She was dead before she hit the floor. Most of the back of her head was gone. Croxon got nothing. The place went wild, and he split. Our finks located him and we scooped him alive. All the time he was on trial, all he said was 'killing her was her fault. If she hadn't of panicked, I wouldn't have had to kill her.'

"*That's* the part I mean when I say the street is changing. There are kids out there, there isn't anything they wouldn't do. Old ladies get murdered for pension cheques. Young women get their faces blown off for nothing. And all you'll ever hear from the killers is how it wasn't really their fault, or how the bitch asked for it. We have killers out there now like little robots. A life is nothing to them. People are like kleenex to them. Use them and throw them away.

"The part that gets to me is that, as a cop, you get to see the aftermath. The consequences. On TV when somebody dies, the camera fades out to a commercial. In real life, you're sitting in the office and the phone rings. There's been a hit out in Outremont. A teller is dead. You scream out there and the place is all tangled up with cops and barricades. On the floor behind the counter there's a body with no face. Sometimes, in a head shot, the heart will go on for a while. There's lots of blood. Guys in business suits are going around with little plastic baggies, scraping bits of bone and brain off the filing cabinets. Over in the corner the office girls are crying. The manager is shaking with anger. On the street people are excited and curious. Right in the middle of all this, but past it, there's this body on the floor. The dress has run up a little. She has nice legs. Her body is kind of sprawled, in that rag-doll way bodies have. As if they had no bones. She's dead forever.

"If you're lucky, you get to go and tell the family. In this case, the Croxon thing, the trial was over for a good year before the husband stopped telling himself his wife was just in the hospital and she'd be better soon. I had him in this office, sitting right there, talking about when his wife got out of the hospital he was going to take her to the Caribbean to recuperate. He was a stockbroker. They were going to have a family. All of that got cancelled in a second, by a kid with no feelings, by a bug. Croxon will be out in fifteen years. The girl will be dead forever. Her husband lost his job, his home. He's just now putting himself back together. It's the *cost* of everything that wears you out. Croxon didn't have to pull the trigger. Nobody was threatening him. I think he wanted to. To see how it would feel.

"That's what is new on the street. Something we hardly ever had before. The new breed of criminal. The bugs."

* * *

DuRoche's hard-nosed attitude towards the criminals he opposed as an Armed Robbery detective was typical of everyone I spoke to on the Montreal force. Perhaps because Montreal has had a violent history, the policemen who dealt with the street were different from other men and women I had met in other cities. There was little theorizing, and less patience for psychoanalytical apologias for criminal behaviour. The lines were clear-cut and final. There were bugs on the street with guns, therefore the police would be on the street with guns. The system for controlling bank robberies in Montreal, which has affected a fifty per cent drop in the rate, has been so successful that softer cities such as Toronto and Vancouver are seeing an increase in their bank robbery rates. It's a good system. DuRoche walked me through it.

The force maintained an independent unit whose sole function was surveillance. Information from finks, or informers, who were out on the street and mixing in the bars, would be analysed to determine the most likely targets for surveillance. Anyone with a history of robbery, anyone who seemed to be going through the motions of assembling a group, anyone who looked ready, was placed under full-time twenty-four-hour surveillance. I suspect that phones were tapped, and that FM wires were installed in apartments and cars. Everything the target did or said was taped, photographed, observed, and analysed. Surveillance briefs were delivered to members of the Armed Robbery Squad, who may have had three or four different men on their files, marked for observation. Experience had shown the operators that targets getting close to a bank hit exhibited certain signs. They tended to stay in one place. Members of the team might arrive for a final discussion. Sometimes the robber would buy a woman, or some drugs, or do something else that was suggestive of a man under tension. Since it was often impossible to determine which bank was targeted, the surveillance teams had to stay on the man wherever he went. If the hit looked imminent, the surveillance teams would notify the Armed Robbery Squad.

Montreal police had recently completed a major effort to persuade the management of the Big Five banks, and the trust companies, to install video camera monitoring equipment in their branches. Almost every branch in the city of Montreal was now equipped with this gear, which ran automatically and which taped every transaction taking place in the bank during public hours. The infinite re-useability of video tape made it possible to record the action on the bank floor cheaply and reliably. More importantly, it sent a clear message to anyone casing the bank for a possible hold-up: cameras running here.

The tactical effect of this was two-fold; first, it meant that anyone hitting a bank so equipped would have to accept the fact of being photographed in the crime, something that made subsequent protestations of innocence rather Kafkaesque; and secondly, anyone wishing to keep his face off the screen would have to come into the bank masked. Masked men entering a bank are rarely agents of the Lone Ranger, a fact with which all bank managers are familiar. Tripping a silent alarm is often a matter of moving a toe three inches under a desk and pressing a button. Sometimes, it's a matter of *not* pressing a button when a certain cash drawer is opened. The systems are varied and subtle. Side-stepping such security systems takes time, diligence, careful thought, and a wealth of inside information. These commodities are not often found in the new breed of robber described by DuRoche. So cameras in a bank provide solid evidence in the commission, and also present tactical problems to the robbers. Having established these systems in the Montreal banks, the Armed Robbery squad was able to devise a solid suppressive tactic for dealing with robbers.

When the surveillance team notified the squad that a suspect was nearing the hit, DuRoche and other men of the squad would pick up their weapons and head for the scene. The weaponry was usually composed of automatic riot shotguns firing number six shot, standard Smith and Wesson Police .38 Specials, some high-calibre small arms such as the Colt Forty-Five, the Browning .9mm, and the Colt .357 Magnum, "varmint" rifles with scopes for long-distance sniping, one or two M 1 Carbines, firing semi-automatically, loaded with thirty-shot clips of .30 calibre cartridges, and the Smith and Wesson .9mm machine gun the older cop had dropped on the table in front of me, a formidable weapon capable of full auto fire. Full auto machine-gun fire is something that has to be seen to be appreciated. And heard.

Aside from this weaponry, the team members carried Kevlar body armour, pocket FM handsets, and handcuffs. All the men were big, muscular, and oddly gentle in their manner. Everyone was in typical plainclothes detective clothing, a business suit, shirt and pull-away tie, trench coats, rubber-soled shoes. They would pile into four ordinary-looking unmarked sedans and head out for the scene of the impending robbery.

If everything ran according to plan, the surveillance team would already be in position near the bank. The disguises worn by this specialist team ranged from street vendors to hydro workers. There was always a central Observation Post set up somewhere within the line of sight of the bank. The OP, which could be in a van or the second floor of a hotel, contained communication gear, video cameras, still cameras with telephoto lenses up to 2000 mm, infra-red sensors, video-taping gear, and some classified gear. The robbery squad would pull up within a few hundred yards and identify themselves on the FM tactical channel linking them with the surveillance team. While the robbers were pulling into the area, the robbery squad and assisting uniform cars would move to seal off various avenues of escape. Then, everyone would wait. If the teams are skilled, an entire city block can be pinned down and controlled without a single citizen becoming aware of the operation. I've seen it done, and it's amazing how little attention the average citizen pays to activities on the streets around him. On any downtown street in any Canadian city, there are under-cover, plainclothes, and security service operations going on almost all the time. It's fascinating to watch the strollers wander through sections of the street that are being filmed or guarded or simply monitored by OP's in various locations. It's also a little disturbing to consider how effective the process is, and how difficult to detect.

Everyone holds his or her position until the robbers are in the bank. The aim of the team is to do nothing to provoke a shoot-out at this point. The people in the bank, if there has been time to do so, have been warned of the attack impending. Plainclothes men will be stationed inside to control any excesses on the part of the robbers. But the aim of this phase is to allow the men to rob the bank and get safely outside onto the street. At that point, the police will have obtained irrefutable evidence of the crime and the actions of the men involved. In-branch cameras will photograph the men in the act. Cameras and sound gear from the OP van will also record the action. Squad members will observe the details and provide witnesses for the Crown in later court actions. It's not the aim of the team to blow the robbers into oblivion in a spectacular shoot-out on a public street. The point of the thing, as DuRoche put it, is to "jail the bastards, not nail the bastards!"

Once the robbery has been completed, the men will usually head for the front doors in a rush. If the job has been broken a long time before, they may be unwittingly carrying FM traces and ultra-violet inked bills. All through the crime, members of the police squads keep up a running commentary on the movements and actions of the criminals. The man with the ultimate responsibility for dealing with unexpected alterations in the scenario is the Sergent de Détectives of the Armed Robbery squad whose finks turned the crook in the first place. As he listens to the action, he has to assess the progress and to plan the final stages.

When the robbers get to the doors, two things are possible. They may split up and leave in different directions, trusting to the crowds and the streets to cover their escape. Or they may get back into the car and roar away from the scene as fast as they can. If they split up, there are men in position to tail, trap, and arrest them on the street. If they run according to custom, they'll get into the car and try for an escape that way. This is where the driver comes into his own; he's been chosen for his knowledge of the streets and his nerve. Everyone in the getaway car is on the edge, nervous, exhilarated. If they sense the slightest thing wrong with the street, they'll panic. Given the standards of violence demonstrated by most of the new criminals on the street, that panic will probably result in a wild shoot-out with a high likelihood of injury to innocent bystanders. So the squads stay out of sight while the robbers make their moves. Nine times out of ten, they climb into a car and drive off. Now the last stage begins.

The surveillance teams drop away. The uniform cars, responding to the tactical direction of the Armed Robbery detective, clear the path in front of the getaway car. The Armed Robbery squad commence a flanking and tailing operation designed to get four of their cars, with two detectives in each car, positioned on parallel side streets, and ahead and behind the getaway car. This process can take a little while, and it's always difficult, unpredictable, and vital. What the men in the four cars are waiting for is an opportunity to make one sudden and unavoidable assault, boxing in the getaway car, preventing a high-speed chase. It's a practice in Montreal to give the robbers a few blocks to calm down, to congratulate themselves, to relax their vigilance. Carrying out this kind of a process on the crowded, twisting streets in Montreal calls for a variety of skills, not the least of which is self-control.

Finally, the car will come into an assailable position. A stoplight, a narrow underpass, a street wide enough to allow a rapid movement of the flanking cars. In an instant the men in the getaway car will find themselves surrounded by four unmarked cars, one in front, jammed up to the grillwork, one in behind, pushing up into the trunk, and one on either side, so close that they can't open the doors. Men in trench coats are everywhere, guns out and shotguns aimed. This assault is over in less than five seconds. The getaway car is at the centre of a circle of weaponry and hard-faced men. If the operation is a success, the men in the centre of this circle will arrive at the conclusion that any attempt at resistance would be suicidal. Nine times out of ten, that's the way it happens.

On the tenth assault, people die. There's no middle ground.

"It's a hard business," DuRoche told me, as we ruffled through a sheet of wanted men. "These new guys, they aren't easy to predict. You have to be ready to shoot, because they sure as hell are ready to shoot you. If you can't live with that, you should quit and apply for Community Relations or Traffic. Me," he slapped his chest with a folder, "I'm here for good. I'm a thirty-year man. Like Roger. Years from now I'll call you up and tell you how *great* it used to be. Right now, they hate us on the street. But Montréal is my city, and nobody is going to run the streets in this town but us."

CHAPTER SEVEN

Drug Squad in Vancouver

The Blackstone Hotel on Granville Street in Vancouver is to heroin trafficking what La Scala is to opera. Setting yourself up in the heroin trade in Vancouver can be, and usually is, accomplished in the following manner. An enterprising young man or woman from one of the eastern provinces, usually departing his home town under something of a legal cloud and trailing a confetti of Non-Returnable Warrants can arrive, penniless, in downtown Vancouver. He, let's say he, because it usually *is* a he, checks into one of the flophouses on Granville Street near Davie or Drake, a third-floor cold-water flat with one army cot, one cream-coloured dresser, one overhead forty-watt bulb in a wire cage, one window overlooking a brick wall, one plasterboard door with a bolt-lock, uncounted multi-pedal room-mates, and a wash-room of unique design a few steps down the hall. Having been briefed by previous scouts, he cleans himself up and takes a bus over to the nearest office of the British Columbia Human Resources office. A concerned counsellor will conduct a short interview, during which he will convey the impression that, although he has recently fallen on difficult times, he truly wishes to make his mark in the new land by dint of honest labour, thusly to rise above the humble station an inimical fate has decreed for him and lay the modest foundations of what will become, given vigour, courage, and the help of God almighty, a new life – none of which either party will actually believe but which will allow the weary counsellor to enter the supplicant's name on the welfare rolls, a very long list, as it happens. If the supplicant is crafty, and they usually are, he will sign a form claiming, with a steady eye and an unblushing cheek, that he has been residing in British Colum-bia for a period of better than two weeks. This harmless fiction can, if he's lucky, produce for him in a matter of hours a cheque in his name for a sum of money somewhere in the region of $350. Step One is now complete. Step Two is rather more complex. Step Two takes place around the Blackstone Hotel. These are deep waters, dirty waters. Crowded waters.

* * *

More rain. It was sliding down the windshield of the Monte Carlo, running in the gutters beside the window, drumming on the vinyl roof. Ike, the Drug Squad cop I had last seen in an alley way over on Davie Street, the one with blond hair and a tough good-looking face, was sitting motionless in the passenger seat, trying to keep the front door of the Blackstone in some kind of focus. We were parked tight up on the curb, engine off, lights off, in a dark stretch of Granville Street south of Helmcken. It was nearly nine o'clock. The shops and clothing stores and fast food places were winding it up for the night. Across the wide street people were arriving at the Blackstone, a mixed crowd of street toughs, local people heading down to the bar for a few beers, some Indians and some blacks, lots of single men of varying ages, strutting, shambling, some of them even staggering this early in the season. The centre of our attention was an addict named Hoppy, one of the Drug Squad's semi-mascots, who was making a very tentative foray in the direction of the hotel doors. The rain on the screen was making it very difficult to watch Hoppy, and watching the addicts was the whole purpose of the exercise. Ike picked up a handset radio from the seat beside him.

"Finn . . . yo, Finn . . . this is Ike. We have our buddy Hoppy on the street. Looks like business is about to get done. Watch for him in your sector." The radio popped, hissed, and a dry voice answered: "Copy that, Ike. Nothing doing here so far." Ike's partner, a big dark bear of a man whose name was Burns, shifted his weight in the blue velour, sent me another unfriendly look over his right shoulder, and said to Ike, "This is bullshit, let's go in and look around."

Ike hesitated. "Sure, let's show him the Blackstone."

Burns, looking away, said, "I mean you and me, Ike. He can wait."

Burns was making it clear that my presence in the backseat of the surveillance car was an irritating breach of police solidarity and would lead to nothing but grief. Frankly, I couldn't blame Burns; a year before this the Canadian Broadcasting Corporation had convinced the department brass to let them send a mobile camera unit out on the road with the Vancouver Drug Squad. The Squad was famous right across Canada for their skilled and relentless pursuit of small-time and medium-grade heroin dealers on the streets of the city. The RCMP, who literally own all major drug-busting operations nation-wide, used the men and women of Vancouver's Drug Squad to give their own rookies on-the-job training. It was pretty well accepted that there were no better street cops on that job in any other spot in Canada. The CBC's instincts had, as usual, been correct; the Drug Squad was good juicy stuff for the market. The Chief had ridden down the resistance of the men in the Squad, who, being policemen, found the job hard enough to do without slamming into observers and hang-abouts every six yards. This difficulty can be described in terms of the Heisenberg Uncertainty Principle, which maintains that a basic problem of any research scientist is to find a way to closely observe every aspect of a phenomenon without allowing the means of observing to affect in any way that which is being observed. As a writer I found it hard enough to get in close enough to follow the action with nothing in my hands but a small black notebook.

The CBC crew had been as unobtrusive and discreet as an amphibious landing in a wading pool. Under orders to co-operate, the Drug Squad teams had somehow managed to carry out street-jumps, kick-ins, and difficult surveillance work in spite of the complicating effects of the Heisenberg Uncertainty Principle. The CBC emerged relatively unscathed with several hours worth of pretty good stuff; gritty, street-level, atmospheric as hell. For reasons difficult to posit from afar, they chose to concentrate on one disastrous kick-in where members of the Squad, nervous and jumpy with strangers on their heels and lights glaring in their faces, lost their grips and their tempers. A woman who was in the house and who got into the way of the rush was slightly roughed up – I've seen the tape and it was slight – and pushed out of the way. Edited *a posteriori* as only the television news boys can, the Vancouver Drug Squad arose into the bright light of the news world as a muscle-bound herd of maniacal oafs charging about the streets of Vancouver kicking in the doors of innocent civilians and thumping their womenfolk off walls like a team of squash-playing gorillas. The camera crew won national kudos. Back at home several members of the Drug Squad found themselves back in uniform and working in Evidence storage or Traffic records. The Chief, who values his image, stuck a few figurative cop's heads on stakes outside the Public Safety Building and publicly disavowed any knowledge . . . as the phrase goes.

Given all this, it takes no quantum leap of the intellect to discern the roots of Burns' resentment against the Press in general. Ike, who may have felt exactly the same, was one of the most good-natured and charming people I've ever met and had difficulty maintaining this level of mistrust with anyone short of a convicted murderer, so he treated me as if I were an honourable man and waited to find out if I was not. To this day I have not been able to figure out why they let me go along in the first place. No one had ordered them to do so, and I had been commanded not to push the point. The fact remains that I was right on their heels when Burns and Ike climbed out of the light blue Monte Carlo on that rainy evening in Vancouver and we all walked together across Granville and into the Blackstone Hotel.

One of Claude Rains' best lines in *Casablanca* was "Everybody comes to Rick's" and it was there in my mind when we pushed inside. Under a long back-lit sign in Gothic letters what may once have been an art-deco entrance had been reduced to flat brick walls slanting inwards to a pair of oak doors. Inside, the main bar was little more than a huge high-ceilinged hall inadequately lit, smoky, suffused in a feverish yellow light. Tables were scattered around the perimeter in a rough U pattern, more or less facing a four-foot high stage on which a five-piece Country and Western band was enthusiastically dismembering an old Fats Domino tune called "I'm Walkin'" without any discernible opposition from the few old rummies and their understudies slouching at the tables, elbows wet in the spilled beer, eyes as empty as holes punched in plaster. The place was filling up fast, though. By the time we completed a couple of circuits there were close to a hundred people ordering up tray-loads of attenuated draft from the tough-tender waitresses, all of whom looked like serious casualties of the gravity wars in elastic chinos and sensible pumps. They went at it with a will, however, rushing from table to table, hairstyles firmly laquered in place, smiling big smiles through out-of-register lip gloss, pale white cheeks dusted like cold-rolled pastry, the sinews on their already sweating forearms pumped up by years of carrying tin trays to the celebrants. The floor was a mixed-media triumph in parquet, tile, astro-turf, and old vomit, much sinned against by the patrons. It was a bad bar no different from ten thousand other bad bars in Canada, distinguished only by its reputation for heroin traffic and the odd creative murder. It could jump late at night, however; it was possible to have the best night of your life in a bad bar. Who could you possibly outrage?

On the way out I asked Ike why the city didn't simply close the place down. I had seen enough by-law infractions to close the Chateau Frontenac and I wasn't half-trying. When he smiled his face broke up into a fan of deep lines around his eyes, which were a kind of quick-frozen blue. He slapped me on the back and pushed me through the doorway. I bumped into Hoppy on the way out.

"Now that bar back there is a den of iniquity, I agree. Most of the people in it are just having a good time, no harm intended, just getting plowed on a Saturday night. Great National Tradition. But there are rats in there, using the bar as a market place and your point, which is well-taken if a bit benighted, is that we should close the whole bar down because a few rats are living in it. By that reasoning they were right to drive the *Titanic* into an iceberg because they drowned a multitude of rats by doing it. I'll ask you a question in return . . . where would you rather have rats, *if* you had to have rats somewhere? Would you like to have them running all over your living room and poo-pooing on the Bokhara or would you like to keep them in a box in your basement? Granville Street is the box in Vancouver's basement. We learned our lesson with the hookers here. Last year we started busting them like mad, giving them hard times, on the orders of the city council. The hookers were giving Granville Street and Georgia a bad name. So what happened? They all went over to Davie Street. I understand you spent some time there. Not an improvement. We're not thrilled with the crowd on Granville Street, but at least we know where the sons of bitches *are!*"

His partner had walked ahead to the car. As we got to it, Burns rolled down his window, "Get in – we've got something happening here." Ike and I were hardly belted in before Burns had the car rolling.

"A couple of uniforms called in. They think there's a buy going down at the McDonald's. Sherman and Bradshaw are on a couple of hypes so they want us to check it out." Burns swung the car hard right and cut up a rear lane behind the shops. Ike was on the handset. "Finn . . . we're going to check out that call. Anything happening in the room?" The handset always hissed once. "Finn here. Ah, that's a roger. Nothing doing here yet. Keep in touch." Burns pulled the car up at the top of the lane. Over to the right, across the street, a group of kids were bopping in and out of the orange-and-red plastic eat-o-matic barrens of the franchise store, skull-faced and bleached out in the fluorescent glow. The kids were all boys, pushing and shoving and laughing. There were no patrolmen in sight. When I asked about that, Burns growled.

"There's no point in having an unmarked car on the spot if you have uniforms crawling all over it. That's why we told you and your partners to beat it over on Davie Street. They know better than to get close to us. The point is to remain inconspicuous, not prance around the streets with bells and whistles on. That's what the uniforms are supposed to do." That was more than I'd heard from him all night.

"Lookie lookie," said Ike, grinning. "Is that numb-nuts, what's his name, the guy we busted last month, the French-Canadian?" He was looking at a group of three men leaning on the counter of the McDonald's, heads close, hands moving. Burns leaned over for a better look.

"Yeah, yeah, that's him. LaFreniere. That look like a buy to you?"

Ike considered for a moment, watching. "Hell of a stupid place for it, under the lights. Is LaFreniere that stupid?"

Burns literally snorted. "That dork has a sheet on the ceepick longer than my – " Ike punched his shoulder. "Consider the Press, buddy. Let's control our speech. What's the first thing they taught you in policeman's school?" Burns laughed. At least sounds came from way down deep in his chest that could have been laughing sounds.

"You know that . . . the scum rises and payday's Thursday!"

"Not that . . . the *other* rule. If you can't say something nice . . . ?"

"You must be a sergeant. Nah, that's no buy. Not a hype in the room. Let's go do an alley. It'll be an hour before the shooter gets on the street. Those uniforms are worse than hairdressers." He hit the starter and drove straight out onto Helmcken, chuckling softly to himself. His hardcase shell was cracking.

Ninety-nine per cent of all police work is boring as hell. Routine is just a word until you've spent twenty hours in the back seat of a stuffy cruiser smoking bad cigarettes, drinking bad coffee, listening to everybody bitch about the brass or their wives or the goddamned government, with nothing to break the monotony but a blacked-out apartment window over a storefront that you are supposed to keep unswervingly in view until your relief comes. This process is known as a stakeout. It constitutes a great deal of the work in Drug Squad detail. Stake-outs can go on for weeks, months, hours, minutes, leading to one of three things: a large overweight zero and flack from management, an ulcer and a weight problem, or, occasionally, another unit of information that may or may not lead eventually to a police raid and a decent drug bust. Men on details such as this spend more time with each other than they do with their wives, if they still have wives. It takes a very special type to put up with the drudgery, the constant suspension of life, fast food eaten on the fly, the pettiness, the gossip, the slow painful accumulation of particles of information that might lead to a case. Every young constable dreams about the Drug Squad. Everybody on the Drug Squad dreams about time off. Ike and Burns had just come off a three-week stake-out that had led to the closure of a restaurant on Granville run by a dealer named Jerry. The raid had taken place a few days before. When we drove by the place Ike and Burns would grin and chuckle. They had kicked the doors in, the whole Drug Squad, all twelve of them, along with a bunch of uniforms. People were flying in all directions, plates, glasses, waiters, customers. Jerry hid under the bar until Ike had dragged him out by the heels, shaken him upside down for a while. Out in the street the hypes had tears in their eyes. It was as if someone had closed down Eaton's. After things settled down and the paddy wagons were pulling away, Burns had pinned a sign on the glass door. It read: "Closed By Order Of The Drug Squad!" Somewhere in Jerry's Grill the cops believed he had hidden almost thirty grand in cash. They watched it every night, just to see if Jerry sent anyone to get it.

"Jerry's was a joy to nail." Ike passed me a chicken wing and a cup of Chinese tea. We were sitting in a restaurant called the Blue Eagle, on Hastings Street, in Vancouver's China Town.

The Blue Eagle is a tiled box, leading back through greasy glass windows about fifteen feet tall, over a tile floor and under an old-fashioned tin-plate roof painted dark brown. There are two blocks of booths, one double, one single, constructed on solid walnut. The lighting is overhead fluorescent tube, long banks of them suspended by wires from the tin roof. It was put together in the Thirties and it hasn't changed much since. The cream-coloured walls have old Korean calendars on them, faded and bleached-out portraits of mountains and ports. The owner has stopped putting doors up in the bathroom because the Drug Squad guys have kicked in every one of the last nine. The owner has one of the worst faces in Vancouver, which is going some, a grizzled pock-marked mud-coloured wobbling mask punctuated by two narrow black eyes that slant upwards and out into a network of laugh-lines and wrinkles as dense and as finely-cut as the underside of a tobacco leaf. He used to have a lot of trouble with the street kids who came over from the skids on Abbot and Cordova to break up the "chinaman's" grill. Ike was a rookie patrolman then, about seventeen years back. His beat was Hastings. He and his partner made it a point to "assist" the owner in controlling the toughs. They "controlled" the problem so well that the Blue Eagle became a kind of unofficial club house for the Vancouver police. The little owner bobs his grizzled head and frowns every time they walk over to the cash. Ike has to push the money into the till himself. Burns reveals an heroic capacity for apple pie and ice cream. The chicken wings come with a sweet-and-sour glaze as pure as tiger's eye. Even Burns gets worked up over the kick-in at Jerry's place.

"There are dealers and there are dealers, understand?" Burns had a trick of setting his jaw and inclining one ear, just so, waiting for an answer. It gave him a belligerent air.

"Well, Jerry's was a big operation. Heroin in British Columbia ain't what it used to be, as the saying goes. Back in the late Sixties, early Seventies, we had heroin in this town the best in the world. And a lot of it. They were making million-dollar busts every second Tuesday. Naturally, Vancouver gets the rep for dope nation-wide. That's fine for the RCMP. According to the statute, only the RCMP has the legal jurisdiction to fight drug traffic in Canada. Any buy over five hundred dollars has to be okayed by the RCMP. They literally *own* the drug war. It's *their* territory. To tell you the truth, they can be a major pain in the ass about it. But that's another story. Anyway, you know about CLU? The Combined Law Enforcement Unit. That's us, and Major Crimes, a few other departments. We were formed to work with the RCMP, to get together and control the heroin traffic in Vancouver. Some kind of treaty had to be worked out, otherwise you never knew if you were busting a genuine dealer or some RCMP undercover operator. Even now, they only tell us what they want you to know. They play it close to the vest. Anything really big belongs to them and them alone. I'll tell you the compost really hits the air circulation system when we step over that line. Like a bunch of sorority girls in a panty raid. Don't tell 'em I said that. Oh shit, go ahead. Anyway, about Jerry's – "

"Finally!" Ike was laughing at Burns' sudden talkativeness.

Burns shot Ike a hot look, which Ike ignored. Burns went on. "Jerry was dealing right out of his storefront. It was like a stage show. The hypes were having a party. It was lousy stuff, stepped on eight, nine times. But it was still dope and it was going for ten bucks a capsule. Jerry was so cocky about it we thought maybe he was fronting for the RCMP. That's *not* impossible. Last year they had a new dealer around here. I hated the guy right from the start. He was a real maggot, filthy clothes, smelled like a dead buzzard, always shooting his mouth off.

He was in from Quebec, had a string of priors, some Non-Returnable Warrants from Quebec. Set himself up in the drug business here on welfare money. He was up and down the street, always hustling and trading. We street-jumped him several times, and whenever we did, he kicked and punched. Now *that's* against the rules. Most hypes, once you've got them, once they know they're not going to be able to fix, they go limp, relax. They can always get another cap later. *This* guy, he'd kick like a bastard. I learned to hate him deeply and truly, which isn't something I usually do. You let yourself hate in this job and it's a ticket to ulcerville. For this guy, I was prepared to make an exception. This went on for some time – knock it off, man, this is *my* story!" Ike had been trying to break into the conversation, obviously bursting with an internal need to drive his partner right up the wall. Burns ignored him.

"Finally, there's a humungous RCMP CLU bust, something I know *zip* about," and he sent Ike another accusatory look, "and we're sitting in the court house when who should appear but this maggot I'd been thumping all winter. He was an undercover cop. Every time I smacked him, he'd get in stronger with the hypes. I *made* that turkey's case for him." Ike was chuckling into a black coffee. Burns was silent for a moment.

"You know what, though. Even after all that. I *still* hate that kid!" Something started to squeal in Ike's jacket.

"Ah hah! *Attenzione*, troops . . . the enemy approacheth!"

* * *

"Roger Finn . . . we are in position. What's happening?" We were back in the car, sitting in a delivery bay off Granville. We could still make out the door of the Blackstone. Burns was talking to another squad man, apparently one carrying a wire standing inside the bar itself. He was known as the Spotter. From his position in the crowd, he was responsible for detecting the transfer of a cap of heroin from a dealer to a hype. The dealers in Vancouver rarely held the caps themselves. The system worked as follows.

A dealer would "come down" from some major drug hiding place with a shipment of heroin. The heroin was sold in small gelatin capsules, after being diluted about eight times with milk powder or sugar. The dealer would meet an accomplice at a bar, usually the Blackstone or the Drake or a grill like Jerry's. The accomplice was known as a "shooter", a "banker", and his job was to actually deal off the caps in singles or doubles to any hype with ten or twenty bucks. The dealer arrived at the Blackstone with the heroin stored somewhere on his body. Actually, to be frank, he arrived with it stored somewhere *in* his body, not to put too fine a point on it. Internal storage of this nature was known as "suitcasing" the stash. Men had one option. Women had two. Women could "suitcase" the heroin, or "overnight" it. The caps were contained in rubber safes or party balloons. When the dealer had checked out the bar, looking for obvious undercover types, anyone new or anyone acting too interested in his activities, he would go to the washroom and, ah, shall we say, retrieve, the party balloon full of heroin caps. The number of caps would depend on several factors; the demand on the street, the supply available, the dealer's need for cash, his health. Once the balloon was in his hands, he'd wash it and pocket it. Sometimes, the dealer would put the balloon in his mouth, resting it in a cheek. That method made it tricky to jump him. If a Drug Squad team attempted to bust him on his way to the "shooter", the dealer had only to swallow the balloon and he was safe. Sort of. The police were required to find evidence of heroin possession on his person. If they came up with anything solid, even a trace of powder, it could be enough to justify a "body search". Body searches are intensely intimate. Few people who have been body-searched in this manner care to repeat the experience. It is also in matters of this sort that one acquires a greater respect for the difficulties presented by some aspects of police work. It's hard to imagine a sufficient cash reward for anyone required, in the line of duty, to conduct this sort of inventory. It's not that the body search will reveal that the dealer has swallowed a party balloon full of heroin caps. That's not the point. The point is that a body search takes time, and time is a commodity that the heroin dealer with a party balloon of heroin in his digestive tract has very little of. At the station, he will be required to sit for a long time while the Drug Squad men "sort through the paper work and send out for pizza." While the police are nibbling away on pizzas, the stomach acids in the dealer's tummy are nibbling away at the rubber walls of his party balloon. The dealer would very much like to go back to his apartment, take some maalox and castor oil, and allow nature to speed his investment back into the light of day. If the dealer is somehow prevented from doing this, he may well suffer a severe overdose of heroin, heroin that he has stoutly maintained, in the face of considerable persuasive arguments, that he does not have anywhere about his person. This is, as one can readily understand, a consummation assiduously to be avoided. So the dealer who is on his way over to his "shooter" at one of the tables in the Blackstone has a lot on his mind. The waters are deep and dirty.

Ike later told me that I had missed their spotter inside the hotel, although I had looked right at him. He was an undercover member of their team, sitting at a table, apparently dead drunk, wired with an FM transmitter, and in a position to see everything that went on. Since most of the dealers were known, and most of the hypes were unmistakable, the spotter's job was to identify the actual moment when the "shooter" passed a cap or two of heroin to a hype. When he was sure that a known hype had just made his "buy", he called out to the teams waiting at various points around the surrounding blocks. All of the teams were in radio contact on a special tactical channel. Tonight, the shooters had started to deal while Ike, Burns, and I were sitting in the Blue Eagle eating chicken wings and discussing methodology. The spotter inside was a man they referred to as Finn. It's unlikely that Finn was his real name. Finn's voice came over the handset oddly muted, as if he was speaking through cloth or into his sleeve. The image was slightly bizarre and I laughed softly picturing it. Ike swivelled in his seat, wondering what I was chuckling about. I told him.

"Boyo, you don't know the half of it. When we walked you through the room, did you notice a table near the door? Three guys sitting at it? One guy with long hair, a scar over his right eye? Another guy in a brown suede hat. And the third one, an Indian, in a beaded thong vest?" I had seen them, but I hadn't paid a lot of attention. They had all been staring at us as we passed and I had found that staring back was sometimes provocative. "Well you *should* have noticed them. They were staring at us, right? Each one of those guys is a fink, an informer. We pay each of them fifty, a hundred, five hundred bucks for information about drug dealing in Vancouver. Each one of those guys is a hype. All hypes will rat on their grannies if it will kick loose some cash. The thing is, not one of those three guys has any idea that the other two are finks. When I walked by, each of them was hiding his face from the other two and giving me a negative signal, no dealing yet. Nothing going down, no shooters in play. No horse in the house. I almost laughed out loud. Ah, buddy, it's all a game."

"Yeah, well, half-time's over, all right!" Burns was trying to get back to Finn. So far, Finn hadn't answered.

"Christ, you don't think anybody's made him, do you?"

Ike wasn't worried. "Nah, nobody'll make Finn in *that* rig. Relax, man, you're going to worry yourself into an ulcer."

"Too late," said Burns.

"Copy this copy this Ricky Rye's on his way over to Joey. I think a buy, something happening. Damn!" Ike and Burns sat upright, tensing.

"What, Finn? What's happening?" Ike was speaking into the handset in a low taut voice. Finn must have had some indetectible means of receiving these transmissions. No one was willing to tell me how it was done. I imagine that a bone transmission speaker behind his ear, under a heavy mat of hair, would do the trick. Finn came back fast.

"No problem, just a waitress in the way. Rye's on his way out. You should be able to see him in a second."

Ike strained to see through the rain. In a few seconds, a short bald man in a black leather jacket swung out onto the street and went off south.

"Bingo – roger Finn we've got Ricky Rye. Sherman, Smith, Bradshaw. Do you copy this?" While Ike checked through the surveillance posts dotted around the area, Burns kept his eye on Ricky Rye all the way to the next pick-up station.

"Roger, Ike, this is Bradshaw . . . we have Rye now. Do you want him?"

"Nah, forget it. He's going back for some more. We'll have some action now . . . it looks like Joey Fine is the shooter. Finn, anything?"

The handset crackled in his palm. A minute passed while the three of us waited. On the street a group of schoolkids hurried past us without a look. No one pays any attention to the inside of a parked car. The handset crackled.

"Action here . . . Joey and Grey Eyes are talking. Damned light in here. Okay, there's some business going on . . . yok it up guys, that's it . . . come to papa . . . *bang*, it's Grey Eyes he's absolutely holding! Look for him, no . . . he's sitting down."

Ike whispered to me. "That's unusual. By the time a hype buys he's really hungry. Not in pain. The shit on the street hasn't been good enough to get anybody hooked, really nailed into a habit, for years. But they get jumpy, and when they score they shoot it fast. The longer Grey Eyes holds it the better his chances of losing it. He'll – " The radio broke in.

"Okay Grey Eyes must have been checking it out or something. He's up and . . . and he's heading straight outside. The front door, Ike, he's yours. He's out in a second."

Ike rolled down the window on his side a crack. Burns picked up the handset. "Roger Finn we're on him." A minute passed in absolute silence. Several people came out of the front doors of the Blackstone but no one in the car made a move. Another minute. "Damn," whispered Burns, "where *is* the bastard?"

"There!" said Ike, as a tall lanky man with shoulder-length black hair pushed out of the entrance and walked directly across the street, passing in front of us and almost fifty feet down. He had his head up, he was alert, his eyes shaded by their brows were black holes in his face. So far, he seemed not to notice the parked car, although we were very close. Ike spoke into the set.

"Okay guys, we have Grey Eyes dirty on Granville just outside the Blackstone. No direction yet everybody hold."

Grey Eyes stopped on the sidewalk, less than forty feet from our grillwork. He looked down the street away from us. Burns swore.

"He's sweeping! Get down get down!" The three of us slouched down below the dashboard line. A long minute passed. Burns put his head up. "All right . . . he's . . . oh christ here he comes stay down." We held that crouching pose for a short while. Steps came up level with us and passed by the front of the car without changing rhythm. Ike looked out his side window. "There he goes . . . he's heading for the hotel . . ." he put the radio to his mouth, "all right Grey Eyes is on his way north up Granville heading for the Nelson all units respond." He sat up and looked at the two of us, crouching in the dark. He grinned fiercely.

"Well come *on* guys . . . time is money!"

We got out of the Monte Carlo and slipped out into the street. Ike had a radio in his hand. Nobody had a gun out. As a matter of fact, during the whole exercise I don't think I saw anyone with a gun in his hand. Grey Eyes was about a half-block away, his head up, hands in his pocket, striding through the people on the street, his legs jutting out stiffly, his heels hitting the sidewalk with a visible jolt. We worked our way up Granville after him, keeping him in sight without dogging him too closely. There seemed to be a correct distance, far enough to be just another figure in the crowd if he looked back, close enough to make sure he couldn't make a fast move and lose us. Ike and Burns stayed apart, one on the opposite side of the street at all times. Ike kept on the handset, always letting the other mobile units, none of whom I had met or even seen yet, know precisely where we were. At the intersection in front of the McDonald's I got a chance to ask Burns how many of the units were going to follow Grey Eyes. He shrugged, and then said, "I don't know, probably no more than three. That's six guys. It's really up to Sherman. He's the senior man. Then Bradshaw. Ike and I are just detectives. The management line is sergeant. Now wait!" Ike was running back towards us.

"He's in the Nelson . . . come up fast. Copy this Grey Eyes is in the Nelson let's go let's go!" By the time Burns, Ike, and I had run up to the door of the Nelson Hotel, there were four other men standing waiting for us. I hadn't seen any of them on the way up. We nodded to one another. Ike went inside and over to the desk. He put a hand on the desk phone, leaned over to say something to the clerk. He waved us in.

"All right he's on the fourth floor room 409. He stopped to talk so we're right on his tail. Let's go." Ike turned and headed up a flight of stairs. The old hotel was falling apart. Green paint flaked off on my hand as I stepped carefully up the flight behind the unit men. The stairwell reeked of wet linen, bad plumbing.

We were on the fourth floor within a matter of a minute. The halls were carpeted, in a manner of speaking. Two of the men went up another floor and down the upper hall. A back-up team covering the rear exits. Ike, Burns, a mammoth brown-haired cop aptly named Sherman, Bradshaw, another Hollywood cop, irritatingly good-looking, like a muscular Terence Stamp, and I went down the fourth floor hallway literally on our toes. The numbers on the doors descended. 415. 413. 411. Just as we got to 409, the door opened a crack. There was something breaking the light behind it. Ike, Burns, Bradshaw, and Sherman, reached the door in a milli-second. Sherman hit the door with his shoulder, an impact I could feel in my chest fifteen feet away. The door flew back on its hinges and the four cops burst into the room. As I ran up I could see Sherman and Bradshaw throwing a plump young woman onto the chenille bedspread. Ike was in mid-air, his black shadow chasing him crazily across the walls in the light from an overhead bulb swinging on its cord. Flying, he hit a tall Indian male who was frantically fumbling with a needle and a glass of water. Burns reached him a second later. He had taken the long way, around the bed and not over it in mid-air. The two cops wrestled Grey Eyes to the ground. Ike had his thick-fingered hands clamped around Grey Eye's throat. Nothing was going down that throat right then but a small amount of air. On the bed the woman was already in handcuffs. There was a short struggle on the floor next to the half-open window. And then it was over. Everything suddenly stabilized, no one was struggling, and the raid was complete. Time elapsed was perhaps ten seconds. It was frighteningly, superbly efficient. Oddly, it wasn't brutal. As soon as Grey Eyes and the woman realised that the cops were on them and the heroin was gone, they gave up. It wasn't long after this that the room became downright social. The woman, a plump, sexy brunette in a black tee-shirt and blue jeans, shook her hair out of her eyes and said to the cop straddling her, "Do you think you could get off me. I'm getting to like it."

The policeman, Bradshaw, laughed and climbed off the bed. She sat up against the headboard, shook her clothes back into order as much as she could with handcuffs on, and literally smiled at everyone in the room. Ike and Burns pulled the Indian to his feet and brushed the hair out of his eyes. The Indian, whose name I assumed was Grey Eyes, wasn't thrilled but he wasn't sending out any murderous waves either. Sherman pulled the bed out from the wall, took a small penlight flash from his pocket, and got down to search the floorboards and corners for hiding places. He was not alone down there. I didn't envy him the job. At that point, the woman spoke up.

"Are you giving us a summons?"

Ike, who was writing in a pad, looked up at her with a broad open grin, his quick-frozen blue eyes glinting in the wavering overhead light. "Well I'm not selling tickets to the policeman's ball, my darlin' . . . of course I'm going to give you a summons. I'm writing you out a summons for Possession of Heroin and that will be a three hundred dollar fine." The woman shook her head impatiently.

"I *know* all that shit. What I want to know is for when?"

"When? When what?"

She smiled what was probably intended to be a seductive, hypnotic smile. Under the rolling light, and considering the fact that her hands were cuffed, the effect ran rather closer to Caligari than Bacall. "The thing *is* I have to be in court on April 15 so I was hoping that you could make this one for the same day?"

Ike stared at her for a while. "What are your other charges?"

She had the blush down pat, which showed real dedication.

"Soliciting, actually. The cab fare's a bitch!"

Everyone in the room laughed. Even Grey Eyes. Thirty minutes later the woman was out on Granville Street in a tearaway skirt. Thanks to the Drug Squad, Grey Eyes was down fifty bucks and two needles and he needed to make it back.

* * *

We did that again. And again. Finn would call the deal from his table in the Blackstone. The shooter would deal the caps out from a balloon in his mouth. The hype would make his play, stash the caps in another balloon in his mouth. Out on the street he ran the gauntlet. They had to know the Squad was on the street. You could see it in their bodies, in the jerky, frightened way they'd hurry up the street, eyes always searching the street and the sidewalk and the alleys, with that precious cap stuck somewhere and their works in their flat or their car or at their mother's apartment. The shooter shot for a full hour and a half and I don't think one hype got through. It was a duck blind. Finn could not hit the shooter, Joey Fine, inside, or he'd blow the operation. Fine would not leave the hotel until he'd dealt away all the heroin. If he did, he'd be street-jumped and choked and relieved of every cap. And his charge would not be simple Possession. Not that he'd do hard time, either.

"No boyo, it's sad but true," Ike raised a beer to me in shared commiseration. "The problem is with the judges, you see. They sit in that chair for hours. They are *bored.* The first ten thousand heroin charges they see they say *O my God heroin* and they nail the creature to the court-room door. Statutes provide for up to ten years in the slammer for Possession Third Offence, and Trafficking carries twenty-five to Life. The judge would give them every inch of that, the old darlin'. But *then* the heroin busts just keep on coming and the faces go round and round. Pretty soon, old mister judge he thinks 'hey this is no *fun* any more' and he say to the Crown 'yoo hoo Mister Crown you run another heroin bust by this bench and I will fall *fast* asleep' and sure enough, after a while, Possession gets you a three hundred dollar fine and trafficking will bring a hundred and eighty days Community Service, which is mowing the lawns at City Hall. Oh, the big busts will still get their attention. That's why CLU concentrates on main supply. But damnit, we can't let the hypes think they own the blasted streets. They *don't.* You want to know who does?"

I thought I knew, but I said 'who' because he wanted me to say it.

* * *

Three different shooters made three different plays that night. It may be that, here and there, some of the heroin addicts made a few connections. We jumped a man in the doorway of a dry-cleaning shop who had the needle jammed into his upper thigh, broken at the tip, some of it buried in his muscle. He had seen the car slow, and he'd made the impending jump. He skin-popped it, a last desperate attempt to get some of the heroin into his system before the Drug Squad took it away from him.

A while later a big black-bearded motorcycle outlaw put up a pretty good stand in an alley behind the Drake Hotel. He'd paid good money for his hit and he was damned if anyone was going to take it away from him, cop or no cop. They took it away from him anyway, without a gun showing, toe to toe in the lane. He went in for the night on charges of Resisting Arrest and Assault. He would have walked if he'd left it alone; heroin possession was a walking offence, no more serious than theft under fifty in other places. A ticketable offence. It took me a long time to get used to seeing addicts in possession of heroin take their summonses, make a few bad jokes, and hit the streets again. Grey Eyes made another play over at the Drake, on another shooter's deal, but I didn't see it. I did see his woman climbing into a big Lincoln over on Davie Street, near the Sylvia Hotel.

One incident stands out. Ike and Burns had jumped a wiry little kid from out of the province, a French Canadian by his accent. He had scored off Joey Fine on Ricky Rye's play, failed to make the spotter as he headed out the back door, dirty, as they say on the street. Ike and Burns and I caught up with him at Helmcken, a street-jump he had never seen coming. After the ticket had been written out, as the kid was running a dirty black rat-tail comb through his modified duck cut, checking out his reflection in the side mirror of the Monte Carlo, smacking his lips in and out in a repetitive, nervous, maddening kind of tic, Ike walked away a few feet and put the kid's name through the ceepick – otherwise known as CPIC or the Canadian Police Information Computer. The kid rang quite a bell downtown. He was wanted in Ontario and Quebec. In Quebec he was being sought by the Montreal Police on charges of Break and Enter and Assault. In Toronto, Ontario, the same boy had been charged with Aggravated Assault, Sexual Assault, Break and Enter, and one count of Fraud. He said he'd been in Vancouver for a month but in his wallet he had a recently cancelled bus ticket showing that he had arrived from Edmonton only three days ago. He had a welfare card and approximately three hundred dollars in cash. While we were taking his heroin away, he had it trapped in his cheek, but he had figured that Ike wouldn't put a finger in there to check. He bragged that soon he'd be inside dealing. Ike just grinned at him. The Warrants on the ceepick were all Non-Returnable. What that meant was that the young man had gone up on the charges listed in both provinces and a trial date had been set for each. Judging from the boy's path, it was likely that the Quebec Warrant had been issued first. A judge had issued a Warrant for his arrest after he had failed to show up for his hearing. The judge had made it a Quebec Only Warrant, Non-Returnable from anywhere else. If the boy was picked up in British Columbia, the Province of Quebec would *not* pay for his return flight to that jurisdiction. The Ontario Courts had done the same when he got into trouble there. Another Non-Returnable Warrant. The Province of Ontario would *not* pay for the boy's return to their province, either. Since the boy had no outstanding Warrant valid in British Columbia, Ike let him go. I watched him walk out of the laneway and into the street, thinking about the woman he had sexually assaulted in Ontario, a woman who probably thought the law was out looking for her attacker. Ike and Burns watched him too.

Burns walked over to me and pushed me softly.

"Don't take it so hard . . . we'll see him again. He's the type."

*　*　*

We were ready to wrap it up outside the Blackstone when the handset came on again. "Guys this is odd . . . do we have any horsemen on the street tonight?" The set hissed while Ike and Burns looked at each other, puzzled.

"Negative, Finn . . . what have you got?" This sounded like Sherman, at his post behind the hotel.

"Well, I have this dude in a black mohair trench coat, very dapper, one of those prince John beards and thin moustache. He's just sitting there drinking right now, but. . . ."

"But what?" This was from Sherman, a spur to Finn. Get to the point.

Ike whispered, not to anyone in particular, "Finn's good but he *do* go on. He and Smith are the worst for that. But what the − " the radio was on again.

"It seemed to me that Ricky Rye can't account for all the action here tonight. He's just not that good. I'm wondering if this mohair dude might be a new boy on the block."

"Do you want to take him?"

"No way . . . he'd be as clean as a vicar's wicker. Let's not shut it down right now, okay. Give him some time to feel at home."

There was an extended silence while Sherman weighed the odds.

"Okay, Finn. Thirty minutes. Copy that all units."

We waited.

Twenty minutes later, Finn came on. He was excited. "Listen Mohair's on the move and I think he's delivered a suitcase. We can stay for the shooter or we can pick up Mohair. He's definitely on his way out. Sherman?"

There was another silence while Sherman thought it through. We had six men available at this moment, three teams in three cars. Most of the action was over. The hypes were home or roaming. The bars were closing soon. But if this Mohair was a new dealer, there would be a whole new play any minute. It had been too busy for an average night. Granville Street was a small world. The new man, Mohair, was something worth looking into. Sherman would have been briefed about all RCMP undercover cops on Granville, and he'd been given no word about Mohair. He must have gone through all of this in seconds, because he came back in a soft voice, deciding on a risk.

"Finn, this is Sherman. Come on out. We'll pick up Mohair."

"Good idea, because he's just paid up and he's on his feet. Ike, Burns, he's coming right out the front door . . . stay on him!"

And we did. Mohair came out the front door of the Blackstone Hotel at twelve fifteen in the morning. The rain had stopped and the air was ripe with the scent of apple blossoms and a salty burn off the sea. Mohair started north on Granville, stopped, looked all around him, went back south about ten yards, stopped, put his back up against a wall, looked all around him again.

Ike was delighted. "Christ, the guy's James Bond. Burns, is that a guilty conscience at work? You tell me!" Burns laughed outright.

"You oughta know a guilty conscience when you see it. You shave one every morning. *Whhoops*, here he comes. . . ."

Mohair started to move again, this time north on Granville. He stayed on Granville until he reached Helmcken, then he suddenly cut left and west. Ike decided that he should be followed on foot, so we parked the car on Helmcken and got out. Sherman radioed that he and Bradshaw's car would stay mobile. Ike, Burns, and I went softly after Mohair, splitting and reforming, staying about half a block back, keeping the short nervous man in the black coat in sight. Mohair was not easy to follow. He kept doubling back, or stopping in the middle of the street, changing sides, cutting down alley ways, stepping into doorways and popping out again a few minutes later. If the men on the Drug Squad had been clumsy or careless, Mohair would have made the tail at least ten times. It was rapidly becoming obvious that Mohair was *not* simply out for an evening stroll. While Ike and Burns tracked him through the laneways and streets, they speculated on Mohair's purpose.

"He could be meeting a gay lover. This town is famous for that."

Ike shook his head. "No gays in the Blackstone . . . they'd sooner die than be found in that place. Maybe he's a fence?"

"What's he fencing? And why all this crap? Dodge, duck, in and out. Guy's acting like a very suspicious man. He has something naughty on his mind."

"A buy?"

"Possible . . . maybe just a prelim, a meet to test?"

"Alone? Not possible."

"*Look* at the son of a bitch! God, Ike, do I look like that when I'm bopping around the streets?"

"No way . . . he's too good-looking. Your kind of ugly is easy to spot from a distance. All the leaves die."

"There he goes . . . back into a door. Tricksy tricksy."

From Helmcken he went to Burrard, and along Burrard to Davie Street. At Davie and Burrard he picked up speed, stopped his jerky, nervous motions, and stalked away down the hill. Ike and Burns and I had to jog to keep up with him, parallelling him from the lanes that ran up behind the stores, relying on the two car teams to hopscotch by him on Davie and keep us informed. The handset was always hissing and popping with snatches of data. He was westbound on Davie. He was in a Becker's Store. He was leaning on a pizza parlour window. He was eastbound on Davie, but walking on the opposite side. At one point we had to pass within ten yards of him as he came back up Davie Street. Ike and Burns leaned into an open car, studying the decor, while I dithered stupidly in the middle of the walk. Mohair didn't even glance sideways. Which didn't mean he'd missed it.

But he kept on going. In the hour and a half that we tracked him, he covered several miles, all of it on foot, from the Blackstone on Granville, up Helmcken, along Burrard to Davie, down Davie to Bidwell, up an alley way on Bidwell, back out through a parking lot to Davie, back up along Davie to Hornby and along Hornby to Nelson and, slowing, up Nelson to Burrard again. At the corner of Burrard and Nelson he walked onto the grounds of Saint Andrew's Wesley United Church and stepped into the shadows beside it. We froze on the opposite side of the street, in the dark. There was no way that we could cross without giving it away. It was almost a quarter to two in the morning and Burrard Street was a wasteland. Nothing moved. Far above us heavy clouds were slipping over the sky with an almost audible hiss. My heart was thumping in my chest. Ike and Burns were panting. By this time, there wasn't a man on the Squad who wasn't absolutely convinced that Mohair was a nervous dealer getting ready to make a very big buy. The fact that he'd stopped in the churchyard was another good sign. Deals go down in rented hotel rooms. The Saint Andrew's Wesley Church was right next door to the Century Plaza Hotel. After a complex foot and car surveillance chase covering several miles and an hour and a half, the Drug Squad was still all over Mohair and he had not made a single man. As surveillance goes, it was a tour de force and I was as impressed as I've ever been in my life, and that is *very* impressed. Ike stepped a little closer to me.

"He's making a final sweep. He's been assuming a tail for the last hour and he's been trying to lose it. He's now checking out the scene. He has just about bought it. If he doesn't have a big buy set up in the Century Plaza, I'll personally eat a dead bat. Look at him, his little heart is bursting."

Mohair was just visible in the middle of a shadow, under one of the descending buttresses of the church. If we hadn't watched him step into the spot, we would have never known he was there. We held our positions and waited him out. Ike switched off the handset so that no trace of cross-talk could slip out in the motionless landscape and alert Mohair. After a wait of ten minutes, Mohair moved out of the shadow.

"Sherman this is Ike Mohair is on the move again . . . he's off the churchyard and he's going south on Burrard."

"Roger Ike. The mobile is now on Helmcken at Hornby we'll put it into the parking lot opposite the hotel. Meet us there."

"Roger Sherman . . . Burns how are we going to deal with Mohair if he goes into the hotel?"

Burns had obviously been giving the matter some thought. "Look, *if* he's making a buy in there, he'll have to take a room. Odds are that he has one already picked out. Sherman's got a tie and a jacket. We put Sherman and Bradshaw in the lobby or the bar with wires. If Mohair goes to a room, we flash the shields and get the room number from the clerk. Then we give Mohair enough time to get the horse on the table and we kick in . . . simple." Ike laughed.

"Sure, department citations all round, right man?"

"Rock solid cinch . . . that writer's good luck. We'll give him something to remember us by, right buddy?" Burns was smiling at me. They weren't so tough. I liked them both at the time, and nothing has happened since to change my mind. Cops were like that; you couldn't resist the bastards. A Monte Carlo was pulling into the parking lot across the street. Mohair was walking up the curved driveway of the Century Plaza Hotel. He was going in. We had him solid.

Ike wasn't looking at Mohair. He was standing very still and staring at something in the parking lot.

"Hey, Burns . . . whose car is that, in the lot?"

Burns turned away from the lobby, where Mohair was talking to a clerk at the registry desk. He squinted his eyes. "The grey Monte . . . that's Sherman, dipstick, who do you think?"

Ike shook his head, once, a dismissive gesture. "I know Sherman's Monte, for god's sake. He just pulled in. But there's a car in the back of the lot . . . do you make it? The green Valiant?"

Burns and I looked harder. Yes, just at the edge of a tree shadow, far away from the circles of light under the street lamps, you could just see the green car, at least you could see a car and assume it was green. Ike was still staring at it. "Burns, is there somebody *in* that car?"

His partner looked for a long time in absolute silence.

"Yeah, yeah, I think you're right. I make one . . . two guys, in the front seat. You think Mohair has protection?"

Ike's face was getting stonier by the second. "Buddy, you don't want to *know* what I'm thinking." He put the radio up. "Sherman this is Ike is that you in the Monte?"

"Copy that of course it's us in the Monte . . . why?"

"Sherman, have you made the car in the back of the lot, about six o'clock from your position?" Even from our distance you could see Sherman's head swivelling in the front seat of the Monte Carlo. There was a long silence. Then, "Bugger this . . . I think we'll check this out. Stay on Mohair." The Monte Carlo started up, no lights, and reversed across the lot towards the car parked under the tree. Sherman stopped it in front of the other car. In the red glow of his brake-lights it was possible to discern two solemn faces in the front seat of the Valiant. There was a brief conversation. Ike, Burns and I watched it take place. Then Ike put his hand up to his face. "Shit . . . shit I should have known. *Shit shit shit*." Burns paid no attention. The radio came back on.

"Ah copy this all units this is mobile five let's pull off the job here that's a negative on Mohair. Call it off, men, let's go home." Sherman's voice was tired and barely controlled. He had been kept in the dark and he was angry.

"Horsemen . . . goddamned horsemen . . . I *told* you something was wrong!"

Burns didn't answer him. Ike shut the radio off and walked away a few feet, swearing softly to himself. Burns was still looking at Mohair. The suspect was taking a key from the clerk. Mohair was going upstairs to make a buy. I didn't understand. Burns seemed to sense this.

"It's the RCMP . . . I guess Mohair is their fink. They've got a listening post all set up in the Plaza and Mohair is working for them. He's setting up a big dealer, would be my guess. Only the horsemen never bothered to tell us about it."

I asked him why not. He shrugged. Ike was still swearing over by the curb. Sherman's Monte Carlo was heading over to pick us up. Burns smiled.

"To tell you the truth I think the horsemen don't trust us. The RCMP don't trust *anybody*. They run their own show and they don't give a shit who doesn't like it. They let Mohair run some small operation over on Granville, he makes a few bucks dealing to a shooter, playing off the hypes, and they protect him from us because he's working on really important stuff, too important to let us know. So we piss away two hours and for what?" Ike came back over to us as the grey car stopped at the curb. He was smiling.

"Yeah, you're right. But if we don't know the horsemen are taking care of Mohair, why we just might make a big mistake and jump him some night, just for some small-time shit like dealing on *our* street. What do you think, buddy?"

Burns was smiling at Ike. He had a good smile.

CHAPTER EIGHT

Casualties

Champlain put a boat ashore on the rocky peninsula where Halifax now sits back in 1605, but no one came to live there permanently until Cornwallis founded the city of Halifax in 1749, the British-built headquarters for their Imperial Army and for the Dreadnoughts of the Royal Navy. This military and naval beginning has marked the town forever. Halifax became the most heavily-armoured fortification in the British colonial empire.

The Citadel on the high rolling slope of ancient granite is still the highest point in the city, visible from almost any point in Halifax, always easy to find from the northerly side of the Eastern Passage, where Dartmouth wanders along the shoreline in and out of industry and residential areas. The rock foundation is nowhere far from the surface; the North Atlantic has five thousand miles of unfettered and unbroken ocean before the big grey rollers hit the rocky shoreline. Waves that last saw land in Cornwall break here in salty white foam, shattering on the rocks and the sea grass, rushing in through the channels and bays as if no wave had ever come here before. The winter storms are awesomely unmitigated; ferocious assaults on the old wooden frame buildings and the stunted trees along the coast. Much of Halifax gives the distinct impression of being huddled into the stoney ground, gripping the peninsula as if the next good storm would rip it from its foundations. The fall starts early here, and passes quickly. The winters are long and bitter. The water in the passages and back in Bedford Basin never freezes. When the thaw comes, you'll get a wind off the basin that smells like a tide flat rotting, that heady mix of salt water, seaweed, rotting wood, and the ammonia-and-blood scent of dead fish and churning muddy water. The port is littered with freighters and tugs; fishing smacks and cutters dart into landfalls as far as the Bridge, oil tankers put in here, cargo ships outbound for Liverpool, Ostend, Bremerhaven, Marseilles, the Gold Coast shift in the tidal flow, butting up against aging wooden pilings like old bulls rubbing fences. Naval vessels weave in and out of the ocean-going freighters, lean grey-wolf shapes, heavy with guns and battened down tight against the heavy seas that lie close in to the harbour mouth. Gulls wheel and fall in the pale blue sky, their cries faint and harsh across the choppy water. A flock of hundreds chase a packing boat in from the harbour mouth, fluttering about the fantail like a horde of Arab beggars.

The town itself, the city proper, as they call it, is an odd mixture of old red brick and stone houses, wood-frame storefronts with rippled glass in the window, and ponderous British Imperial structures holding down immense stretches of scrubby lawns. Along the shoreline below the Citadel there are several office towers just beginning to block the view; commerce will ruin Halifax and save Nova Scotia sooner or later. The people are small and dark-haired, wiry Celts with bony faces and strong hands. They give you the feeling that it all started here, that anything further west is a fad, like silk flowers. There are only about 150,000 people in the city, and another 100,000 in Dartmouth and environs. The town is full of soldiers and sailors, able-bodied seamen, fishermen and stevedores. They carry the same names that are slowly wearing off the soot-stained granite slabs in the old cemetery in the centre of town. Like the Newfoundlanders, they have a short, nasal, and abrupt way of speaking, as if they paid cash for each word and you were going to drop the best ones on the floor. Under this salty surface there is an earthy eastern fatalism and a great deal of humour. Fatalism and humour are good traits in anyone. In a policeman's wife, they're indispensible.

* * *

"My husband was a policeman in Halifax for many years. He's dead now, and I will be soon, I suspect." She literally cackled at this, although she was not so old that death was anything other than a slightly more defined terminus than it would be for a thirty-year-old. We were sitting on a bench outside the grassy walls of the old fort. Down below us the channel appeared in slices between several new office towers. The sky overhead was blue, but there were thick grey clouds off in the western horizon. Spring was just getting started. Down in the town, the sidewalks were hot where the sun caught them, but up here on the Citadel it was chilly under the fragile warmth. I was talking to a lady who had been the wife of a Halifax policeman for twenty years. He had died a couple of years ago, within months of his retirement. This had come as no surprise to his widow.

"It's hard for an outsider to understand how a man can get caught up in police work. In the first place, there are the strange hours. My husband would get up in the afternoon for the evening shift for a month, and then he'd get up at six for the day shift. We never ran on the same schedule as the folks in our neighbourhood. Even in those days, people acted oddly around policemen. It wasn't considered proper to be one, in the first place. We had some rough men on the force, too. The Halifax force was started in the 1860's, just to take care of the sailors and whalers in the old town. The policemen were as bad as the sailors, too. My husband's father was a policeman, up in Sydney, and his father was a sailor and *his* father was in the army, back in England. My husband always said that the men in his family were born in uniform. He joined the Halifax force when he was twenty, and he never left it. So of course, when he had nothing left to do but change the earth in the flower boxes, he decided to die. They mustn't think about life too much, the policemen, you know?"

I didn't, and I asked her why.

"They're just like machines, after a while. They have to deal with such unpleasant things. He hated violence, but he had to fight quite a bit. He wasn't big, so the tough guys would pick on him. Right from the start, he had to fight. He even fought his own men, sometimes. He was really quite soft, inside, you should have seen him with the niece. But policemen can't stay that way. I watched him get mean sometimes, as if he had two souls. One soul was for the family, and the other was for his work. That's what I mean by a machine. He was trained, just like a guard dog, to act in a certain way. Over the years, it got so that all he could talk about was his work. When I used to ask him what he wanted to do after he retired, he'd stop and stare at me, as if I'd said something in another language. He never thought about that part of his life. If we'd had children, maybe, but we didn't. So when he got old enough to have to think about it, he died. That was just like him, too."

She stopped to smile about that for a minute. There was a cold wind moving over the hillside. Down below us the Old Town clock whirred and a bell sounded the half-hour. Several starlings flew off the gable roof. I was trying to place her age. She had the skin of a mother superior. If she had ever used make-up, there was no tint of it any-where on that seamed face.

"He put everything he had into it. Every day when he left his boots were gleaming, and he soaped all his creases, so they'd stay all day. He had a thin brass sheet with a cutaway in it, that he slipped in under his buttons, to let him put polish on the buttons and keep it off the fabric. His leather got neat's foot oiled twice a year. His shirts were always ironed at home. The younger men got theirs cleaned at the dry cleaners, but he always said that was hard on the material. The gun he cleaned every week. The salt played up the finish all the time. He'd curse if he found rust on it. He was always complaining about the younger men, too, about how they had so much to learn. They don't know how to stand up at parade, he'd say, or they march like chimney-sweeps. To hear him go on you'd think there wasn't a good policeman born after 1935. We went on a vacation once, to Montreal. Do you know what he did when we got into the hotel? He called a friend on the Montreal police force and he went out that night on a patrol with him. Got back at dawn, sick as a baby. I wasn't going to let him in, but he kicked up an awful fuss in the hall. I learned after a while that I was just one part of his life. If I was going to stay with him, I had to accept that. I got involved in the YWCA and the church. Have you found that policemen's wives are always doing something for the church?"

She wanted me to say yes, so I did, even though the world had changed a little since then. Most policemen's wives I had met were working to support the family.

"You must make a life outside the marriage. He belongs to the force first. He'd have men over after the shift; you had to be charming at four in the morning. Make tea and scones. Look pretty on three hours sleep. Never lose your temper. And be able to listen to the worst stories in the world, tales to frighten the dead, and make light of it. They hated it if you took things to heart. Even if someone got shot, as one of his closest friends did. They had the funeral and then they had a wake to shock the devil. And after that, you couldn't say the man's name out loud without getting such a look from him."

I helped her out of the bench and we made our slow way down the steps by the clock and onto the street below. Out of the wind, it was warmer, but she looked tired and cold. I offered her some tea at a restaurant.

"No ... no, thank you. I don't see how my blithering could help you figure out a policeman. I always thought they were like priests, in a way. They took Holy Orders in the Law, and they could never get that mark off their souls. Once In, Never Out, he used to say. Well, he's out now."

I wondered about her friends. She smiled at me through blowing grey hair, and pulled the fur around her neck. I caught a faint scent of something on the wind. It was Chypre, on a lace cloth in her sleeve.

"Listen, young man, don't patronise me! I've been patronised by the best. I miss my husband, but not enough to cry over him now. I have lots of good friends, and a niece in Cherry Hill. I play a mean game of bridge, and next year I'm going to Paris. I served my time as a policeman's wife, and I intend to enjoy my retirement. Good day, young fellow. Send me a copy of your book."

She reached up and kissed me on the side of the cheek. She had to stand on her toes to do it. The Chypre scent was stronger. Then she turned and strode briskly down the hill towards her apartment. At the last corner, she waved. She knew I'd be watching her, and of course she was right.

*   *   *

I was in the main dining room of the Barrington Inn on Barrington Street. There was a heavy snow falling outside. The day before had been just like spring. I had been sitting on a bench talking about policemen to a policeman's widow. After twenty years with a policeman, she was still a fan. The woman I was meeting with here had been referred to me by mutual acquaintances at Dalhousie. She was in her third year there, and planned to take Law. She was a very positive young woman; there's no shortage of positive young women in university. Her father was a lawyer "for the oligarchy" as she put it. After our filets and bordeaux, she sipped a cognac and got down to the issue. It was all a matter of dialectic.

"Look . . . have you ever read Jack London's *The Iron Heel*. You should! It's an absolutely brilliant book. Incisive, devastating . . . a perfect dissection of everything that's wrong with modern capitalist society. It's out of print, you know. Everybody's read *Call of the Wild,* but *The Iron Heel* is nowhere to be found. Well, the Iron Heel in this city is the Halifax Police Department, and the RCMP Detachments here and in Dartmouth. They recruit special types. They have tests to isolate the right kind of cop . . . he has to be smart enough to remember orders and to carry out simple instructions, but not smart enough to figure out that he's being used. Really, the Baader-Meinhof and the Brigada Rossa and the rest, they have a legitimate point. The police aren't going to drop their weapons and join us on the barricades. They're too indoctrinated. The only thing that will convince the elite to change is force. It's like with that rapist and the victim. If she's a beneficiary of the system, then she has to pay the price of that benefit. A society that creates criminals will create victims for the criminal to use."

I raised the question of poorer victims of rape.

"Sure, sure, there'll always be victims in the underclasses. The man who is a victim of capitalist oppression doesn't always know how to pick the right target. The function of the police is to keep the middle classes safe from this struggle. The police create violence simply by being there. If there were no police, we would have no criminals. It's as simple as that!"

I thought that was pretty simple, and I said so.

"It's a demonstrated fact that eighty per cent of the prisoners in Canada's jails are non-violent offenders, people who pose no threat to society at all. But we keep them locked up as part of the propaganda campaign to convince everyone that the police are the only thing keeping us from the raging beasts. Police create violence by carrying guns and clubs; they are conditioned to react with violence to any challenge of their power. Ninety-nine per cent of all police activities are confined to the enforcement of an outmoded morality on the streets. Laws against prostitution, against harmless drugs like marijuana, cocaine, or hashish, laws against so-called sexual deviates like homo-sexuals, these functions of the police forces are simply a means for the police to demonstrate their power over the powerless. What harm comes from prostitution, other than the affront to an outmoded Judeo-Christian morality?"

Although I was relatively certain that was a rhetorical question, it seemed singularly apposite to describe some of the Davie Street life-forms. She listened with her breath held, lips tensed across two thousand dollars of first-rate orthodontic skills, polishing her rebuttal while I droned on like some feeble don at the campus buttery.

"Nonsense! The problems on that street result from the *laws* against such things as prostitution and drugs, not from the things themselves. If there were no laws against heroin, the hookers wouldn't have to sell their bodies to buy it at black market prices. And if the Vancouver Police would only do as they have done in Amsterdam, create a red-light district, then the prostitutes would become merely another utility, like the cabs or the fire department."

Reeling, I asked her if she had ever been to Amsterdam.

She tossed her hair again, a contemptuous dismissal.

"I consider that irrelevant . . . I've never been to the moon, either, but I can describe the *Mare Serenetatis*. It's a known fact that red light districts in Amsterdam have virtually eliminated prostitution in that town, and all major sex offences!"

It struck me that legalising something was not the same as eliminating it, but she was on a roll.

"The essential point I'm trying to make here, and as a journalist you should feel this more acutely than anyone else, is that the police are nothing but the Zomos of this fascist state. They exist for no other reason than to ensure the safety and survival of the upper classes and the stability and submission of the underclasses. Crime, violence, poverty, suffering, they are all merely symptoms of the elementary evil of this social system. How can a man be blamed for criminal behaviour when he is born into a system that constantly exploits and abuses him without holding out any possibility of redress? The police have complied with this policy because it allows them to establish a sphere of power and influence as the strong arm of the ruling classes. The individual cop may seem like a nice guy, he may even *be* a nice guy, but his bosses know that they control him, and in the crunch he'll do what they demand. That's why cops are militarised, to reinforce blind obedience, to make robots of them all. The worst crime a cop can commit is to think for himself. My suggestion, if you're interested . . . ?"

Interested was one word. I waited, but not for long.

"Eliminate all police forces and prisons. Establish block counsellors and store-front legal aid stations to help the returning prison population re-integrate with society and receive assistance in un-learning the old violent and self-destructive patterns. Ensure that everyone has enough food to live on, and decent places to live. The money could come from all the police forces that have been disbanded, and the prisons that have been closed down. Once the prisoners realised that violence was not necessary, they would become peaceful. If they had no fear of the cop's brutality, they could develop as nature intended. Look at films of the Chicago Police Riot in 1968. That's the true cop at work, the conditioned Zomo running wild with a club. Have you seen films of that?"

One of the drawbacks to getting older is that undergraduates will quote your history at you out of context and distorted beyond recognition, and then settle down to tell you how it really was. I just nodded.

"Absolutely unprovoked assaults on harmless children. And they loved it, you could see it in their faces. The Sixties were the first years of true revolt, the rising up of the underclasses and the enlightened children of the oligarchy. That's my hope, that someday it will happen again. The Zomos put it down this time, but the Sixties will come again, and once again the masses will be on the move. Led by – "

Don't tell me, I said, the enlightened children of the oligarchy. Did that include her?

She nodded around her éclair.

"Yes, I suppose, the burden of my privilege. The educated must lead."

* * *

In a lounge chair in the bar of the Chateau Halifax, I sat back and listened as a recently divorced woman told me why she had left her policeman husband after careful consideration. The divorce was not recent, but the pain seemed fresh. She was nearing thirty and handling it well, a brunette with grey eyes and a tan fading away under a forest-green ultra suede suit.

"He wore his job on his sleeve, I guess. The department makes them wear their hair just so, and they all have this college jock look, running to fat around the jawline. Anyway, everybody knew he was a cop so anytime we went anywhere it was . . . tense . . . sometimes. My friends were college crowd, they used a little grass now and then, and they had this view of cops. My girl friends could never understand why I got mixed up with one. I was always such a hellion. But he had something, a kind of simplicity? Not stupid, he was smarter than me by a couple of blocks, but he was clear. He always acted as if he knew what was good and what was bad and what was in between. He had that kind of light? Well, we had it pretty good for a while. My friends either got used to him or drifted off. Then that miserable strike came up . . . you know about that?"

I did. Wage and contract disputes had brought an unprecedented walk-out by the Halifax Police Force. Chronic underpayment was at the edge of it, but municipal intransigence and complacency cut the deepest into the force's morale. The strike was over in a few hours.

There had been some vandalism and some wildness in the city centre, before the RCMP arrived to act as stand-ins. Largely, civilisation had run on in its grooves while the police stayed home. They had struck in Fredericton later that year, with similar results. The story would have stayed at the local level if the *fact* of a striking police force hadn't been so monumental. The networks carried it nationally. The Halifax police were still smarting under the accusations of public irresponsibility and mendacity. Municipalities like to wrap themselves in the flag of fiscal restraint whenever it's inconvenient to pony up right away.

"Yes . . . everybody remembers. Anyway, the strike was over fast. But leaving the street . . . that part was very hard for him. He always thought that his duty, that was the word he used, his duty was to protect the citizens, to stay on the job in any weather . . . I used to kid him about sounding like a postman. He and his buddies argued ferociously about the strike. Should they? Shouldn't they? A lot of friendships were broken. My husband lost a couple of buddies from the college. They just stopped speaking. The sergeants were pretty hard on the men, as well. The whole idea of striking burned him. But he also had to stand by the members. There was an issue at stake. Either they were serfs or men, was the way he put it. Anyway, you know what happened. They went out on strike. And he changed literally overnight." She punched out her cigarette. A gold chain tinkled musically on her slender wrist. She blew out the last of the smoke and sighed.

"He lost that light. It was as if somebody had reached inside him and pulled a plug. I thought he'll get over it eventually, but he never did. Such a stupid thing, too, a silly labour dispute. Who cares about strikes these days? But it wasn't the strike that bothered him, not directly. I think what was eating at him was the fact that everybody had walked off the job and left the city unguarded. I think the poor kid felt that staying on duty was some kind of sacred trust or something. Imagine! In this day and age! A genuine point of honour. He never said honour, but I think that was what was preying on him. Well the light went out of him . . . he got very tiresome. No fun to have around. Nothing bright to say. He just went to work and came home. After six months, it got on my nerves and I told him I wanted him to cut it out. It was useless. He wasn't carrying on or anything . . . it was just that he wasn't the man I married. He was just too noble for his own damned good. After a while, I left him. Really, can you blame me? It was like he'd lost his virginity. I finally decided he was a lost cause. The world is just too complicated for men like that. It gobbles them up. Nobody thinks that way anymore, do they?"

Apparently not.

* * *

The meeting had been set for five o'clock at Thackeray's, a brass-and-mahogany restaurant on Spring Garden Road, in the shadow of the Citadel, in Halifax. I sat in the greenhouse section, admiring a lapstrake rowing scull suspended from the roof, for an hour and a half. I was on my way out when the man in the blue wool topcoat caught me at the door. He was embarrassed-looking, but it could just have been his colour. He was very ruddy-complexioned, and his eyes were red as well, as if he'd been standing in a cold wind for too long. He had a strong dry hand and a broad open smile. He apologised for the wait.

"Look, I'm still asking myself why I'm here. You guys aren't exactly the apple of a cop's eye. But you tell the truth at least this once, okay?"

I promised.

"All right . . . it starts out slowly, so slow you never notice it. I mean, it's a tradition for the cop to be a hard-drinking man, isn't it. Hell, it's a tradition for the writer, and I see you're having a double right now!"

I found this observation disturbing but secondary.

"Maybe it is. I was on the street for years. Good at it, too. I had several partners, and we never drank on duty, even in those days. Halifax is a rough town. Like any port city, we have some wild bars. ABS's fight like demons. They have all that money and so little time. They'll work over a hooker, or just start up a punch-out for fun. We got the calls. It was like that every Friday and Saturday night for at least six years, for me. And when it was over, I'd stop for a few drinks with the guys, at the clubhouse over by the channel. Rum was my drink then, in honour of my daddy, who was a captain over in Saint John. I used to pride myself on the amount of rum I could handle. There was always this feeling, that if you were a hard man you could drink all night and work all day and never weaken. Lord knows where it came from, but we all believed it. I'm prepared to put a little money on the table tonight that says you yourself have been drunk nine nights out of ten on this book, and every night was with a cop. Am I right?"

He was close enough to make an objection pointless.

"Sure, I can see it in your face. You *look* like you've been doing a lot of drinking. It's good fun, isn't it? Nobody has a better time than an off-duty cop. I should know. Now and then, my wife would kick up a row over it. I'd come home late, smelling like a rum barrel. The guys would drop me off on the steps giggling like fools. One night, she opened the door to catch me standing there, relieving myself all over her periwinkle plants. Hell to pay, of course. Anyway, this went on for close to six years and I never thought anything of it. It was just part of the routine, and routine is what the job is made of. Habit. Work the street, get pissed. And then one day I realise my sergeant has been dropping hints about my shooting. We have to qualify each year, and your scores are marked down. I had always been one of the best in my division. I was proud of that. I even have some trophies. I was a marksman. I used to feel good inside when the guys on the squad would say 'you can always tell what Pete was aiming at by what he hit!' I never used the gun but once on duty, and then only to warn. But it's no easy thing, to shoot well, and a man can be proud of himself if he can. The devilish thing about it is pistol work calls for control. I had control. I could steady up like a stone and the sights would never waver. On rapid fire, I brought the barrel back on line like a machine. One year, in just one year, all that left me. I couldn't shoot for shit. The sergeant got onto me about it. I took some kidding from the guys. But I never made any connection until my kid says to me 'daddy show us the *chugalug*' and it comes to me that I'm famous with his friends as a drinker not a marksman. I got mad at him. My wife and I had a real row. I finally walked out of the house and went to a bar to cool off. That was the first time I started to think of myself as a man with a drinking problem. I had some friends there, we went back a few years. I told them my wife thought I was a man with a drinking problem. They said that was crazy, I drank, I got drunk, I fell down – no problem!" He laughed at that old line. The table in front of him was empty. He still sat like a man with a drink in his hands, his elbows resting on the wood, forearms slanting in to the spot where his glass would be, but there was no glass there.

"I'll make this part short. I was so used to drinking after work that it never occurred to me that I should cut down. I'd been hitting the rum for six years and it had never hurt. Anyway, a man needed something to cool the nerves. Some police nights are horrendous. Even barricade duty at a homicide can be nasty. Accidents we see a lot of. Haligonians pride themselves on their talent to hold booze and speed. The weather on this rock is something you have to see to understand. Nights come along that could sink the whole city; nothing left above the waves but the old fort. There you are on the street or in the car slipping all over the road, freezing. I started to carry a small flask in my coat, just to keep the chill off. A tot of rum to burn my throat. No harm in that. I'd get kidded by my friends, but no one would ever tell the sergeant. Policemen don't do that. Booze was just a tool of my trade. It kept me alert."

The waiter stopped by for second orders. There weren't any.

"Two years ago I was drunk on the job at least half the time, and useless almost all the time. My buddies carried me. My collars slipped away to nothing. Now and then, some guy would feed me one or two, just to help my sheet. Funny thing was, I knew the work was slipping, but I thought I was only going through a bad time. I had trouble at home during this period. For some reason, my wife and kids were getting on my nerves, always at me for some stupid thing. Do this, fix that, fix this, wake up. In the fall I slapped her so hard it broke a tooth. I stood over her lying on the kitchen floor, swearing at her about how it was her own stupid fault. I wanted to hit her again. The scene looked so familiar to me but the point of view was all wrong. I should have been standing in the doorway, in uniform, trying to get this stupid drunkard to stop beating his wife. I knew then that I *was* the drunkard. I didn't stop."

This story didn't come out all at once; he worked at it. I admired his backbone. Telling me this story was half news, half penance.

"Towards the end, I had bottles in the locker, in the trunk of the cruiser. If I was on foot I kept it in a carton in an alley. I knew people who'd sell it on Sundays. I was never without. I started losing friends. No one wanted to partner me; I was just too sloppy. I jumped a couple of kids once, for nothing. I had to be pulled off. I should have been fired. In any other field, I would have been sacked a long time ago. But I wasn't."

I had already gathered, from the empty space on the table between his restless hands, that there was an ending to this story I wouldn't be sad to hear.

"Finally the sergeant hauls me into the station right off the street. Just him and me in the office, nobody else around. 'You,' he roars at me, 'are a fuckin' disgrace to the uniform. You have a choice; dry off or get out. What's it gonna be?' The guys were outside listening. I thought about how I was still mad at my wife, and I thought 'shit, maybe I really am a drunk!' I said I'd dry off. The sergeant says to me 'You're off the street until you do. In records.' I knew he was giving me a break. They dumped me in AA and there I stayed. Half the time I was in AA I told myself that I didn't belong there. I fell off three times. My wife moved out twice. Finally, I just never took that next drink." He drummed his hands on the tabletop. "Christ, Thackeray's . . . I even been pissed in here."

I asked him why he'd named a bar to meet in.

"Buddy, I *work* in bars. I'm a goddamned cop, remember?"

* * *

Thursday, December 14, 1978 was a windfall day for city editors in Toronto, Halifax, Vancouver, and a multitude of small-town dailies in between. The rubric over the banner of the *Toronto Star* for that date said: "Enough Guns Seized 'To Start War' Police Say." The lead paragraph stated: "A vast assortment of weapons seized in a coast-to-coast crackdown against Canada's biggest ever gun-smuggling ring, contained enough material 'to start a small war or insurrection,' police say." On page two the story continued under a large black and white photo of two grim-faced plainclothesmen holding a weapon described as "a miniature bazooka . . . it could knock down a plane." On the floor in front of the two police officers three military weapons were laid out like fishing trophies; an M 1 carbine with a half-moon clip, an FN-FAL 7.62 military rifle similar to the weapon issued to Canadian Forces, and an M 16 rifle such as the US Forces had used in Vietnam. The tone of the report was breathless and portentous. The impression was conveyed, in spite of reasoned statements from Detective Inspector J.F. Savage of the Ontario Provincial Police to the effect that the guns were directed to collectors, that Canada had been narrowly rescued from a coast-to-coast terrorist uprising. This was heady stuff.

On December 27, 1978, the *Toronto Star* ran a full-page report by staff writer Paul King on the nation-wide gun-running conspiracy. It was entitled "PROJECT LEGATO . . . How North America's Biggest Gun Smugglers Were Smashed – and 2500 Weapons Uncovered." The lead line reiterated the quote from an unnamed policeman that there were enough guns "to start a war." Comparing Operation Legato to "a hurricane", King detailed an investigation over six months long conducted by officers of the RCMP, the Ontario Provincial Police, Peel Regional Police, into the illegal importation and sale of machine guns, military arms, plastic explosives, rocket launchers, including such now-familiar names as Uzi, Ingram, Kalashnikov, and Hechler and Koch. Raids by RCMP forces in Quebec on houses owned by local bikers had resulted in the "discovery" of a "major dealer" in

Ontario. As King put it, "The first strands of the noose were being strung."

According to the *Star* report, RCMP men in Kirkland Lake, Ontario, and Bridgewater, Nova Scotia, commenced undercover surveillance of the "dealer" in Matachewan, Ontario and the "supplier" in Nova Scotia. This surveillance included legal wiretaps, physical surveillance, and the interception of "parcels of guns through the mails from England." As King put it, "The Mounties determined, by surveillance, what the parcels contained: some of the most lethal weapons in the world; in all, twenty-seven different kinds of prohibited firearms . . . among them were two types of assault rifles . . . the FN-CAL . . . the most advanced assault rifle in the world . . . costs up to $300 legitimately, and $1,800 on the black market . . . the other, the FN-FAL costs $700 on the black market . . . the standard NATO and OPP rifle . . . both these semi-automatic weapons are legal in Canada with proper registration since the trigger must be squeezed and released with each shot. However, by installing 'selector levers' (a small bolt-like attachment) the guns could be converted into fully-automatic rifles – firing twenty bullets in a second. . . . "

The report went into great detail about the various kinds of weapons these "conspirators" were importing and distributing. The phrase "black market" turned up repeatedly, with all of its clandestine resonances. Further down the page, the *Star* reporter identified the Matachewan dealer as running a "gun and tackle business" but "he wasn't registered." He was alleged to have also sold "everything from rocket-launchers to anti-tank guns, prohibited weapons used sparingly even by select police units."

The article sketched in a picture of men in at least three provinces conspiring to import and distribute to various people described as "gun nuts – men who collect and trade expensive military hardware" in the United States and Canada just about every major terrorist weapon known to man. Throughout the article the word "collector" appeared in quotes; the editorial equivalent of the raised eye-brow and the sly wink.

The operation was described in terms of an illegal drug-dealing ring. The man in Matachewan was said to receive special orders from his "collectors" in various parts of the United States and relay these orders to "a go-between in Sept Isles, Quebec. The go-between took the money to a man in Volger's Cove, N.S. Then, the supplier in Bridgewater, N.S. took the weapons to Volger's Cove and was paid. . . .The man in Volger's Cove then dismantled the guns and mailed them, in several pieces, to the Matachewan dealer – at any one of three addresses. The dealer picked them up, reassembled them, then mailed them to the customers. . . . The task force was able to follow the operation. What they still don't know is how the guns were smuggled to the Bridgewater supplier from Europe. The RCMP and Interpol are now investigating the sources."

Project Legato rolled on through the summer of 1978. The North Bay section was collecting the names of other men across the country to whom guns were being sent. According to King, "As the collectors were identified, RCMP in their area put surveillance on them. Eventually, sixteen different groups were being watched." The "illegal guns" were regretfully allowed to move about the country. The police lived in constant fear of exposure or the outbreak of "bank robberies or sky-jacking." After collecting evidence of this massive conspiracy for almost six months, a go-ahead was finally given to launch Project Legato raids on all parties cross-Canada in early November. After some delays, including an unexpected "amnesty" declared by the Federal government to allow people to surface all unregistered guns and an attempt by the Bridgewater "supplier" to register seven hundred weapons at once, the nation-wide raids finally got under way on December 12, 1978.

In North Bay, men of the OPP Detachment went with six men to the Matachewan "dealer's" house and arrested him. Other men went to the Extender Mine in Matachewan and arrested the caretaker. In the mine's outbuildings the officers discovered "a truck-load of Uzi and Sterling sub-machine gun parts, plus silencers, hidden in picnic coolers filled with oil. Other parts were hidden through the shed. Thirty other rifles, revolvers, and business records were also found in the caretaker's home. . . . In Nova Scotia . . . men raided the home of the Bridgewater supplier. They found two thousand weapons. Guns were stored in every room except the bathroom. . . .

" . . . In total, ten arrests were made in Ontario, one in Newfoundland, two in Nova Scotia, one in the Northwest, one in Calgary, one in B.C. and two in Winnipeg." Among the men implicated were a Captain of the Royal 22nd Regiment, a Chrysler Corporation foreman, an engineer, stockbrokers, firemen. The Van Doos Captain was relieved of two gold-plated Thompson sub-machine guns valued on the "open" market, whatever that is, at twenty thousand dollars.

In Quebec, over a hundred men engaged in thirty-five raids across the province, netting eighteen machine guns and an indeterminate number of machine-gun parts, a hundred and ninety-three carbines, seventy-five revolvers and pistols, five grenade casings (which are grenades without explosive), two silencers, and a great deal of ammunition. Mounties scooped two-hundred weapons in a single house.

The report concluded with this statement: " . . . the task force expects to continue follow-up investigations until the spring of 1979. Officers say that up to a hundred more arrests are possible."

Project Legato made headlines all across Canada. The CBC carried the story nation-wide, as did CTV. Local papers and television stations did follow-ups and context pieces with obvious relish. Nineteen men were charged, eleven with Conspiracy, a charge that could result in fifteen years in prison. The venue was Haileybury, Ontario, a little town near North Bay. All men charged were arraigned there and then released on bail. Any citizen who read these reports or who watched the television coverage would have come to the inescapable conclusion that a crack police investigation had brilliantly intercepted and crushed a clandestine weapons smuggling conspiracy the scope of which was hitherto unknown in Canadian history. The leads into biker gangs and para-military groups in the United States kept the RCMP and other forces busy for another year. The image of those terrible instruments of murder in the steady hands of the police was reassuring. The effect of Project Legato on official funding of other anti-terrorist operations can only be speculated upon. By the time all the leads were tied up and the final raids successfully completed, the actual cost of the project in terms of man-hours and equipment and disbursements approached one and a half million dollars.

In North Bay they made much of the fact that this huge criminal conspiracy had even involved a serving police officer. Almost unnoticed in the lengthy lists of the accused published in various papers on December 13, 1978, was the name of Ontario Provincial Police Constable Ronald Kurelo, aged 29, of Kirkland Lake. Kurelo was charged with possession of a restricted weapon, an FN-FAL assault rifle which he was alleged to have altered, via the alarmingly simple expedient of installing what Paul King referred to as a "selector lever" in the action, in order to convert the rifle to full automatic fire. People in Ontario, and Kurelo's brother officers in Kirkland Lake and North Bay, were "disgusted" and "disappointed" to hear of this corrupt cop in their midst. The trial and punishment of this criminal along with his co-conspirators was eagerly awaited by the good citizens of this country.

Kurelo can still remember the arrest. Men he knew, RCMP Constables with whom he'd shared a glass, OPP Officers he worked with, suddenly turned on him with amazing venom.

"It's a funny life, the cop's life. It's as if there are two lines in the life. There are lines you can cross without being thought of as evil. You can rough up a prisoner in anger, and the guys will shake their heads and drag you off the guy and say 'poor guy's been working too hard.' You can accept a complimentary drink from a friend in a bar and the guys will say 'good old Ron he has the common touch.' You can accept a fifteen per cent reduction from a price tag for a coat from a storekeeper who wants to thank you for being a good cop, and nobody will say 'graft' or 'bribe'." Kurelo puts the glass down on the table and his face locks up. He's still young and good-looking but his eyes are not.

"But if they suspect, even a little bit, that you've gone over that line, it's like you're dead. Your closest buddies will turn on you. Men you've worked with for years will spit on the sidewalk in front of you. Sergeants who've stood up for you in disputes or backed you on cases will curse you in the street. Other officers will threaten you, sometimes attack you. Nothing you can say or do, nothing that ever happens, will ever change their minds. It's black and white. If you hadn't done somethin' wrong, you wouldn't have been charged. You know the expression, 'sent to Coventry'? It's from the old days of the British Army. An officer who was thought to have betrayed the code of the gentleman soldier was declared by all his mess-mates to be in Coventry. No one, under any circumstances, was to acknowledge your presence in any way, not even to insult you. No one could look at you. No one could step out of your way on the walks. No one could eat with you or drink with you or walk with you. Except in the line of duty, you had ceased to exist. It's an experience I will never never ever forget. It was as if I had died but I was still walking around Kirkland Lake. Even the townspeople turned vicious. Small towns are like families, and I'd betrayed the trust. I was part of an international terrorist conspiracy. They knew that because they'd seen it on TV and they'd read it in the papers.

"I tried to tell my buddies . . . they snarled at me. One of them took a swing at me. A guy I'd saved from brawls and backed up in all kinds of tight places, tried to take my head off. No one wanted to hear my side. I was on a tape recording as having ordered gun parts from this dangerous gun dealer in Matachewan, this Peter Wilke guy, and that was all they needed to know. That contact meant I was a crooked cop.

Crooked. Try to imagine how it would be taken if a priest or a minister
or a rabbi had been caught molesting a child. Being a cop who went
sour is that kind of sin. You're marked for life. After a long time, I
stopped trying. They had to listen to me in court. I shut up and
waited."

Kurelo was suspended with pay while Ontario gathered evidence
and the senior officials in charge of Project Legato collated the
information their agents had collected. Ron Kurelo's connection with
the mysterious Matachewan gun broker named Peter Wilke was not
so mysterious, according to the now quite bitter ex-policeman.

"Look . . . policemen deal with guns every day. Some policemen
even collect guns. I had an interest in guns going way back to my
childhood. You do that in the north. Kids learn to shoot like city kids
learn to drive cars. It was no big deal. Cooey .22's were cheap. Every
kid had one. We used to plink at cans, or hunt for ground hogs.
Hunting used to be considered a respectable sport, even in the big city.
I grew up and kept my interest in guns. Being a policeman – and when
I say policeman I mean straight-arrow copper. I was two years in the
RCMP before I went over to the OPP. RCMP guys are the straightest,
most rigid and most convinced cops you're ever going to find – anyway, being a cop, I got involved in military weapons. Hell, the OPP
Tactical Rescue Unit has a five-million-dollar budget every year, one
hell of a chunk of which gets spent on FN's and top-notch military
gear. I became quite an expert on military weapons. Right now I think
I know as much about Russian small arms as any man in Canada. And
all my copper buddies, every RCMP guy and every OPP guy in the
north, knew perfectly well that I knew guns, that I collected guns, and
that I was always interested in getting a good deal on parts. Those
bastards knew all of that stuff, because I never ever made one single
attempt to hide it! Why the hell should I, goddamnit, the shit is all as
legal as hell. Who the christ would have thought that I'd get busted for
doing something I'd been doing all along, right out in the bloody
open – buying and trading and selling military weapons and weapons
parts. It was my goddamned hobby, for god's sake!"

I said nothing. After a long while, he cooled down and poured us
both another drink. Outside in the street a siren dopplered wildly in
the dense night wind. He grinned suddenly at the sound. "Another
poor innocent son of a bitch, I'll bet." We both laughed, but my laugh
was unmixed. His was not.

Ron sat forward and pulled his shoulders tight, as if flinching, and then launched into a narrative on Project Legato. He talked long into the night, the facts ready and vivid and spinning out easily and without pause. I could see that the impact of Project Legato was deep and permanent, a collision with the legal mechanism which had fractured his life and shaken his deepest convictions. Briefly, this is what he said:

– The mysterious Peter Wilke, the Matachewan dealer who was described as the centre of the ring, turned out to be an engineer commissioned to run the Extender Mine during shut-down and who started up a thoroughly legitimate gun-parts importing business to make extra money.

– The "European connection" turned out to be nothing more than mail-order weapons houses any bona-fide dealer can utilise.

– All the "European shipments" were fully declared at Canada Customs as guns and gun parts, and all legal duties paid.

– Everything Wilke had imported through Bridgewater N.S. was imported in complete accordance with importation laws and firearms regulations.

– The "truckload" of parts found "hidden" in the Dry of the Extender Mine were actually legitimate gun parts held as part of Wilke's parts' inventory, and they were not shown to be hidden, but rather "stored", a word with an entirely different shading.

– The majority of the twenty-five hundred "prohibited and restricted" weapons seized were later proven to be legally registered and allowable under the applicable firearms regulations in force at the time of Project Legato.

– The devilish "selector levers" mentioned in the *Toronto Star* report, the ones that could be "simply installed" in order to make a weapon run on full auto, were shown to be only one small item in a conversion procedure that involved fifteen hours of skilled gunsmithing and a well-equipped metal milling shop.

– The network of "terrorists" were demonstrated, to the satisfaction of the court, to be solid citizens with a keen interest in military weapons; an arguably bizarre pastime, but a pastime nevertheless.

– The "miniature bazooka" that "could knock down a plane" was shown in professional military testimony to be the expended fibreglass casing of an M 72 Al, a military anti-tank weapon which can only be fired once and is then discarded, possessing no capability whatsoever of repeat fire, as is the case with a bazooka. Further, no one in the entire conspiracy was shown to possess any rockets that could be fitted to the M 72 Al casing.

– Ordering rifles and military goods from firms such as Fabrique Nationale in Belgium, and Hechler and Koch in West Germany was simply a matter of delivering a certified cheque and instructions to ship, along with suitable customs clearances, to their plant order desks, and then awaiting delivery in customs. The laws have since been altered.

– The extent and demographical breadth of arms collection and use in Canada was shown to be immense, touching all strata of society, and made up, in the main, of ordinary citizens with an extraordinary hobby. The senior officers in Project Legato appeared to be unable to make a clear distinction between a criminal conspirator and a collector.

– Weapons that can be described as military weapons are often sold, by the manufacturer, to private citizens or private dealers, and the simple possession of a military arm does not establish that the weapon was obtained illegally from any army base or arsenal.

Ron rolled on through the charges. Finally, his case came up. The bailiff had gone into the hall and called for Ron Kurelo. After some preliminaries, the Crown got down to the heart of the matter. Hefting a ticketed FN-FAL 7.62 assault rifle, the Crown looked over its glasses at the accused in the box and said, "Mister Kurelo, do you recognise this weapon?" Kurelo said yes.

"And do you admit that it belongs to you?" Yes, once again.

"Are you aware of the charges against you? You are charged with Possession of a Prohibited Weapon, in particular a Machine Gun on Full Auto Fire."

Ron knew this.

"And you are still prepared to accept this gun as yours?"

Ron was.

"And do you admit that you knowingly made mechanical adjustments to this semi-automatic weapon to convert it to a fully-automatic weapon?"

Ron did. Crown glowed. The kill was close.

"So you freely admit that this FN-FAL, which is yours, as you've said, was knowingly altered to fire on full-auto, and that it is presently a fully-automatic weapon? In other words, a machine gun?"

Ron said yes. The room was still.

"Are you aware of the legal restrictions placed on such weaponry?"

Yes.

"And are you aware of the penalties for illegal possession of such a weapon? As a *peace* officer, you *should* be aware. Are you?"

Ron nodded, and then said yes.

"Then I put it to you that you are guilty as charged, sir. I say – "

Kurelo was reaching into his suit jacket pocket. He pulled out a large rectangular slip of paper, and placed it on the Judge's desk. He explained what it was. The Judge looked over at Crown Counsel.

"This man has presented to evidence a Federal Firearms Permit to Possess a Restricted Weapon, one FN-FAL described as firing on Full Auto. It seems to be in order. Crown, what about this?"

There was a great deal of talk. The outcome was that Ron Kurelo was acquitted of all charges and he walked out of the court a free man, carrying his FN-FAL rifle, which he had been entitled to all along, according to the laws of Canada. According to him, the Crown demanded to know why he had not simply told the arresting officers that he possessed a Permit for the weapon.

Ron said, "I've been a policeman long enough to know that when you're being charged with something, you shut your mouth. Nobody ever asked me if the thing was ticketed. They just assumed I was crooked. They *never* asked."

Project Legato, which had cost $1,500,000, finally netted around seventeen thousand dollars in fines. No one ever went to jail. Peter Wilke got ninety-nine per cent of all his gun parts back again, and he carried on as before. What should have been a paper investigation, an administrative examination of paperwork, was turned by some senior police officers into a very costly anti-terrorist campaign. Not out of spite or ill-will, but out of the desire to fight evil. None of the junior men can be faulted for accepting the theories of their superior officers. It's not their duty to analyse the case; their job was to carry out the commands of their leaders. The atmosphere that contributes to mass hysteria, to the widespread public belief that the cities are crawling with gun-bearing killers, that conspiracies abound, is largely the creation of the Press, not the police. If even senior policemen are sometimes affected by this phenomenon, should we be surprised?

Ron Kurelo summed it up at the end of a long night.

"If you're a cop, you're under a scope all the time. You have to be whiter than white. The trouble is, you never know what's going to be the source of your troubles. Suppose I was very interested in muscle cars. Say I bought and sold them all the time, and I was always looking for parts. If I happened to call a dealer one day and say I wanted a Holman-Moody bolt-on, and the guy said sure, I'll send it right over. I get the part, and three weeks later I find out the guy was under a surveillance operation and the RCMP had fingered me as a rotten cop working with a stolen-parts ring. You never know which one of your harmless hobbies is going to turn wild on you. The police are under so much pressure to be honest that even the slightest hint of a crooked cop in their midst is enough to drive them buggy. And as you see they don't want to know you after that. That whole Project Legato farce was strictly an administrative fuck-up, a paper palace. There wasn't one single true criminal in the crowd, just a bunch of poor stupid saps who thought gun collecting was as legal as the rules said. You shouldn't think that all cops know a lot about guns. Most of them know the .38 and the shotgun and that's *it*. When the RCMP brass heard M 16 and AK 47 and oh my goodness a *machine gun*, they didn't even stop to check the rules or the tickets. They just kicked off a huge boondoggle, and the Press rolled right over with them. As far as my job was concerned, it was finished. I *must* have been guilty. Why else would I have been charged? What the court said didn't matter. I was *out*!"

* * *

The bar in the Vancouver Police Club overlooks Burrard Inlet and the mountain slopes of North Vancouver. At two in the morning it's a splendid view across the dark water covered with reflecting lights up into the thousands and thousands of street lamps and home lights of the neighbourhoods. The bar itself is walled in dark wood, with comfortable leather-padded chairs and polished wooden tables. Every evening it fills up with off-duty policemen who need a place to slow down, and a drink or two to help dissipate the emotional charge built up while on the streets. Policemen relax here, away from the sergeants and the public. They joke with buddies, insult their enemies, play darts, put their cards on the table. Policewomen flirt with their partners for the hell of it, and the waitresses flirt with everybody. Behind the barman there are several rows of bottles. Glenfiddich and Glenlivet scotch, Jim Beam, Johnnie Walker Red and Black, Bell's, Irish Mist, Black Velvet, Crown Royal, Smirnoff's, Jack Daniels, Strega, Galliano . . . the Police Club in Vancouver is a well-stocked, comfortable and deliberately exclusive spot. The men and women of the Vancouver police expect to relax here, they expect not to run into lawyers and citizens and civil activists and hoods and weirdos. They expect to sit a while in comfort and down some good liquor while their heart-rates slow. The exercise reminded me of how much attention was being given in the various media to the subject of police stress, to "burn-out". I was sitting at a corner table with some of the men from the Drug Squad. The phrase "burn-out" got a reasonable laugh.

Finn, the undercover spotter from the Blackstone, a man I can't describe, chuckled into his Lowenbrau. "Oh lordy yes! Stress . . . it's a terrible killer around here, isn't it guys? I suffer from it all the time. That's why I drink so much. That's why I have to have nine women every night after the shift. Sometimes ten."

"Sometimes none, Finn . . . don't listen to this, this dork's as married as they come. And so are most of the rest of these guys." Ike was jovial, but there was something underlying his mood that I couldn't quite read. He went on.

"It's the wives, I think, that help the most in this job. I mean, here I am, sitting here having a glass with you . . . it's two thirty in the morning and we've been on the shift since six this afternoon. I know she's probably waiting up. I tell her not to but I know she will. Fourteen years now and she never changes. Finn talks a good game, but I don't know a good cop who doesn't work hardest at keeping a good wife. Not that it's easy."

Burns spoke up. "Too true . . . I'm on my third. Some of them can take it and others can't. I think that a cop's wife is born, just like a good cop is born. You either have the stamina or you don't."

Sherman rumbled from a corner chair, "It's not such a bad life, though. We make good money . . . lots of overtime. I bring home over forty thou a year. We have a good home, a couple of cars. The kids get anything they need, and a lot of things they don't. We're happy."

Ike shook his head, but said nothing. Before I could ask him what was on his mind, someone else spoke up.

"This stress thing, Finn's right. I mean, you do get worked up. Like on Homicide or accidents; some nights you wade through dead meat. Literally dead meat. It may have once been a kid or a wife or a grandmother, but some bug has turned it into dead meat. You get it on your sleeves, you smell of it. The pictures stay in your mind even if you get pissed to the gills for hours. Or the brass gets to you . . . take Smith here, please." Smith looked up from his pitcher of margaritas and crossed his eyes. "Now Smith here was sent out by the department to learn everything there was to know about traffic accidents. He went to a course that cost the department an easy five grand all told. He learned about tire wear, skid mark interpretation, velocities, braking characteristics, road law, acceleration, kinetic and potential energy, crash dynamics, you name it, Smith here learned it. Took the son of a bitch six months, but he aced the course and they sent his ugly face back here a bona fide expert on traffic accident investigations and courtroom analysis. So ask me?"

I asked him the question. Why was Smith on the Drug Squad?

"Frigged if I know! The brass got him back here and bangoed him right into Drug Squad. With all due respect to Smith here, he didn't know doodley-squat about Drug Squad. Smith was a Traffic ace. That's not all! As soon as Smith got back here, the department posted a job opening for Traffic Investigator. Smith applied for the job the force had trained him for and they turned him down! Now that kind of stupidity will give you migraines. So I guess there is stress here. But you don't let it take over your whole life − " Burns cut in:

"That's exactly right! I get a pain in my hip pocket listening to the media go on and on wringing its little white gloves over Stress In The Force and The Burnt-Out Cop, as if we were a bunch of light bulbs. Sure the job's tough. There are lots of tough jobs. Try tree-topping, or brain surgery. Life is tough. But you have to keep the shit under control. You don't wander around the locker room moaning to your buddies about your angst and your cosmic role and your meaning-of-life shit. You do the job, you jump over the shit, you stay away from the sergeant, no offence Bradshaw, and you keep the stress part in only one part of your mind. It's like you have one small corner of your head and in that corner, you are off the goddamned wall. You're a major wacko, a screamer. But it's only a small part. The other parts get pissed with the guys, go kiss the wife, thump the crooks, catch the bad guys, bullshit with the lawyers, and save your cash. That's how cops deal with stress. That's how *anybody* deals with stress. I'm sick of being made to sound like some kind of wimp in the papers. It's a tough job but I can do it. Ask me how?"

I did.

"Rock and Roll and Rhythm and Blues. Ask me what was on the flip side of *Great Balls of Fire* by Jerry Lee Lewis. Never mind. It was

Shake. I think I have the entire Decca label catalogue memorised. Fats Domino, Rufus Thomas, The Bluenotes, US Bonds . . . I collect forty-fives. I probably know more about the original Rhythm and Blues sidemen in this country than any other man alive – "

"Any *cop* alive!" said Sherman, grinning hugely.

"Any *man* alive! Okay, smart ass, you tell the man who was on the first Little Eva cut, for *Locomotion,* and when did it come out? Come *on!*"

The table got into a big debate about this. Like most cops, they hated to talk about cops. Away from their work, they were relaxed, good-natured, opinionated, raucous, cursed with twisted senses of humour, and thoroughly likeable.

I looked over at Ike. This kind of discussion was his bread and butter, but he wasn't saying anything. He was sitting slightly away from the table, stirring his scotch with a pencil, smiling mildly, but apart. I watched him for a while, until he noticed that.

"Sorry," he said, "I seem to be a little out of it."

"What's the problem?"

"Nothing, really . . . well, these boyos, they make the job sound tough, and I guess it is. Mind you, I think we get paid a good price. We work for it. The brass are all crazy, and so are most of your customers. But, this stress thing. It's like a big pike up in the lakes. You know that I mean?"

I had no idea what he meant.

"Look . . . you troll for pike in the early morning. You let the spinner in and you run it out, and then you glide along in the boat over water as flat as the back of my hand. It's so quiet you can hear a robin puking in the bushes. It's so quiet you can hear – anyway, a little while goes by, nothing happens. Then *pow* the line strips off the reel and your spinner flies off up the lake. You never saw it coming. You figure everything, but you never see the pike. Right?"

We were pretty drunk; I figured he'd make his point eventually. He did.

"Our boss, he's a good man. A hard-nose, but fair. Honest. His buddy is a guy, I can't tell you his name right now, he was one of the first guys to open up the street squads. A real old hand, and cool as ice. A thirty-year man. He's got a place up in the interior, a real nice spread, his wife would break your heart. A real colleen, a Black Irish beauty. Kids, a good home. Even a sailboat down by the park. Now all of this is absolutely legitimate. If there's graft in this department I don't know about it, and believe me, with my rep, I'm the one they'd ask. We all think the world of this guy. Look up to him. From our days in uniform. He's the kind of cop you want to be. He's as brave as vinegar. And smart, not just street smart, but intelligent and polished. He had saved his money and made some investments. Cops are always big on investments. I don't know a cop who isn't dabbling in stocks a little. This fellow made good decisions, and he ended up with a fair pile. He is kind of an example to us, something to let you know that it can be done. You can stay honest, you can avoid being a fast-tracker screwing his buddies for a promotion, you can stay alive. And in the end, it will all pay off. You get the brass ring." Ike lowered his voice and his glass, leaning forward in the leather chair until our heads were within inches. Ike was fairly ripped by this time, and I was way ahead of him. I knew what was coming.

"You remember the poem "Richard Corey?" Simon and Garfunkel did it as a single, in the Sixties. Last week, this man, this hero, did a Richard Corey on the department. He walked out of the office at the end of his shift, he drove home and kissed the wife, he had a drink. Then he walked into his library and closed the door. He took the .38 out of his holster and he stuck the muzzle in his mouth and blew the back of his head off. Killed himself!" Ike put his big arms out in a gesture of encompassment, see the madness.

"Yeah yeah some cops eat the pistol sooner or later. The thing is, with most of them, you can see it coming. They've got family troubles. The wife splits. The kids are gone. When he quits the force his life is over. But this guy, we all thought he had it made. When I looked at him, I thought, there's a happy cop. And now he's in a box with half his brains blown out. The thing is, is it like that pike in the water? I think I'm happy. I think I've got it under control. But is the big pike coming up on me? How do I tell, if *he* couldn't tell?"

Ike lifted his tough-guy's face up out of the scotch glass. His quick-frozen blue eyes were not sad but puzzled. I had no answer.

CHAPTER NINE

Hookie-Mal's Run

A cold wet wind was coming in off James Bay, driving low banks of dull grey cloud over the bare pine woods. The black flies were thick around the yellow bulb on the porch outside the old frame house. It was late in the evening, but the long northern twilight was still glimmering far off in the west. There was a new Franklin stove hard up against the north wall of the house. On the wall above it the owner had placed a collection of black and white snapshots of his years in the force. We had been punishing a bottle of Chivas most of the day, and the room was heavy with cigarette smoke and the smell of pine logs crackling in the stove. It was a good room, not too calculated or overdone. It had that kind of masculine solidity that you find in hunters' lodges and the homes of retired servicemen. We had been admiring his vintage Winchester 30-30, found on a Riel battlefield at Batôche. The stock was outlined in tiny nail-heads, decorated in an Indian fashion begun on the Great Plains during the last century. When I put the gun back on the wall, I noticed a photograph of a young Indian boy, smiling out from under a policeman's fur hat. When I asked the man about this picture, he told me this story.

* * *

"Hookie-mal was always a handful. No real bad in the kid, but wild. Reservation Cree, like most of them around Moosonee, Fort Albany. Southern James Bay is Cree country, unless you're asking the Ojibway, who think the Cree eat the dead. The Cree think the Ojibway were born from marsh grass, so you have to ignore a lot of that. I liked the Cree. Most of my partners didn't.

"Hookie-mal was only seventeen when he jumped out the window of the police car. We were taking him in for breaking windows. Not that it was a big charge. There wasn't a hell of a lot to do in Moosonee. The whole town was just a single street, a collection of shacks and houses in wood, propped up on the permafrost. An Ontario Northland Railroad spur, a bad road, the OPP Detachment office, the Hudson's Bay Store, the LCBO. The Cree were good people but they drank. Hookie-mal was no different. Just a small-built black-eyed kid with a funny sideways kind of walk. He carried one shoulder lower than the other, as if he was getting ready to rabbit-punch you, but he wasn't mean. My partner and I had gone out to the reserve grounds, just to visit, really. A bunch of the Cree kids were playing baseball and doing some Le Pages out of a brown paper bag. We jumped on that whenever we saw it. Glue was the drug of choice on the reserve. I hated to see it; little kids eight and nine with their eyes bloodshot and their brains half-cooked. Suicides all the time. Reserves will break your heart if you let them. Anyway, we got out of the Suburban, it was fall, the ground was hard. Hookie-mal saw us coming and tried to hit a ball through the windshield of the truck. It hit the side window, which I just rolled up. Shattered it. We chased that kid for a mile. He was just like a squirrel in the bush, fast and quiet and clever. We cornered him at the edge of a marsh and scooped him up, kicking and biting; a real little wolverine, he was. I would have let the whole thing drop but not my partner. Deep down he hated the Cree. Most of the guys either loved them or hated them. It's funny, really. We take all their lands, even the godforsaken soggy swamp-soaked flatlands around southern James Bay, and we set up our laws and our stores. We sell the poor buggers all the booze they can drink and take away anything they really want. And then we hate the bastards because they turn into alcoholics before they're twenty. Made no sense to me then. Still doesn't. Anyway, I'm rambling.

"My buddy dragged Hookie-mal back to the Suburban and threw him into the wire cage on the flatbed. Everybody stood around and laughed. The women came to the doors and looked out. We must have had twenty kids hanging on to the fender as we pulled away. They bounced off in a bit. We went back down the track. Roads in that part of Ontario are just like a part in the trees. The ground is either marsh or rock, so you just point the 'dozer and drive it through the pines. We were bouncing over the road with Hookie-mal hanging on to the wire cage by his fingers. Frank was doing it on purpose, I guess, just to give the kid a hard time. I stuck my head out the window and told Hookie-mal to sit down, in Cree. The Cree could never get used to my speaking their language. None of the officers did. Cree spoke English and Cree and French, but the OPP spoke English only. Hookie-mal gave me a wave.

"When we got into town we were passing the ONR spur when the gate on the cage popped open. Maybe I hadn't shut it tight. Hookie-mal gave a little whoop and jumped right off the truck. We were doing maybe thirty. He would have been all right if it hadn't been for the hydro pole. He was wiry and tight, like a gymnast. I always thought Hookie-mal could have been Olympic, if only he had been born in the south. And born white. Anyway, that was all over in a second.

"He flew off the cage into the air, grinning from ear to ear, his hair flying in the wind. Frank hit the brakes. In the dust I could see Hookie-mal in the air. This telephone pole flicked by in the corner of my eye and hit Hookie-mal right in the side, under his ribs. He got all wrapped around it. We slid for a bit and then I ran back through the dust. Hookie-mal was out cold. When I picked him up there was blood in his mouth. We took him to the clinic.

"He turned out all right. These Indians are the toughest people I've ever seen. I've known Indians to get up off the floor with a bread knife in their chest and fight all afternoon. Hookie-mal had a broken rib, some bleeding inside. The blood in his mouth was from where he had bitten through his tongue. And he passed blood for a week or so. The only lasting thing was that he had bad back pains. They made him walk like a crab, sometimes. He'd scuttle when he ran, and he could never stand up really straight; he was always just a little bent. I hated to see that, but he never said anything about it and after a while you just learned to ignore it. Anyway, he didn't like you to talk about it. The village kids rode him hard about it, though, so I sort of took him under my wing and let him hang around the detachment house. Now and then we'd give him a job, let him sweep up or cut wood or go to the store for beer.

"There were only three of us in the detachment at that time. Frank, myself, and a corporal. Frank and the corporal were big guys, six feet and more, and they weighed an easy two fifty apiece. I was small, five ten, and I never weighed more than 165 in my life. We were together long enough to figure out that you couldn't act like a big city copper in the north. You learned to talk your way out of trouble. You used the people to help. If you tried to act like an asshole, throw your weight around, you'd get an early morning call from some guys and they'd waltz you around the woods for a while. You either figured it out or left town. Small town cops are just a small part of a family, even if they don't like to think of it that way. You can't disappear into the big city anonymity the way southern cops do. What's the point of concealing your badge number when you live two doors away from the man you're hassling? Frank and the corporal didn't really like the idea of having Hookie-mal hang around the station all the time, but we were good enough friends that they never made an issue of it. All the corporal asked was that I made sure Hookie-mal got out of the way when the sergeant flew in for Inspection. That was fine with me.

"A couple of years passed. Life went on as usual. They changed our old truck for a new GM Suburban complete with a red flasher on top and a hand-cranked siren. There was talk about giving us a radio the following year. Up in the north, you understand, we're about twenty years behind the south. When they buy new gear for the OPP boys in Barrie or Downsview, they send the old worn-out crap up north to Hornepayne and Hearst and Moosonee. Even the men don't mix. Men who love the northland don't make it in the cities. To us, Kirkland Lake was Palm Beach, and Toronto was a tropical jungle full of exotic natives. I went down to Toronto once; I left in two days. The air is like a smokehouse fire, and the people look like prisoners. Nobody was meant to live like that. I've never been back, and I never will. Anyway, Hookie-mal became sort of a mascot around the place. Even the ONR guys, when we got together for poker or a dance with the clinic nurses, they'd bring along something for Hookie-mal's people. He was trying to support them at the time. Hookie-mal's father had died the year before in a fishing accident out on the Bay. His mother was a lady named Ruth Little Basket, as pretty a Cree as I've ever seen. Hookie-mal was downright handsome, sort of a brown-skinned Fonzie, you know, from that *Happy Days* show. Hookie-mal even started wearing his hair like The Fonz, and he had this trick of hitching up his chinos and putting his head off to the left, just so, right, and saying '*heeeeyyyy – watchit!*' in a kind of Bronx Cree. Broke me up every time.

"I think it was in the Flood Year that it all came to a head. You look around outside, what do you see? Tundra and muskeg as far as the eye can see, and a thin fur of bush pine everywhere. Under the forest, we have swamp. James Bay doesn't exactly stop at the shoreline in this part of the province. It's all marsh and swamp and scrub pines and rock for two hundred miles inland. We had a heavy snowfall the winter before, and the run-off came early, before the ground got properly melted. So we had water everywhere. Nobody was dry. The black flies were as thick as pepper in the air. Tempers were short. We had brawls with the guys from the Forces base; I personally punched out two men from the Ontario Northland Railroad. People started packing shotguns in the trucks. Even after the water went away and the black flies settled down to normal, the whole town was on a knife-edge.

"Jimmy Kameladsit and his brother went fishing on James Bay and only Jimmy Kameladsit came back. He said his brother had gotten drunk and fallen overboard. Jimmy Kameladsit's cousins came down from Winisk when they heard about the drowning. We tried to keep them apart, but what can you do when you're all alone in a cabin with twenty Indians all as drunk as lords? The week after the Kameladsits came down, Jimmy Kameladsit was found in back of his cabin with his head beaten in. His skull was flat as a frying pan on one side, so it was reasonable to assume that someone had done him in with a frying pan. That's what homicide was like up here and I'll tell you it hasn't changed. We have ten men and cars where we used to have three men and trucks, but the people are still the same. You get an average of one murder per thousand people in the north, and most of the murders are solved by racing out to the shack when you get the phone call and taking the murder weapon out of the hand of the killer while trying not to step in the victim's blood. The Kameladsit murder became known as The Frying Pan Murder. We caught his cousins on the way back to Winisk and they were sent south for safe-keeping. They later got two years less a day for Manslaughter, I think. Anyway, The Frying Pan Murder started a real fad.

"Nobody kills in cold blood in the north. Most of the deaths are the end result of three-day drunks and reservation blues. A wife will cancel her man with an iron. The husband loses his temper and hits the nephew too hard. A young blood flirts once too often with somebody else's girl at a church dance. You get a call in the middle of the night to get out to Charlie Joseph's place or the freight yards and when you get there, half the time they've already tied the killer to a tree and whipped the billy out of him. You don't need to be Hercule Poirot to solve northland killings, and the ones you don't hear about don't count. Because you can bet you don't hear about fifty per cent of them. And if you do hear, sometimes you get out there and they say 'hey we buried him out in the bush' and they can't tell you exactly where. Do you want to know what the great white law machine can do about that? Nothing, my friend. Nothing. Want another drink? I'll have one too. One thing about single malt; it keeps the permafrost out of your toes. Anyway, where was I?

"The summer passed like putting your hand over a match; just a brief passage of warm weather. The days lasted most of the night. The sun just drops lower and lower but it won't disappear. Then there are geese way up there in the sky and you get up one morning and the water in the rain bucket has a thin sheet of ice on it. The wooden seat on the privy is frigid again. You feel the old big cold coming back over everything. Winter never really goes away, it just goes underground for a few weeks.

"It was in late November. Winter was back for good. We had two feet of it in the street and it was blowing up every day. I was alone in the detachment shed when the phone rings. Johnny Jumps Up and William Sinclair had been drinking out at the shoreline and they got to fighting. Johnny hit Billy with a firelog and Billy laid Johnny out with a frying pan full of pike. Johnny's brother had stuck Billy with his hunting knife.

"No one was around when I got the call, so I left a note and fired up the truck. Once you got it going, you never turned it off. I was on my way down the road when Hookie-mal jumped onto the hood and made a face at me through the windshield. He wanted to come along. I figured, what the hell, he can help me clean up the mess. When we got there, no one was around but Johnny Jumps and Billy Sinclair. They were both dead. It was freezing up fast out in the Bay, and the sky was dark with a big blow from the northwest, where the bad storms come from. We couldn't get the truck up to the shore. Hookie-mal and I sat down between Johnny Jumps and Billy. I had on my parka and all-weather gear, but Hookie-mal was only wearing a ski jacket and his toque was back in the truck. Hookie-mal put his back up against Johnny Jumps and snuggled into his stomach. Johnny Jumps was still warm, he said, and he smiled at me with that silly-ass Fonzie smile of his. Billy was still warm, too. They weren't by the time Hookie-mal and I had lugged them back to the truck. We put them in the wood-house to keep. There was no way we'd be able to bury them until the spring. Robert Robitaille, Johnny Jumps brother, came in about midnight to confess and we gave him some hot coffee laced with whisky and locked him up in the cell.

"Christmas was a bad season, too. There was a brawl out at the reserve and Jimmy Kedakwabit got killed with a rock. Magistrates came in twice a year to deal with local crimes, but we had to send the murderers south on the ONR. The bodies stayed behind; there wasn't much need for autopsies in cases like this. By mid-January, we had four stiffs in the wood-house behind the detachment office; Johnny Jumps and Billy, old Charlie Joseph, the Elder who died of natural causes, and Jimmy Kedakwabit, or Jimmy Catch A Rabbit, who got a rock in his temple at the Christmas party. Jimmy's killer had almost joined the group in the wood-house. His name was Jonah Walks Far, but he called himself Jonah Walker and tried to pass for white down in Kirkland Lake. He had an eye on a girl named Grey Eyes, a Cree doe with skin like buttermilk. I liked her myself. Jonah made a serious attempt to rape her at the party, which was the reason for the brawl that killed Jimmy Kedakwabit. By the time Frank and I got out there, old Jonah was lashed to a tree in the ballpark and he was bleeding all over his head and shoulders. When we picked him up, sheets of frozen blood cracked off his jean jacket and fell onto the snow. They looked like the candy stuff they put on candy apples, or like stained glass. Justice was like that up here; they handed it out themselves unless you got there fast. I remember one fall, they caught another rapist up in Lake River. They left him tied to a tree for the OPP to come and get. When the man got there, the black flies had bled him half to death and his eyes were swollen shut. I'm not sure you handle your rapists down south any better; maybe if you tied them to trees and left them there, you'd have fewer rapists. Anyway, there I go again.

"The point of this whole rigamarole is that we ended up in mid-January with four big Indian corpses in the wood-house. You couldn't bury them because the ground was frozen. Hookie-mal, who was trying to be helpful, said we could pile rocks on them and leave them like the old marker cairns from the whalers that you see sometimes up around Cape Henrietta Maria. The corporal put that one down fast. We had tried that one year up in Winisk. The wild dog packs had dug up the bodies and dragged them out onto the ice floes in James Bay. We had God's own time trying to get them all back. When you bury somebody, you don't usually want to see them again a few months later. Finally, we agreed that the carpenter should bang up some boxes to make things neat.

"Things hadn't progressed much past the planning stage when the bush telegraph was hopping with the news about our sergeant coming up on Austin Airways for a surprise inspection. This happened once or twice every month during the good weather, but it wasn't often he came north from Kirkland Lake in January. Austin Airways was the carrier. We used to call it Austin Scareways. Anyway, the rumours were usually true, so we set about getting the detachment ship-shape for the sergeant's inspection. We gave Hookie-mal the job of getting the stiffs all fixed up with pine boxes before the sergeant got there. That was a mistake.

"Sergeant arrived two days later. I was clean-shaven and in full uniform. The corporal looked like Napoleon. Even Frank had his shirt tucked in and a tie on. Everything was going smooth as silk until we got out to the wood-house. Hookie-mal was standing at attention outside the shed. The sergeant nodded once to him but said nothing. The sergeant was about fifty and he hated Indians with a passion. There was a rule in the Northland OPP that any man with an Indian girlfriend was a squaw-man and unfit for promotion. This was a real source of pain to me since I was heart-and-soul in love with Grey Eyes, the girl that Jonah Walks Far had tried to rape last Christmas. I'll say this; Hookie-mal had come up with the nicest pine boxes I had ever seen; all bevelled corners and good clean wood. They even had brass door pulls along the side. Hookie-mal was at that time cherishing thoughts of being one of the first Native policemen in Ontario, much to Ruth Little Basket's disapproval. The sergeant walks over to the coffins all laid out on the floor and he says 'I thought you had four bodies up here. Where's the fourth?'

"I'll tell you the truth, I had been so impressed with the boxes that Hookie-mal had come up with that I simply forgot to count them. I tried to look calm as I checked out the shed but there was no fourth body in sight. I thought 'God I hope Hookie-mal hasn't put one of them outside because the 'coons'll be at it for sure, frozen or not.' Finally, the corporal walks outside and asks Hookie-mal to come in. He steps in as smart as a grenadier, back as straight as he can get it, chin tucked into his ski jacket, grinning. He had even combed his long hair back under his toque so that he'd look neat. The sergeant growled at him 'where's the fourth body?' and Hookie-mal's face lights up. He walks over to one of the boxes and kicks it with his mukluk. I feel my stomach roll over slowly.

" 'In here!' said Hookie-mal, and he even hiked up his chinos and was half-way into The Fonz before he noticed that everybody was staring at him. The sergeant turned to the corporal and told him to pry the lid off. Sure enough, there was old Charlie Joseph, dumped in on top of Johnny Jumps. It had been a tight fit for Charlie Joseph. I think

Hookie-mal had found it necessary to bend old Charlie's left arm the wrong way to get him to fit.

"Hookie-mal wasn't being disrespectful. To the Indian, dead is dead. They know there's nothing left in the body when the spirit is gone. They don't think any more of a dead body than you would of a candy wrapper after the chocolate was all gone. He'd been able to find three good boxes, so he improvised. But that didn't matter to the sergeant. Not only was this a desecration; it was an Indian desecration to boot. He took one giant step over the box full of stiffs and cuffed Hookie-mal across the side of the face. Hookie-mal tumbled back into a woodpile and stared up at us while his face got redder and redder. Then he just got up and ran out of the shed. We caught holy hell for a good hour.

"At dawn the next day there was an awful crash down by the Hudson's Bay store. By the time the town turned out, somebody had gotten in through the front window and stolen a Winchester Pump shotgun, six boxes of shells, and two cartons of Milky Way chocolate bars. When Ruth Little Basket phoned in to say that somebody had stolen their skiddoo during the night, I knew that Hookie-mal was gone. Since Hookie-mal was my friend, I was told to go get him, and not to come back until I did.

"This all happened around the end of January. You have to understand that January around Moosonee is the cold heart of winter. Being from the south, you have no conception of cold. I headed out of town about two hours later on the detachment Bombardier skiddoo with a puppy full of supplies and all the heavy outergear I could find. The snow was frozen on top and maybe three feet thick under that. The world was as flat as a nun's pulse from the east to the west and from the north to the south, except maybe it's a little flatter out on the pack ice in James Bay. Hookie-mal's skiddoo tracks were easy to follow. The sun was up. The sky was blue. I felt pretty good; I was sorry about what had happened to Hookie-mal, but he had to come in and face it. No sense hiding, and anyway I'd stand up for him in front of the magistrate. He might get a few months or even probation if he kept his mouth shut. All I had to do was settle down onto the skiddoo and catch up to him.

"His trail led north along the shoreline in the direction of the Albany River. I figured he'd skirt Fort Albany if he got that far, but I didn't really think he'd try for it. Fort Albany is almost a hundred miles across the flattest, coldest and most-godforsaken piece of land in

America. The skiddoo was good for fifty out and fifty back with a spare tankful. My guess was that Hookie-mal would think it over and be waiting on the trail a few miles north.

"I got over that idea by dark. I wasn't thrilled about spending a night out on the snowfield but I had a good arctic pup and a coleman so I was sitting pretty good. I even enjoyed that night. The quiet is something you have to experience to understand. If you turn off the coleman lantern so that the hissing doesn't distract you, you can sit and listen to the north groaning under all that ice. James Bay has tides and sometimes they break off a floe and drag it out of the pack. The whole field will moan and creak; the sound carries for miles in the sub-zero weather. It's so cold that if you spit it will freeze solid before it hits the ground. On a moonless night, the stars are as thick as city lights and twice as bright. When the moon is out, the whole icefield will shimmer in the light. Even softer than moonlight is the starlight on the snowfield. It looks so beautiful it's hard to believe that you can die out there ten miles from home if even the slightest thing goes wrong. I went to sleep listening to the wild dog packs howling out on James Bay.

"Hookie-mal must have been travelling all night. I knew the machine he was on and mine was much faster. His belt had a line of cables running loose. They left a trench in the snow path each time they made a circuit, so his trail was impossible to lose if I crossed another skiddoo. I hit the trail at dawn and jogged all morning without seeing anyone at all.

"It's useless to scan the horizon in a snowfield. There isn't one. It just looks like a huge sphere of white and you're in it travelling nowhere. You have to be pretty sane to keep your bearings. According to my compass, the trail was curving very slowly to the northwest. It looked like Hookie-mal was really going to try for a point west of Fort Albany. I couldn't figure what his ace-in-the-hole was. He had to be nearly out of gas. He had relatives in Lake River but his chances of getting there without being picked up were slim. The sergeant would see to that. Anyway, as soon as he got to Lake River, we'd scoop him. Austin Airways flew into there. It seemed to me that he was just running into nowhere.

"The second night on the snowfield wasn't nearly as peaceful. A big wind came up and stirred up the flour snow. I found myself in a white-out by dusk. I had to set up the pup in a freezing white dust cloud so dense you could hardly see your hand in front of your face. The whole thing had to be done by touch. When I went outside to relieve myself I had to string a cord from the tent to my wrist. Inside the tent the windsound was enough to deafen you. I ate cold beef jerky by the coleman lamp and thought nasty things about Hookie-mal and the OPP and life in general.

"In the middle of the next day, while I was filling up the tank with the last of the gas and calculating the distance to Fort Albany, I heard a skiddoo motor in the distance. I stood up on the seat and strained to see where it was coming from. Way off to the southwest I could see a black dot running on a course that would take it across my trail. I jinked the snowmobile back around and headed off to intercept. I figured Hookie-mal was tired of running.

"It wasn't Hookie-mal. It was an Ojibway trapper checking lines. We knew the same people in Fort Albany so he was almost an acquaintance. He had heard all about Hookie-mal and the police sergeant. They were talking about it in Fort Albany and Lake River. It was on everybody's tongue along the shoreline. In the north you got used to this; the Indians always knew what was going on. I called it the bush telegraph. To this day I don't know how it worked and I don't want to guess. How could gossip travel where there were no phones and no roads and no one could run there? But the Ojibway knew. He hadn't seen Hookie-mal yet, but he'd cut a skiddoo trail three miles back, running due west. And it had a trench mark. This was great news. It meant that I could cut across the diagonal and intercept Hookie-mal within a few miles. Hookie-mal seemed to be heading back to Moosonee. The only thing that worried me was that so far I hadn't seen any sign of a camp. Had Hookie-mal run non-stop for two nights? If he had, that trail the Ojibway saw would be ancient history. But that wasn't possible either, since the white-out last night would have covered any trail left there yesterday. Hookie-mal also seemed to have plenty of gas; I cursed myself for not asking Ruth Little Basket if she was missing any gas cans.

"Hookie-mal's trail had led me a fair distance out onto the bay. As I headed back south and west, the treeline came back up ahead of me, a thin wavering black line. There was no skiddoo sign anywhere, and since I had cut off the trail of Hookie-mal's machine, I was running on faith that I would intercept. If he altered his course in between, I'd have to cast for it. I was still worrying about that when the skiddoo went through the ice.

"Well, 'through the ice' is an exaggeration. I hit a heave, a place where the icefield had cracked under the pressure and shifted up.

You'll get a floe riding up on top of another one. That's what causes the groaning sound you hear at night, ice floes grinding up against each other. I didn't see it because everything was covered in snow and any way, to be honest, I wasn't really looking. I was looking for Hookie-mal and I stopped paying attention. I hit the fault at the bottom and damn near shoved the machine right through and into the bay. I tumbled over the handle bars and cracked my head on the ice. I thought I'd killed myself. I sure as hell killed the machine.

"The nose was all pranged up, and the treads were slipped. It could be fixed, but not by me and not out here. All of a sudden, I was on foot. I wasn't too worried. If I couldn't make it forty miles back to Moosonee with all the supplies I had with me, then I didn't deserve to be out here at all.

"I took everything of value I could carry or bury off the machine. I had a pennant I should have been flying, and I tied it up on a stick so that we could find the machine again. What I couldn't carry with me, I hauled off a few hundred feet and covered up with snow. There was a good wind blowing up and I figured that my tracks would be covered soon. Of course, so would Hookie-mal's. It looked like Hookie-mal would win this round, thanks to my carelessness. I wasn't looking forward to listening to the corporal when I got back.

"Forty miles out from Moosonee is a five-day hike for a healthy man, four days if you want to push it. I tied a lot of my supplies up in the tarp and ran a cord from the tarp long enough to go around my waist. No sense carrying what you could drag. I made a compass check and started walking back to Moosonee.

"I kept the shoreline about fifty yards off and figured to make a good seven miles before I had to camp. If a wind came up worse than the one I was walking in front of, I could dog it for a while in the trees. If it blew up real bad, I'd just set up the pup and wait it out.

"I had gone maybe four miles when I happened to look back and saw five, six, maybe seven black dots way off in the distance. I was having a tough time because the snow was deep here and I kept breaking through little wind holes into soft flour. If I hadn't been wearing snowshoes I wouldn't have made it at all. The improvised travois was heavier than I thought and all in all I was getting pretty tired. When I saw those black dots way off to the north I knew what they were. Wild dogs, nothing really dangerous. There were far easier pickings for them than man. It wasn't likely they'd come any closer, and if they did I had my service revolver and lots of ammunition. As a matter of fact, a little wild dog started to sound good; I was getting sick of beef jerky and powdered eggs.

"I made a camp that night in the shelter of the trees. The dogs were still on my case but I wasn't worried about them. Mainly, I was thinking about Hookie-mal and the corporal and wondering what would happen. Maybe, way down deep, I was just a little worried. More scotch? I'm a little dry from all this talking.

"In the morning there were snowshoe tracks all around the pup tent. I hadn't heard a blasted thing. I didn't know the tracks; could have been some Ojibway trapper or a Cree out hunting, but why not stop in and say hello? Nobody with an honest purpose ever passed by a stranger in the bush without stopping to share some jerky and coffee. After a long while, I figured it had to be Hookie-mal. That was when I started to get a little worried.

"You can live in the north, in the bush, all your life. You can drink with Crees and Ojibways and breeds five nights out of seven. You can even marry an Indian woman, as I did. But deep down it's almost impossible to feel one hundred per cent sure of how you stand with them. A lot of history has gone down the pipe between us and the Indian. As a policeman I was always aware of the tension there. It was our job to keep them in line, to push the white law down their throats. Was it possible that I didn't even know Hookie-mal? It seemed stupid to think like that, but who else would sneak around my camp at night and never wake me?

"In the morning it was bright and sunny overhead but the horizon in the north was furry and indistinct. That meant a blow was coming. It was useless to try to out-run it. I had to stay in the tent and let it roll over top. I'll always remember that day and night. I only used the coleman light when I found the dark too creepy. The wind rolled and stroked and screamed all over the tent walls. It flapped and rattled and bumped. Anytime I went outside I was blinded by blowing snow and darkness. I was beginning to feel jumpy and disoriented, and after a long while listening I began to hear voices crying in the wind. It was like the voices those old whalemen used to hear when they'd be lying in their bunks at night while the ship rolled through the sea. They'd hear wailing and calling. They thought it was the voices of drowned men calling to them. I began to feel like that. It was getting to me that there was an Indian out there running from the law, maybe a little unbalanced, and maybe he wasn't very far away. I got more paranoid by the hour. What was happening was that I was getting 'bushed'.

" 'Bushed' means that the wild is creeping up on you. Men weren't made to live alone in the wild places for long. They needed other people. I was letting my imagination run away with me, having hallucinations and silly dreams. Hookie-mal was just an Indian boy and probably scared stiff, trying to get up the nerve to go home. I was ashamed of myself, letting the bush get to me as if I was some downed greenhorn stockbroker from Sudbury. I shut the coleman off and tried to get some sleep.

"The dogs woke me up. I could hear them snuffling around outside the pup tent flap. One of them even brushed up against the side of the tent. The wind had dropped off. If I looked away a little, I could see things faintly so it must be that hour when it starts to get light but it's not yet dawn. The nights went on forever but they had to stop sometime. I could hear two of the animals growling at each other about three feet away. I moved as softly as I could out from the bag and got my revolver. I guess one of the dogs sensed me moving because I could hear a definite threat growl outside the flap. A muzzle pushed right up against the flap, straining at the zipper. I figured five, maybe six; the pack must have been very desperate to come this close to a man's camp. When I drew the hammer back, two of them started barking. I jerked the zipper down about a foot, stuck the barrel right up this big grey sonovabitch's left nose and pulled the trigger. The whole left side of his face blew off and everybody else hit the road yelping. I couldn't get back to sleep so I dressed the carcass and packed him in the tarp. I didn't figure to see his buddies again, and I didn't.

"I never saw Hookie-mal's tracks again. The wind stayed off my case and I made good time. The load got lighter as I got closer to home. I had wild dog for dinner. It was good; stringy and leathery, but not too spicy. I kept his teeth to give to Grey Eyes for a necklace. The days were fine. It was the nights I was having trouble with. I was a cop. I was supposed to be hunting for a fugitive. But I couldn't get rid of the idea that Hookie-mal was out there, not too far away, and that Hookie-mal was playing some kind of strange game with me. I never heard the sound of a shot, so he wasn't hunting anywhere nearby. He had that big Winchester with him, wherever he was. That gave me trouble too. He could stand back out of range and blow me into red snow if he was crazy enough to do it. I couldn't see him changing a lousy B and E charge to a Canada-wide manhunt for a cop-killer, but you could never figure Indians. It was possible that he was bushed too; I had heard of that happening to Indians. I thought too much about what

Hookie-mal was doing. Finally, I got pissed off and decided to track the kid down. I was the law here, for what it was worth. Hookie-mal was going in if I had to call in the planes to find him. I sacked out that night, maybe half the way home and three nights away from the wracked-up snowmobile. When I woke up in the morning the snowfield was one huge sheet of unmarked white. I had slept all right since the wind had been quiet. I heard nothing all night. When I was taking down the pup tent, I found a Milky Way wrapper stuck on the centre pole.

"I guess I was in kind of a panic then. I acted crazy for a while. I jumped away from the tent pole like it was a cobra. I ran back and forth with my gun out, looking for something to shoot. I cursed and swore and jumped and swore some more. Finally, I calmed down. I packed up everything and piled it into the travois. Then I stood on that and slowly traversed every degree of the horizon away from the treeline. I inched myself around and looked through the binoculars as if I was looking for a periscope. One circuit took me more than an hour. There was nothing out on the bay. Then I got off the pack and crouched down beside it, putting it between me and the shoreline. I rested the glasses on the top of the pack and I studied every foot of that treeline. I looked for a clump of branches, I looked for a dark spot, I looked for a white hump, I looked for a break in the snow, I looked for a figure in the branches. I looked until my eyes watered and my head pounded. I saw nothing.

"All of a sudden I was up on my feet and screaming with rage. I put my hands up to my mouth and I called his name over and over again. I called it until my voice started to crack. When I stopped there was nothing but the wind on the snowfield. I've never felt that alone in my life. I would have been glad for a shotgun blast, a rock, a goddamned arrow! That Indian was playing a game with me!

"I came to my senses after a while. All right. So the little shit wanted to play that game. Fine. It beat me all to hell how he had gotten up to the tent during the night without leaving tracks. But it wasn't impossible. I hadn't really been alert. When I got up I could have missed something. He could have dragged a branch across his tracks. He could have come up quiet as soon as I was asleep and put the wrapper there, and then he would have had the whole night to let the wind clear the traces. One thing I knew; I wasn't going to stay out here in the open and let him track me from the woods. Because I was sure that he was in the woods. There was nowhere else for him to hide. Somehow or other he had ditched the machine and he was now in the trees not far from me. If he was in the trees, he was leaving some trace. All I had to do was cut his trail and follow it right to his hiding place. Hookie-mal was no *wendigo*, no bloody forest spirit. I'd gotten plastered with the son of a bitch. We'd thrown up together in the detachment house. I'd carried him to the clinic when he bounced off that pole. I had seen his blood. As you can see, that Indian was really getting to me.

"I'll make this short. I chased around in the woods after that kid for almost twenty hours. I stowed the gear at the shoreline and set off by the compass straight into the bush. I went a good mile due west, another one due south, and another one due east again. Then I cut back up along the shoreline to my stash and in all that time I never cut his trail and I never saw a single sign. I never saw a sign of fire, or a place where he might have sheltered. I never saw any droppings, or a place where he might have buried droppings. In the last of the light I made a big arc out onto the ice of James Bay, swinging from south to north. I found no trace of anything. There were no heaves big enough to hide behind, and no holes to drop into. I was absolutely alone.

"I had wasted so much time looking for Hookie-mal that I had to get a camp ready in the dark. I kept it dark, too. No coleman lamp to mark my position for Hookie-mal out there in the night. There were stars out and they gave me enough light to see what I was doing. I popped the tarp and spread the pup tent out on the ground about fifteen feet from the treeline. There was a Milky Way wrapper stuck under the yellow cord that bound the pup tent up. There was no way on earth I could have missed it when I packed up that morning. I would have had to put it there myself. There was only one way for that wrapper to be there and that was for Hookie-mal to put it there, and the only chance he would have had to do that would have been while I was blundering around in the woods trying to cut his trail. I pulled out the coleman lamp and lit it up. The Milky Way wrapper didn't fade in the glow. It was real. I wasn't imagining it. As impossible as it was, Hookie-mal was somewhere close.

"I set the pup tent up as quietly as I could. My hands were shaking. It was getting colder. The stars were as bright as headlights. I got the tent up and I put my gear inside it. I lit the lamp and stuck it inside the tent. I backed away from the tent about fifty feet and lay down in the snow. I put my service revolver on my forearm and stuck a piece of jerky in my mouth. If Hookie-mal came out of the ground in front of me, I wouldn't have been surprised. I held that position without moving until the coleman lantern ran out of fuel and the little island of yellow light faded out. The night was all over me. It was like I was floating in space. It was as cold as space. I think I slept for a while. Anyway, I was all of a sudden aware of this strange sound, a hissing and popping sound, only very faint and coming from all around. I realised that my head was down on my arm. I grabbed the revolver off my arm and crammed my finger into the trigger guard. The gun was so cold that it burned me even through the gloves. I got myself steadied up, and then I jumped up on my knees with the gun out. The ground was shimmering with light.

"I looked up into the sky and I saw where the hissing noise was coming from. The whole northern sky was filled with huge shimmering curtains of soft violet and blue light. Red lights, green lights, yellow lights. It was like I was lying on my back under these huge luminous curtains, only they went up for a thousand miles into the starry sky, waving and drifting. I don't have the words for it. It was huge and beautiful. They hissed in the sky with a sound like silk rubbing against silk. I could feel the hairs on my wrists stand up and tingle. It was the Aurora, the Northern Lights. You see them all the time in the north. But never like that.

"I was kneeling there on the snow with that stupid gun in my hand, scared white, trying to set a trap for a ghost. I was the law, I thought, and I started to laugh. I sat back on my heels for a while and I just felt good, I don't know why. I laughed some more, and I wasn't frightened at all. I did know that I would get home. I knew that somebody would find Hookie-mal. I just knew that it wasn't going to be me. I had reached the limit, that's all. I was so used to being a cop that it had never hit me before this that there was a limit to anybody's power, even the power of the law. Hookie-mal had gone outside, over the line. Even in this year, even with all the science, there was an end to towns and cities and even an end to policemen.

"Later on, much later, I married Grey Eyes and quit the force. I never saw Hookie-mal again."

CHAPTER TEN

Winnipeg Major Crimes Division

Thirty thousand feet over Manitoba it's easy to believe that Columbus was wrong. The Prairies slide away under the wing to a luminous blue horizon as flat and as straight as the edge of a prism. Far below, the ground glitters with glare ice dulled in sections by a thin sifting of fine snow. At the outer limit of the northern plains the lower shores of Lake Winnipeg are little more than an arc of ice like the cutting fan of a glacier. When the plane banks to starboard a tiny cluster of buildings rolls into view. Surrounded and ringed with a delicate tracery of streets and secondary roads, shimmering in the fading light from the west, Winnipeg looks like a bullet hole in a windshield.

The best thing Winnipeg had going for it in the last century was room. The planners used as much of it as they felt like in the gore between the Assiniboine and the Red. People who settled here were mostly farmers, here for the black earth and the spaces, solid Dutch and German men and women with heavy shoulders, straw-coloured hair, flat hard faces with pale blue eyes. In the western part of town they built block after block of wooden frame houses painted white and green. These flicker by like the wooden blades of a millwheel, each street short and straight, every house with its back into the wind that slides across a thousand miles of prairie from the glaciers of the Northern Rockies, getting colder and drier with every acre it passes. Winnipeggers don't talk about this wind. There's something arrogant and grim in their refusal to recognise a force that drives visitors off the street and that can shatter an engine block on three or four of the worst days in the winter. Winnipeg makes no sense to an urban planner. Divided into three wedges by the twisting Red and the Assiniboine, encircled by the Trans Canada Highway, the streets jog and tangle in a crazed and haphazard pattern, reflecting the fundamental anarchic inclinations of the Prairies. Few of the buildings are taller than ten stories; visitors get the impression that anything bigger would present too easy a target for the wind. Myths about the gales that blow around Portage and Main turn out to be fine illustrations of western moesis born in a mordant wit. In March, the cold and the wind are strong enough to dull the mind, a relentless assault on your nerves, as if you had been forced to stand at the edge of a cataract for a month.

Winnipeg is really a rural supply town, a trading post adrift on the sea of the Great Plains. Lumber moves through it out into the true west, and coal, and steel from the mills at Hamilton and Gary. Winnipeg gets back grain for the packed grey cities of eastern Canada and the Yankee states. The ruling government is NDP and rabidly socialistic, but the people are forthright and honest. In the streets they have an unsettling tendency to look straight at you as they pass, free and careless of the eastern obsession with isolation. Here a hastily averted face is a signal for further investigation and not a means for declining public contact. The young men wear peaked caps with names like Deere and GMC on the crowns, and they walk with a loose-jointed saunter in faded blue jeans and heavy scarred Kodiak boots. The women have unlikely hair in odd styles, but their faces are fresh and none of them show the armour-plated antagonism that passes for insouciance in Toronto or Montreal. To an outsider, they seem at ease, happy. The streets are wide as any boulevard in Paris, although the shops are rough and the selection limited to clothes that were slipping off the fashion pages two years past in the east. Even in the downtown streets pick-ups go by with 30-30 Winchesters racked in the window and bales of hay wired onto the flatbed. Winnipeg has a ballet and theatres and an excellent art gallery, but these things are like the clothes a gentleman farmer will wear going east to argue with politicians, something fine that comes off quickly if he's pushed. Underneath the polish Winnipeg is a tough little plains town not too different from Butte or Abilene. Carl Sandburg would have liked this town, or Norman Mailer. It sits at the junction of two great rivers and takes up as much room as it bloody well pleases, and there's no one around to dispute the matter. At least, not any more.

Outside the Princess Hotel the music from the bar is loud enough to feel in your chest. Overhead, the green neon sign had a couple of letters knocked out. The entrance doors had been broken so many times the management had simply boarded them up. Over the years the doors had been pasted over with hundreds of rock posters, political handbills, ads for itinerant gurus, until the lobby made a kind of archaeologist's relic heap of local street history. The endless bitter wind of the plains was rolling down the centre of Main Street like a Mississippi of liquid nitrogen, but the crowds were jammed into the doors as if it were a soft spring night on the Wabash. We were outside on the street. Our job was to get inside, where just maybe a young Indian male who had raped his brother's wife was sitting at one of the tables.

In Winnipeg they expect their police to do everything. There's no Homicide Squad separate from Rape or Fraud or Armed Robbery. The Winnipeg Police Force had an all-purpose unit they call Major Crimes, and the men and women on this unit operate as roving investigators into just about everything the streets have to offer. Which, in Winnipeg, is likely to be brutal, sudden, and shocking. I had been assigned to a pair of plainclothes detectives known as Holmes and Harper. Holmes was younger than Harper, about twenty-eight, and new to Major Crimes. He was a solid full-back type with meaty shoulders and he carried his two hundred and fifty pounds as if it were eiderdown. Earlier in the day I had watched him press four hundred and fifty pounds in the police gym while carrying on an argument about some new city hall committee he referred to as Penner's Pansies. He had a beefy body, but huge corded muscles writhed under his skin like groundswell. Holmes was something of an anomaly in Major Crimes since he had been made a detective quite early in his career. He had solved an extremely complex and viciously unpopular homicide in the face of opposition from senior staff and his friends on the force. When it looked as if the murderer was a cop, Holmes had fastened on the hunt with what I was told was a truly frightening intensity. It hadn't been that he wanted to catch a cop, I had been told, it was that he just hated bad cops more than anything else in the universe. He'd caught the man, too, and instead of being ostracized, for once he had been rewarded. He and his partner had been together three years. Holmes had a number of odd characteristics, the most striking of which were his eyes. They were clear and dark brown, very large and round, like the eyes of a gun dog, very expressive and reassuring. Set in the middle of his hardcase facade they were as out of place as his smile, which was manic and slightly insane and intermittently outrageous.

Harper was the perfect counterpoint to Holmes' bulky grace. Greying and sharp-featured, he'd spent time in Vietnam, an experience which seemed to have cut more deeply into his face than it had his sense of humour. He was lean for a Winnipeg cop, a force which has some of the biggest and toughest cops in Canada, weighing some-where around one hundred and seventy-five pounds. He dressed like an investment counsellor. The day I met him I'd swear he wore a Sulka tie and a tailor-made Oxford cloth shirt in descending half-tones of soft grey. His suits were always perfectly cut, but he created the impression of absolute indifference to his clothes. When amused, he had a sudden short barking laugh something like a steam piston. His lean face would break up into tiny deltas of leathery skin when he smiled, except for his left cheekbone, which bore a thin white cut-line that truncated the lines fanning out from that eye. In fine, he looked like a Lascar pirate. He was as pointed and impulsive as Holmes was restrained. For reasons I later understood, he hardly ever wore a gun. He used to say that covering fire was his partner's job; he was "point man". "Point man" was a Marine Corps term. It referred to the position assigned to a rifleman in a platoon when they were advancing to contact in enemy territory. The "point man" was always put far out in front. It was his job to uncover the ambush, to clear the path for the platoon coming up from behind. Harper had fallen into Vietnam roughly the way he'd fallen into police work, and he did the job with the same kind of casual grace.

Neither of them was delighted to have me alongside as we stood out on the frigid street in front of the Princess bar and considered the massive back of the last man in line in front of us. I suggested that we might go in another way. Harper looked at me briefly with cool dislike and put out his right hand, tapping his fingers in the long black hair of the man in front of us. The man jumped and spun around, his face puffy and dark. He was an Indian, maybe a Cree or Ojibway, and he had once been beautiful, but that was a long time in the past. His eyes were a dull black. The whites were the colour of ancient bone and chased with bloody marbling. He knocked Harper's hand away and moved in to hit the detective with a short looping left hand which never landed. Harper just followed the Indian's direction, passing him through in a kind of capeless veronica, delivering a coup into the man's right kidney as he lumbered past. I felt a puff of moist beery breath as the big Indian's face went by my shoulder on his way to the ground. He hit it with a loose aspirant thump, the way big men do, and would have gotten up again with his knife in his right hand if Holmes hadn't pinned the Indian's arm to the ice with a boot. Aggression and hatred flared up in the man's face for a brief time, and then slowly dissipated, like blood in water. He had recognised the detectives. He forced a smile over his wolfish features and I was struck by the whiteness of his teeth against the roughcast redstone of his face. Watching him get the smile all the way across his face was like watching a magician pull a silk stocking across a straight razor. I could see he had decided not to fight. Harper wasn't even watching this; he had immediately turned into the rest of the line and was now shoving his way past the other men and on into the dark interior of the bar. In the corpse-light green from the neon sign overhead I could see that every man and woman in the line was an Indian. Harper was shoving them out of his way. One older man slipped on the wet tiles and fell against the wall. It occurred to me that there were more amiable ways to get inside a bar, and I said something along these lines in a whisper to Holmes as we followed Harper's wake into the maelstrom of lights and noise. There was a strobe light pulsing just inside the entrance. It lit up rows and files of grim dark faces hunched over draft glasses, black eyes like beads tracking us inside, radiating dislike. When Holmes turned to answer me, the strobe made his face look like a scene from an old silent movie, but I could just make out his words over the tortured shriek of a Fender Stratocaster.

"Fuck you," he was saying, and smiling that manic smile.

* * *

A couple of kids from Quebec City were trying to jump-start a fight in a far corner of the bar, but Harper wasn't looking at that. His face was old-looking in repose, although I knew he wasn't past forty. Harper was making a point about professionalism, as we stood leaning over the bar.

"Something you civilians don't realise is that the quality of hoods has declined one hell of a lot in the last fifteen years. It used to be that we all understood the rules. I'm not talking about the punks, you understand? A punk is a punk and they never change. I'm talking about the professional crook, the man who has decided that robbing banks or B and E's are his career, that kind of man you don't run into much any more. They were a pleasure to do business with. They knew the rules." He looked at me for a sign that I understood. I nodded, trying to concentrate. Harper could see I didn't.

"Look, we had a guy here once . . . what was his name?" Holmes gave him a name. "Yeah, that was it! Now, he'd been doing banks and stores in this town for years. He was always reliable. He'd do his homework. He knew the systems, he'd study the cruiser schedules. He'd spend months looking the place over, he'd meet the people inside and get an idea of how they'd react to armed robbery. He always knew where their pieces were, and what pieces they had. He'd think about it and work out every detail. When to hit it and how to hit it. How long to stay in. He carried a little timer device that would buzz after three minutes or ninety seconds, whatever time he had decided was safe. And he knew before he went in just how he was going to get out, and he had secondary routes, cut-offs. He always worked alone, so that he had perfect control. He never shot anyone, and he was cool on the job, so nothing ever went sour. Took us years to get him, and then we had to trick him into the bag. Well, he pulled some hard time for Armed Robbery and he served it like a gentleman, so of course he was out in a third. Being a pro, he set about his business. We knew he was back in action, simply by the way the jobs went off, but we were under-staffed and we couldn't put full-time surveillance on him, so he'd get away with one or two jobs. Sometimes we'd pick him up, grill him a little at the office. But he was the kind of guy, you could bounce him off the walls until you got tired and all you'd get out of him was a GFY. That was another thing about him. There are kids working this town now, if you raise your voice to them they'll wet themselves and faint. Kids who need a skinful of speed just to get out of the car with a piece in their hands, assholes who'll shoot up the whole fucking place because they don't have any control, because they're stupid enough to pull the job but to gutless to do it clean. But this guy . . . he was a pro. You didn't bounce him because it was useless to bounce him. Even if he knew you had him, dead on, the gun, the stuff traced right back to the bank, eye-witnesses, even if his mother was turning him in, he'd just sit there in that goddamned chair and speak nice and soft yessir Mister Harper well I don't think I want to comment on that sir until I see my lawyer sir. One time we did get him, and when he got out he comes by the station with a forty-ouncer and invites us to get pissed with him. So we were sitting in the Charley, he's paying, and he's saying you know you bastards you almost had me on the TD bank job, I really thought you had me, but you were just bullshitting me. We'd laugh about it, understand? Anyway, finally, he settles on this Safeway job. It was a soft hit. Plenty of cash. Bugger all security, and dorks for guards. He looks it over and over and he even finds out that one of his old school buddies is working there as a clerk. He takes the guy out for a drink and pumps him about the store. He had this job laid out like a train set, all the parts chugging around in their tracks. Careful. Neat. Complete. Like a jeweller. Guy was a joy to behold. The day of the hit, he climbs into his party clothes and he checks out his piece, he had a nice .357 which I don't think he ever fired on the job, did he?" Holmes shook his head.

"Anyway, what happens is that he walks into the place and pulls out the .357, he's got his ski mask over his face and he's standing there pointing this gun at his school buddy, who has gone very very pale, and the buddy is stuffing the bag full of cash when someone grabs at the guy's ski mask and gets it half off, just enough to show part of his face. He sees the school buddy and he knows the guy has made him, right?"

"Right."

"So . . . does he grease him, like any one of these little shits in here would do? No, he doesn't. He backs off and pisses off to his place. He pours himself a scotch. He packs up a few things. He mails a deposit off to his bank. He moves some chairs away from the front door and he takes up a spot with a clear sight line to the doorway. Then he pulls the coffee table over and he sets his drink down on it, along with a fresh forty-ouncer. Next to the bottle he lays out his wallet, a toothbrush, and the .357. He unloads the .357 and he lines up the six brass cartridges in a row on the table. Then he waits. He waits because he knows the guys are coming for him. I think Ray Johns picked him up, right? Anyway, a half-hour later the guys are banging on his door. He says 'it's open, guys' and they go in. This guy has his hands spread out on the coffee table, empty, and he's saying 'Christ, what took you guys so long?' Now, that's the way a pro would handle it. Out of every city, you only get three or four guys who play that way. Used to be more, but the young ones have no class."

By way of illustration, the two kids from Quebec finally got their fight going as Harper finished his story. Holmes watched it develop with his big bear detachment but Harper didn't even bother to look. A middle-aged Indian woman strolled out from behind the bar with a bored expression on her face while the people at nearby tables shouted encouragement to the combatants. They were on the ground in a puddle of spilt beer and broken glass, kicking and rolling, fingers locked in each other's hair. The onlookers backed away as the Indian woman arrived. She stepped over the pair and grabbed one of the boys by his ear. I could see her shoulder jerk from across the room. The kid yelped once, twice. The crowd closed in around this scene but you could see that it was already over. Up on the stage the band lurched into an old Marty Robbins song called "El Paso" and I was thinking that bars were no different right around the country.

* * *

When things calmed down a little Holmes tried to explain the situation for me. His manner was warmer, and for the first time I felt the presence of considerable charm and a careful intellect in the big man.

"You pissed me off, when we came in. I guess you knew that. You were bugged about the Indian, right? You think we should have been polite. Harper should have tapped real nice on the guy's shoulder and asked him to let us through, right? You pissed me off because you don't know shit about this town. We are sitting in the middle of the biggest Indian reservation in Canada. In the hotels around here I figure any night you could count five, six thousand Indians, men and women. Up north at Crane River or Duck Bay or up at The Pas the RCMP has to baby-sit thousands more – Crees, Ojibway, some breeds. Ask anyone who deals with Indians and he'll tell you the same thing; they're crazy, sad, rough. They have a problem. Ottawa, and the local brass, in their infinite wisdom, sold the tribes a bill of goods. Indian Affairs says to the Indian: 'You're not Indian any more . . . you're a Native American and we've got all sorts of great plans for your people. We're going to make you just as good as white folks!' Well, you and I know this was just simple bullshit. It's just a story we told these poor bastards to get them to hand over land and liberty. We've been looting from these people for three hundred years. It's still going on. We fuck them over for mineral rights and we jerk them around for welfare qualifications. Up at Crane River one native kid in ten will commit suicide before he's thirteen. Suicide! The reservations are a killing ground. The trouble is, they're such trusting bastards. Ottawa sends them workers and advisors and counsellors and administrators and all these people are supposed to do is keep the Indians quiet. That Minaki Lodge bullshit over in Ontario is a prime example. Take their balls and give them money. What's *really* going on here is genocide by neglect! For chrissakes, look around this fucking bar, man! Just look!" He swept his massive arm in a huge arc. In the heavy air, lit by forty-watt bulbs in the ceiling, pounded by the bar band, perhaps three hundred Indians were sitting around tiny tables in tight circles, talking, drinking, fighting, while their lives ticked away. "These poor bastards are here every night, drinking away their money, kicking each other to death, raping their brothers' wives, knifing, cutting, throwing up in the alley, beating the shit out of each other, killing each other. Oh, we white folks, we're sharp as hell. Stick them in one place, give them just enough money to get pissed on and never enough to save. Bullshit them with stories about how white they can be. Shit, Custer was a saint. He just shot their ponies and their women. This is nothing but genocide, not just here, but right across the country." Holmes said all this in a rush, looking at the bar and downing a boilermaker in the telling. I can't say, even now, why he had opened up like this. It was always a puzzle to me, this odd duality in all policemen, the struggle between their insularity and mistrust of any outsider, and the surprising need to be understood. It was a kind of vulnerability they all shared. It made you feel protective of them, as if you knew more about the subtle evils of the world than they did.

"The trouble here is that I feel all this stuff about them, but I'm a cop. It's my job to stop people from beating up each other and raping each other. It doesn't matter how I feel about what's happening to them. I have to do my job. You can see that, can't you?"

I said something about brutality. His fist hit the table.

"You still don't see it, do you? What do you think it is that keeps people inside the law? You think most people keep the law because they understand the social contract? They keep the law because they have something to lose, because they want their lives and their Cadillacs and their cottages at Keewatin and Black Hawk. What the hell would you do if someone had taken away everything you held close, even your self respect, your love of life? We've robbed these people of everything worth having and now we're surprised that they don't give a shit about life. I'm a cop and I tell you my life wouldn't be worth squat in any alley or bar in Winnipeg if the breeds didn't know I was even meaner than they were. There's only one thing left that these people respect, and that's power. You go be kind and gentle. They'll feed you your liver. I treat them like men, like they were braves. All they see when you soft-soap them is another lying white man trying to fuck them over. When they come up against us, they get treated like men, like people with some power. It doesn't matter then that they've been cheated for three hundred years, or that now the boys in Ottawa are trying to finish them off with welfare money and tricky native rights legislation; what matters then is that we respect each other. So we throw them around when we have to, and they fight us from time to time. I've had stand-ups with some of them, out in the back lanes. Bare-handed and no police bullshit. I've lost some and I've won some. I've knocked them around. Then I've gotten pissed with some of them. But I treat them as if they were dangerous, as if they were men. They say if you have strong enemies you are a strong man. Maybe, in some crazy way, that's the one thing you leave them with, after everything else is gone. You leave them some pride." He stopped, suddenly, as people do when they remember where they are, and who they've been talking to. I could see in his face that he expected to be betrayed, that his honesty with me would somehow come back to mock him. He shrugged, and ordered up three boilermakers. I knew that nothing I could say would change his feelings.

*   *   *

Harper and Holmes and I sat silently for a while over in the Charley bar off Main Street. The band cranked up a Ry Cooder ballad called "The Borderline". It had a lyric melody something like a Mexican love song. The guitar went before it with a steelhead blues chord progression, clearing the way through the smoky haze. A sodium spot flared out from somewhere over the stage and pinned a circle of hot sulphurous yellow light on the guitarist's hands as they slid along the fretboard. Not far from the stage the light caught an Indian couple at a table. The man was older. He wore a red polka-dot bandana around his forehead, pinning down his shoulder-length black hair. He had a good face. His skin was the colour of copper. The woman was sleeping on the table, her hair spilling out across it. The man was listening to the music.

In the last days of the Indian Wars, before the Battle at Wounded Knee in South Dakota in 1890, the American Indians sustained themselves with a delusion that a Paiute medicine man named Wovoka was in reality Jesus Christ come back to the earth to drive the white men off the plains. Wovoka told the Indians that he knew the Ghost Dance, which was a spell dance that would make this happen. The Indians in the Dakotas, in Saskatchewan and Manitoba, and in Montana, all fell under this man's influence, and because of their belief in him, they refused to fight the white man any longer. Instead, they danced and drank and listened to the music of the Ghost Dancers. Nothing had changed.

"Is that our boy?" Harper whispered to Holmes, as "The Border-line" went on. He was looking at a young Indian male, about five eight, who had just come into the bar. He was dressed in jeans and a plaid shirt. He looked something like the mug shot I had seen in Harper's notebook. The man they were looking for had been asked to care for his brother's wife while his brother served a month in jail for petty theft. On the first evening, the young man had called on his brother's wife, had drunk all the liquor in the apartment, and then beaten and raped the woman, before falling asleep in the bedclothes. The woman, bleeding, had run next door to a friend's apartment. From there, they had called the police. At three that morning, the police patrolmen answering the call had kicked in the flimsy chipboard door with their guns out, but the young man had disappeared. In the morning, Major Crimes had been handed the assignment. Incidents such as this one were commonplace in the area, not limited to Indians or any other single type. Poverty, drink, hard times, and growing unemployment, tended to grind away the veneer of ethical or moral standards. It was pretty much as Holmes had called it, people who care about laws are usually people with something to lose.

The kid hesitated in the doorway for a brief time, his shaded eyes scanning the bar for trouble. We wouldn't be hard to miss, three white men in shirts, ties, tan trenchcoats, nicely-polished shoes. Earlier in the day I had asked the head of the department why no one was in jeans, rough clothes, anything that looked like something the public in the bars might be wearing. The man's name was Pike, an Inspector, tall and lean, a handsome man in his early forties. As most cops do, he had a handshake like a pipe-bender and he fixed you in place with a hard stare, right into your eyes, assessing you in a matter of a moment and filing the impression away. No policeman I had ever met had been anything but politely distant on first meeting. They sized you up on the basis of a number of things; the feel of your grip, whether or not you could look them in the face, and if so with what manner, how long you held the look, your carriage, your voice and, perhaps most impor-tantly, the way you dressed. Clothes are the most reliable indicator in a cop's world. They govern how you are first seen. Whatever my street clothes usually were, I found out early that it was best to dress like them, and to stand up straight when we met. I had the impression that first impact was probably final and eternal. I also knew that, no matter how much I may have been liked during the visits, they were all going to wait and see what I turned out to be. Pike was that kind of man.

"Major Crimes detectives aren't undercover cops. That's not the job for most of our men. We have roughly twenty men and women in the department. We have to cover all of the major crimes that take place in our jurisdiction. Outside that, it's up to the RCMP. It's not the job of our men to look like punks in the street. They wear suits and coats and ties on the job because we want everyone they run into to know exactly who and what they are. When they make a call on a suspect, everybody in the neighbourhood knows that the police have come to call. The same in the bars. It makes for better understanding all 'round. Part of our job is to be visible, to let everyone know that the cops are there, that the law's on the street, the law's in the bars. If somebody starts trouble with our boys, we know he's not under any false impressions about who we are. Sure, some of the guys in the bars don't like it when we come waltzing through. They say it puts a crimp in the festivities. They say they feel harassed. I hate to hear that. It hurts me. I lie awake nights, thinking about it."

Holmes watched the Indian as he stood in the doorway with the same kind of look a piranha gets when somebody dangles his fingers in the tank; a look of pure unadulterated anticipatory glee, barely restrained by his desire not to betray our presence to the target. He changed, in a matter of a tenth of a second, from a laconic, vaguely disgruntled young man passing a slow night with friends, into a unit of concentrated purpose, as focussed as a laser. Harper told me not to turn around, but I couldn't see any way that the Indian boy could possibly miss us. We stood out in that sea of black hair and hooded eyes and blue jean jackets like signal flags. How could he miss us? He didn't.

But he didn't run, either. His eyes slid over us without a waver, and he ambled over to a table full of people at the far side of the bar. Harper got up with elaborate insouciance, grinning at me wolfishly, while Holmes stepped away from the table and moved to close off any means of retreat. "These boys have always got a knife somewhere – you have to watch their hands," Harper informed me, as the two men headed across the room. I followed behind, tensing slightly but intrigued by the casual attitude of the two detectives. There was no sense of melodrama, none of the TV cop storm-the-beachhead bravado. This was just business, and there was no point in getting everyone excited. At the far table, the man was picking up a draft, his back to the detectives. Neither of the men had a gun out, nor did I see any signs that one was about to appear. Holmes had his hands down by his side, and he looked like a stroller calling on a friend. Harper was more taut, but not excited or aggressive. When they got within a few feet of the table, one of the Indians facing us leaned over and said something in a low voice to the rest of the table. A rough peal of laughter went around the table, carrying over the torrent of rhythm and blues coming from the stage. The detectives had to snake their way around the small circular tables, packed in as tight as the by-laws would allow, while people watched their progress out of flat unfriendly faces. I began to see the sense in a discreet non-violent approach. It was a slow Friday and most of the bar could go up like a shout of spears if anyone had given them half a reason. Scooping one of their kind in a melee of overturned chairs and struggling bodies would be considered more than half a reason. I wondered why the Indian boy was so relaxed. Rape convictions in Manitoba were not lightly treated; they valued their women in that part of the country.

The two cops arrived, from different quadrants, simultaneously at either shoulder of the young Indian at the table. He did not look up. Holmes put out a hand. It settled on the kid's shoulder in an odd mix of amiable threat. Harper stood a little away from the scene, his eyes moving over the people at the table, watching their hands and their eyes. The Indians were still grinning, but there was nothing friendly in their faces. "Let's see some ID, my friend," said Holmes, not really watching the boy under his hand, smiling that crazy smile. We stood in a ring of tables with at least fifty men and women waiting to see what would happen. I was thinking about my chances. I hardly expected the two detectives to take care of my body in a brawl with all of these men. I tried not to let anything I was feeling show on my face. The boy swung around in his chair until Holmes' big hand clamped him down. Leaning under the weight, he looked right at Holmes, still grinning. The detective slumped just a little. "Ah shit!" said Harper, from across the table. "That's not Jimmy." Holmes knew it already. He dropped his hand away, and his manic grin got even wider. The Indians smiled but did not laugh. Before he turned away, Holmes reached out his left hand and patted the kid's cheek. The gesture was another hybrid mixture, this time at once challenging, patronizing, and affectionate. "See you again, boys. Enjoy your night," he said, and we moved out of the crowd. "Could be his goddamned brother," was all Harper had to say, his disappointment obvious. Holmes walked with us slowly, his attention on something else. I asked him what.

"I hear one son of a bitch laughing out loud back there and I'm going to make them eat the table." But nobody laughed.

* * *

With the possible exception of the Diamondback Grill in El Paso, the hotel bars in Winnipeg were far and away the roughest, nastiest, and most depressing bars in North America. During my time with the Winnipeg Police Major Crimes Division I got to see most of the bad ones. Of all of them, the Charley was the worst. It had started out life as a hotel with a lounge on the main floor. That was sometime in the Thirties. It had slipped some since then. Most of the Charley was just a big square room filled with round tables. The ceiling was a moot point, since it was rarely visible during working hours. The Charley was always half full of smoke. By midnight, it had reached the level of the table tops. The patrons rose up out of this mist like dinosaurs rising up from a misty swamp. It was hard to make out the furthest walls, and when you did you were seldom thankful. I never saw it less than overcrowded, packed to bursting with three or four hundred people, drinking, fighting, dancing, and the talk fast and loud and always edgy with aggression, threat, anything you cared to find. Most of the people were native Indian, usually heavy-shouldered men with pot-bellies and thick arms, their shining black hair running shoulder length and tied back with bandanas or leather thongs. Some of the men were huge, over six five and easily three hundred pounds. Most were of average height. The women broke down into two types; the young ones, none of them older than fifteen or sixteen or seventeen, who were slim, with smooth tan skin and eyes like black pearls and smiles as rare and sudden as a flash of light off bone china. All of them were beautiful. A few were some of the most stunningly gorgeous women I've ever seen, like Hedy Lamarr in *White Cargo*, quick-walking, small-footed and lithe little girls who flirted outrageously and were dead serious about the consequences. The second kind of woman was the overweight harridan squaw with a face blurred by too many years of too much bad liquor and too much whoring in the back alleys of the Charley bar and the rooms upstairs. For any man to respond to the invitations of these young girls was risky; for a white cop to do so was nothing short of suicidal. We sat at tables in the Charley while the younger women flirted with Holmes, whose solid muscular authority and irritatingly good looks made him irresistible to them. They'd sit at the table and ask him how he was in bed, how big was he, how long could he screw, and how often. Holmes would chuckle and turn them aside. All around us the males would burn like black coals, their anger so dense you could hardly breathe. Violence hung in the air all over the Charley, as palpable as the smoke, something you could reach out and put your hand up against, like a kind of electrical field. Harper would cruise the room, stopping here and there to gossip with men he knew. He was still trying to get a lead on that rapist. I never saw a cop who knew how to stop working, even on an off-duty night as this one was, even after the drinking started. Anywhere you looked around the room you struck a face heavy with threat. Most of this went on in the eyes. I had never before been made that aware of the importance of eye to eye threat. It was as constant and pervasive as white noise. There was only one way to handle it, and that was how Holmes and Harper handled it. Wherever they saw it they sent it back to the source in spades redoubled. It was a mistake to slide off if you caught someone staring at you, and it was a serious mistake to smile your most engaging big-city smile. At the Charley on a Friday night the only way to get around was to look as if you spent most of your waking hours dreaming about a chance to kick somebody's teeth down their throats and that tonight was your last chance. Perhaps this special attention was partly caused by the presence of a man they took to be a new cop on the job, in this case me, but Holmes and Harper saw no reason to get worked up about it. "The usual bullshit," Holmes told me, as he worked his way through his ninth boilermaker, "just stare the fuckers down." I asked the detectives how they got used to the feeling.

"You don't get used to it," Harper put in, coming up to the table with a handful of cold draft beer, materialising out of the smoke and noise and the smell of five hundred men and women in an overheated barn, "you just stop thinking about it. That's one of the toughest things a rookie cop has to learn. Everybody hates your guts. And that's not just down here in these stinking toilets. They hate you uptown too. The lawyers think you're a fascist. The citizens think you're a sadist who loves nothing better than handing out fucking parking tickets. Back at the station, I can think of a couple of brass hats who hate us just because we're out on the streets and they have to ride the mahogany while their butts get shiny! And make no mistake, my friends, about the politicians, especially in this town! Make no mistake about our dearly beloved Attorney General, and make no mistake about those sons of bitches over at city hall, most of whom hate us so goddamned bad it makes their kidneys hurt! Crooks hate us because we bust their asses! The fucking *victims* hate us because the bastard who raped their daughter only got three years or because we can't get his evidence back in time for spring or because the Crown buggered the case or because, god forbid, *we* buggered the case, which happens sometimes! Hate, fuck it, the whole goddamned job is lousy with hate! Man, I think even my wife hates me sometimes, when I come home mean as a snake over some bullshit number the department put us through! *Everybody*," and this part he literally bellowed out into the crowded room, blasting it into the hard copper faces all around us so strongly and so suddenly that they jerked back, "*everybody hates the fucking cops!*" and then he slammed his fist down on the table hard enough to bounce the draft six inches off it, and he leaned over close to my ear, so close I could feel his breath, and he whispered, "And you know what, my friend, my buddy from the Press, you know what? I couldn't give a single solitary sentimental suffering shit about any of these bastards." He held up a right hand, index finger and thumb a millimetre apart, and said, "Not even . . .*this* much of a shit!"

"That's not a lot of shit, is it?" put in Holmes to me, from the far side of the table, in a voice coming from far down in his chest, his face set in an expression of polite interest.

I thought about this very seriously for almost a minute before answering him. "No," I said, "that's not a lot of shit." We considered this statement for another minute, deadpan, until Harper, who was still looking out over the wall of belligerent faces all around us, repeated himself, "Yessir, just a teensy weensy little bit of shit. *Right you goddamned redskin bastards?*" and the whole bar broke into a single toothy grin, white teeth appearing from under thin brown lips like a conjurer's spell, and a laugh started up somewhere behind me.

"Right, you goddamned *whiteskin* bastards!" came from someone on the far side, a voice out of the mist. Quite suddenly, it seemed to me, the three of us were almost paralytically drunk. The big bar churned with voices and sound. Indians were everywhere, grinning at us, offering drinks and talking too loud. We may have danced. Later, in an alley, as Harper performed a creditable Astaire and Rogers tango with his trenchcoat and I tried to keep the cold black nightful of stars overhead in their places, Holmes told me the following story.

"That son of a bitch over there is the main reason I'm still a cop. That man is what is known as a 'partner' and I don't want to sound too, what's the word, too sappy, but he's one of the main things about this job that keeps it good. We were called in once on this bomb scare thing, I think it was in a bank building, somebody had a grudge, right? They find this shoebox full of dynamite. But the trouble here is that the shoebox is full of *old* dynamite. It's all covered with this stuff like sweat, you know what I mean. Only dynamite doesn't sweat water, right? It sweats nitro-glycerin. Can you see this? So they call in everybody in the whole goddamned area including the Bomb Disposal guys and Harper and me. Here we are standing around in the hall while the bomb guys fuck around should we this should we that. Now this is six fifteen maybe six twenty and it's been going on for an hour, two hours, and it's Friday night and we're off at seven? You see? The bomb guys have this shiny new bomb-containment vehicle parked out on the street and the street is blocked off and there are uniform cops all over the place. It looks like a movie set. Roadblocks and barriers. The Press is all over it like termites on a crutch. And Harper and I are sitting on our butts out in the hall while these fellows in Bomb Disposal start jerking around with these long tong things from behind a big shield. Gotta be careful fuckin' nitro goodness gracious me! Enough nitro to level a couple of floors, too, as it turned out later. Okay, I'm happy, I got no beef, as they say. But this boy," he nods his head, carefully, in Harper's direction. Harper is relieving himself up against an election poster. From the care with which this activity is being executed, I infer that Harper is not fond of the man pictured in it. "*This* boy, he's bored. He's bored with Bomb Disposal and the whole shooting match. He looks over at me where I'm pressed up against the wall alongside twenty other poor dumb cops and he grins at me, you know that grin, right? And he says 'fuck this, buddy, I got things to do' and he gets up off the floor and he walks into the room, steps over the bomb guys in their special flack suits and their armour and their stupid fucking tong things and he picks up the shoebox full of nitro. Man, *everybody* got out of his way! People pinned themselves to the ceiling! Oh God oh God oh God keep away from me you crazy prick. It was wonderful. He waltzes over to the elevator and he presses the button, I'm lying on the floor half-crying half-laughing, you see it? The doors open, down this fucker goes out into the street with the crowds all held back. He steps up onto the truck and he drops, I mean drops, the nitro into the fancy containment truck, and he says 'drop your peckers boys the chief is buying!'" Holmes paused, Harper lurched over with exaggerated care, and I tried to keep them both from cloning. "It was crazy, sure, but it was . . . it had greatness, you understand?"

We staggered out of the alley. On Main Street the river of liquid nitrogen rolled over us, an invisible frigid swell that fractured your lips and crystallised your breath in front of you. The bars were dark and the sidewalks were deserted. Up by the Princess our cruiser sat locked in ice and frost. The bricks on the walls cut my fingers like a knife when I brushed up against them. Holmes and Harper stopped in the middle of the street, facing each other. "What about the rapist?" I called to them.

"The rapist?" said Harper, his face a black mask in the cold blue light from the streetlamp, "The rapist? We'll get him. He's here or he's up in Crane River or he's hiding out in Brandon or he's shacked up with his sister it doesn't matter. We don't get him tonight we get him tomorrow, or one of the other teams will get him. Look at them!" Harper spun, his hand out, a drunken but Shakespearean flourish, gathering in the dark streets and the grim hotels and the cold blue circles of light, somehow evoking a mass of invisible people lining the walkways, watching him spin. "Look at those bastards! Out there with guns and knives and heroin cutting each other up and fuckin' each other over. Penner's Pansies and the goddamned Law Enforcement Review Board and the goddamned kangaroo courts and the goddamned mayor. Work work work. I don't give a shit. I do my job. I don't cross the line. And I stand by my partner. I'm gonna live forever! Don't you worry about the little rapist. We'll get him. That's why they call us cops, right?" He slammed his left hand hard up into Holmes' granite shoulder. His fist hit with a sound like a bat striking a ball, a clear sharp sound that bounced off the empty buildings on Main Street. There were uncountable stars in the deep black night overhead.

"Right!" said Holmes, and turned him to the car.

Live Forever, Harper had said. I hope they do.

CHAPTER ELEVEN

The Line

Goethe said that "Only the exhaustive is truly interesting," and I can see that he was right. This book took a year to research and write; it could have taken ten years. Since I left home in my seventeenth year, I have been all over North and South America, on the roads and in the back-country. During those years, I met policemen and policewomen under every kind of circumstance. Most of the time, we got along. Sometimes, we didn't. But the life they led, the risks and the privileges and the miseries, has always held a curious fascination for me. They seemed blessed and cursed together, bound by a terrible oath to act correctly and without hesitation as the symbols and the arbiters of right and wrong on the street. I've wanted to write a book about this terrible oath for years. The problem I faced was a matter of degree and scope. Perhaps I should have chosen one street in one city, and spent all my days and nights on that one street. But the streets were different across the country. Vancouver was as wild as Halifax was slow and quietly dangerous. Winnipeg had Indian problems, and raw strength. Montreal is still unlike any other city in Canada. Toronto is a big city, with the largest and most modern force. In the north of Ontario I found the limits of civilisation and the limits of the law. In selecting critical details here, I have been compelled to pass over equally vital aspects in other places. Not to have included the Northwest Territories strikes me as a serious omission. The growing role of women in the police force had to be only lightly touched upon because I wasn't permitted to accompany any serving policewomen, and to assess them second-hand was contrary to the rules of the book. Homicide, Morality, Vice, Fraud, Community Relations, Highway Patrol, Intelligence Operations, even the Motorcycle Units and the Mounted Patrols, all deserved attention I couldn't give them. Trying to understand the

RCMP and its unique position in Canada is a book all by itself. To draw a limit anywhere was arbitrary, but I had to draw one. I chose The Street.

It is on that street that most of us encounter the police. People who wouldn't know an undercover cop from a juniper bush can spot the foot patrol from two hundred yards. Drivers are as attuned to the presence of a squad car as gulls are to a hawk. Plainclothesmen in their unmarked cars, detectives in tan coats and sensible shoes, uniformed constables watching the picket line, are part of everybody's spiritual landscape. If you're going to meet a cop the odds are high that it won't be a Homicide detective or a Morality decoy. The street cop is the point of contact for all of us, the place where our private lives abut the public good, the visible manifestation of the state. But few of us can see the street cop clearly. We look at him through the filter of single experience, or the accumulated distortion of twenty years of television dramas and media interpretation. According to the shifting tenor of the decades, the street cop has been seen, in Canada, as a pig, a brute, a saint, a buffoon, a dupe, a hero, a lazy incompetent, a fanatic, a zealot, a clown, a Zomo, a tool of the oligarchy, but rarely as a man or a woman. Add to this the increasing inclination on the part of our governments to pass laws that require considerable interpretation from the enforcement branch, and it seemed obvious that any unbiased look at the street cop was not only necessary but long overdue. So, I hit the road in search of the essential cop. For what it's worth, I think I found him.

One of the first things I discovered was that there is a distinct difference between the policeman in the United States and in Canada. Bearing in mind the dilution of truth implicit in all generalisations, I think it's accurate to say that most Canadian street cops were far less ready to use violent and threatening tactics on even the most deserving citizens. On Davie Street in Vancouver I spent hours with many different policemen, of varying ages, and none of them were eager to rough up the frequently obnoxious street people they had to deal with. Even policemen who didn't know I wasn't a cop took a long slow time to think about it before they decided that force was called for. I watched one cop stand quietly and accept five minutes of gross verbal abuse from a drunken tourist on Robson Street in Vancouver. The man cursed the cop creatively and thoroughly for far longer than I would have considered acceptable, and then he left untouched. I can't think of a State Trooper or a city cop in any of the American towns I've visited who would have stood still for half that harangue without striking back. Taking abuse such as that may be part of the job description, but taking it as often and as gracefully as most of the men and women did calls for a genuine commitment to restraint. Officers who carried a chip, who provoked a fight, were openly frowned upon as men without maturity or control. There were men like that, but the peer group pressure they opposed was immense and sustained. The worst insult was to be considered "unprofessional" and a pugnacious cop was always seen that way by his colleagues.

A related distinction between Canadian police and their American associates was their attitude towards the guns they carried. After a year of intensive study, I have yet to find a Canadian policeman who thought of his gun more than once or twice while on duty, and then only because it was sticking into his ribs. Although guns play a large part in the public's image of the policeman, most cops consider it a small and sometimes inconvenient part of the job. No beat cop I was with ever pulled his gun. The Drug Squad detectives in Vancouver, men whose everyday work involved kicking in hotel room doors and shocking heroin addicts, carried out every kick-in with nothing in their hands but radios and flashlights. In Winnipeg, I saw at least eight different plainclothesmen confront various wanted men without a gun in sight. In James Bay the tool was talk, not a pistol. In Montreal, of course, it was different, but their work was armed robbery prevention, and weapons were vital. In Toronto I went up dark alleys with Squad Car officers on calls where we thought there might be men hidden in the shadows and no one was holding a gun. They drew them to clean them, or to present at inspection parade, but other than that, the gun might as well have been a paperweight. This attitude was the result of considerable thought on the part of experienced policemen. The gun limited their options to one fatal act. They never drew it unless it had to be used, and if it had to be used, they were psychologically ready to use it to kill. The public illusion of the disarming shot is just a joke on the job.

Most of the Canadian policemen I met preferred to think of themselves as Peace Officers rather than Law Enforcement Officers. The distinction is an important one. Historically, the role of the policeman was that of a mediator and a symbol of order. Until quite recently, the main work of the policeman was to keep order in the streets and public places, to make the city a comfortable social ground. He was responsible for implementing the neighbourhood consensus of order and peace, a consensus which varied considerably from neighbourhood to neighbourhood. The good beat cop had an instinctive understanding of the life of the street. He knew that most people think of a safe street in terms of freedom from harassment by panhandlers or rowdy teens, and not as a matter of safety from mugging or rape. Violent crime was a secondary consideration for the beat cop. He acted in concert with local people. He was sometimes appealed to as an arbiter of disputes. He sent vagrants on their way. He stopped little boys from breaking windows. He rescued pets and he gossiped with the storekeepers. As a part of the community, most beat cops derived a sense of accomplishment, a feeling of shared affection and appreciation with their beat areas.

With the meteoric rise of violent crime, or at least our awareness of it, pressure was exerted on local governments to root out and eliminate this social problem. This task was, naturally, passed on to the local policeman, who very quickly found that his time was completely taken up with enforcing laws and attempting to capture criminals. His performance as a Law Enforcer was considered more important than any Peace-keeping role. Enforcing law calls for an entirely different set of skills than keeping order.

The Law Enforcement Officer has to keep abreast of changes in any by-law or code. He has to memorise the mechanics of lawful inquiry, lawful search and seizure, lawful arrest. He has to develop the ability to lay out the fluid realities of any street encounter in the concrete terms of the courts. Where intuition and tact figured most, these subtle qualities have been displaced by diligence, exactitude, methodical procedures, in short, by The Book.

As a Peace Officer, much of his role would be considered legally impossible. Discretionary powers are currently considered too vague to entrust to the policeman. But it was precisely those informal, discretionary powers that gave the beat cop his authority and his real power to affect immediate and lasting changes in the street. Call it a Gentleman's Agreement, if you will, but the final test of its worth was that it was genuinely effective. Citizens who live in areas where they see a beat cop on regular duty have a real sense of security. The cop himself enjoys the obvious respect of his neighbourhood, he learns to recognise dangerous trends, and he derives a positive feeling of accomplishment from his work. All these aspects were lost to him when he became a Law Enforcement Officer.

Working by the Book, policemen soon realised that Collars and

Arrest Rates and Crime Stats were going to be the measure of his worth. It followed that Foot Patrols, with their limited coverage and lack of mobility, were poor areas for ambitious men. For quite a while, beat cops were considered inferior, and a beat was punishment detail. "You'll be back pounding a beat" was a catch phrase all through the Seventies. Not surprisingly, a slow schismatic process began. The Law Enforcement function became dominant as crime rates rose and street violence became a priority. Foot Patrols gave way to Squad Cars and Riot Police. The Watts riots in Los Angeles showed the municipal forces that they were totally unprepared for massive urban revolts. The Special Weapons and Tactics Squad was developed by military advisors in California, now famous as the SWAT team. In Canada, just about every major city has one, known by various names, such as the Emergency Task Force, or the Tactical Rescue Unit, or the Emergency Response Team. Guns, rifles, knives, skill in armed combat, courage and ruthlessness were the new paradigms for aspiring policemen. The old skills of negotiation, debate, tact, and personal authority, atrophied and died. Younger officers, boys who had grown up watching *Highway Patrol, Dragnet, Mannix, Adam Twelve, Police Surgeon, Starsky and Hutch* on TV, or admiring Clint Eastwood in *Dirty Harry* and *Coogan's Bluff*, got into police work with a completely different set of expectations than their predecessors. They started to think of the public as part of a battleground, something separate from them.

The public, in Canada as much as anywhere, was quite ready to accept this separation. Canadian streets got very dangerous, or they seemed to be. We were quite ready to see our cops as heroes doing battle on the street, as long as they won the war. The cop in a cruiser, the hard-faced android with the reflecting aviators and the nasty moustache, glowering out from under a stern billed cap, became the new image of the cop. Nobody had names, and who could remember the badge numbers? Just do the job, catch that B and E man, stop the rapist, kill the killer, make the world safe for democracy and commerce. The cop, being human, was quite ready to shoulder the glory along with the load. But the cop, being human, wasn't always successful. And that's where it all broke down.

Now we have cops with dark glasses and numbers, men and women with fearsome reputations, gun carriers and club wielders, voidoids in funny cars who roar past with sirens blaring, soldiers of somebody else's army. And the street crime didn't stop. We had lost the friendly neighbourhood cop, but we hadn't made the world safe for frisbee in the park. As a matter of fact, the park got very sinister indeed. Being human as well, we blamed the cop. We gave him all this power, and he fumbled it.

This schism is at work in Canada now. Just about every cop I talked to was torn by opposing forces within him. They mistrusted the people, largely because most of their contacts with the public were unpleasant, frequently intensely so. Sometimes the public killed them, sometimes they killed members of the public. Isolated from any work with a positive side, they experienced a gradual erosion of their faith in individual members of their society. They substituted a general intellectual commitment to society, to their country, to Canada, as an abstraction, an ideal. They loved humanity. But as Graham Greene said, "No one can love Humanity. You have to love people." Canadian policemen and policewomen feel that they can only safely love their fellow cops. Only the buddies understand. Only the buddies can be trusted. This kind of a schism is self-sustaining.

Canadians seem to be increasingly ready to abdicate personal responsibility, to place the burden of society's problems on "professional" shoulders. We leave our grandparents in nursing homes, we let the poor fall into welfare nets, we create "commissions" and "review boards" and "agencies" to do the things any thinking person once felt ethically obliged to take care of personally. And we surrendered the responsibility for our safety and the safety of our families to the police forces. Having done so, we slapped our collective hands together and walked off to enjoy our peace as something bought and paid for. The fact that the policeman can't do the job alone seems to be viewed as a breach of contract.

That's the Wall we've made. We put a Blue Wall between Us and Them, and we live in the shadow. We've made something unreal and superhuman out of ordinary men and women, with their help. Being thought of as Guardians of the Commonweal and Pillars of the Community is an attractive prospect. Too attractive to be easily resisted by anyone. It isn't until the young man or woman has become part of the Wall that he begins to see the price.

Where are we now?

Most street cops don't like the citizens very much. As Canadians, as a nation of shopkeepers, we tend to think of the police as hired hands who don't do the job well enough. It's a fashion to theorise about the cop, and your attitude to policemen is frequently a telling indicator of your background and educational accomplishments. For reasons which escape most cops, they feel they are hated most vehemently by the upper classes, by college-educated people with fine homes and good cars and fat portfolios. Generally, they return the compliment. Among the senior brass in Canada, the phrase "college kid" is always an insult.

Most teenagers hate the cops. To be frank, most cops don't like the teens much either. Teens are trouble. Teenage boys seem to look upon the streets as a proving ground for their own masculinity, and the cops are the lions. Drugs, liquor, violence, and sex, occupy a disturbingly large portion of the imaginative lives of many street youths. I can understand the sex, but the charm of violence eludes me. Sociologists in our universities are always complaining that the cops spend too much of their working time arresting, harassing, and generally annoying teenage boys, particularly those boys from the poorer areas, and boys of other racial origins. For what it's worth, that's true. On the other hand, boys in these categories are on the street, and wild in the street, in a much higher proportion than, say, investment bankers. If the guys at Dominion Securities or Pitfield, Mackay, Ross started cruising up de Maisonneuve or Robson or Spring Garden Road in wacked-out Toronados, mooning the tourists and tossing beer cans at the hookers, you might see a blip in the stats among investment bankers. I see the prejudice in the cops. It's real, and it's also based on reality.

As an observer, I felt most threatened, most in danger of violent assault, when I accompanied uniformed policemen into upper- and middle-class bars and private clubs. In the bad bars, we were a familiar sight, part of the daily routine in places like the Drake or the Blackstone in Vancouver, in the Charley or the Princess in Winnipeg, in the Gasworks or Stages in Toronto, but we were attacked most often in bistros and lounges where members of the educated classes were relaxing and drinking. In a bar called the Arts and Letters Club, two uniformed officers of the Vancouver police were almost mobbed by well-dressed and well-heeled club members when they entered to eject a troublesome patron at the special invitation of the management. We all got pushed around by men and women who worked as lawyers and executives and entertainers. Perhaps cocaine had something to do with this, but there was a deeply felt outrage on their part that the "cops" should intrude on their ground. I had the distinct impression that we were supposed to be off somewhere less tasteful thumping poor folk and busting street punks.

I felt least threatened when there were no citizens around at all, when the room was filled with nothing but blue uniforms. After a few months, I found it hard to trust anyone who wasn't a cop; I had just had too many nasty surprises from people I assessed as harmless or "part of my circle".

After a while, I also realised that most street cops don't like many of their superior officers. They always had one or two staff sergeants that they admired and/or trusted, but as a rule the constables and the detectives and the sergeants disliked being around senior men, "management", as they called them. I watched this at work in every police station I visited. After a few weeks, I learned to pick out the unpopular senior man on sight. Generally, the brass could be divided into two groups; the administrative insiders, and the good cops. For some reason, the good street cops who made it to management level held the respect of every cop on the force, but the administrative insider, the "fast-tracker", was cordially loathed by all the street cops. In accordance with an apparently natural law, the fast-trackers rose faster than the good cops, and tended to make most of the important departmental decisions.

This usually resulted in the implementation of policy changes which drove the working cop wild, such as the mandatory rotation of detectives in the Vancouver Police Force, a policy which seemed only to strip good detectives from areas they knew and to abandon reliable informers to strange and possibly unsteady hands.

Another side effect of this dichotomy was that most street cops hated to be in the stationhouse, because they ran the constant risk of falling afoul of a fast-tracker with a grudge against them. The degree of gossiping, infighting, back-stabbing, and generally rotten behaviour in police stations can only be rivalled by a Federal Caucus Room or the dormitory of a private school for boys. The jockeying for position was ruthless, relentless, and joyless; there were only two safe places for street cops, on the street or in a bar. Which brings me to liquor.

I saw and assisted in the demolition of more bottles of good liquor while writing this book than I have ever before imagined. Most policemen drink, many policemen drink too much, and some policemen drink as much as writers. The fact that there are any functioning livers on the nation's police forces is a tribute to the resilience of the Canadian metabolism. Oddly, though alcoholism is a problem in Canadian police forces, none of the men I met had any trouble at all controlling their taste for expensive liquor, and absolutely no one drank while on duty. My most memorable drunk was in Winnipeg, with the two detectives Harper and Holmes, and neither of these prodigious drinkers touched a single drop until the semi-duty night had been officially declared over.

It comes down to narrow ground in the end. Most street cops don't feel liked or admired by the citizens, although I think that they are mistaken in that belief. Nevertheless, the suspicion is there. Cut off from good contact with the public, they fall back on family and fellow officers. There seem to be limits even to that. A good wife was valued above rubies, but the men I met must have tried her patience dearly, since we spent a great deal of time in a bar or on the road.

The society of other policemen was largely resorted to in official functions and semi-official league games. The men had one or two close friends, usually other officers, with whom they shared weekend hunting lodges or trips. These friendships were always rooted in mutual experiences, and always honest to the point of brutality. Good friends in the cop's world were the ones who told you the truth; truth seemed to be a scarce and valued commodity.

Cut off from the public, isolated from department solidarity by the rigid hierarchy of the force, and subjected to the relentless assault of crime, violence, and despair generated by the street, the street cop is sooner or later reduced to a handful of certainties in an uncertain and frequently fatal world. They call these certainties The Line. After a lot of searching and talking, I found these three to be the most common certainties, and if the street cop in Canada has a code, it rests in these basic beliefs. I thought they were cliches, when I first detected them, but later I realised they were nothing but simple truths.

Stand by your partner was the first, possibly the premier rule. A man could fail his wife, his children, his parents, and himself, but the loyalty to the police partner was perhaps the strongest social bond I've ever seen. In war, it's a truism to say that a soldier died for his country, but anyone who's been there knows that a soldier dies for the men in his company. That's the kind of loyalty I saw between partners, composed of absolute trust and something so strong it could only be regarded as a kind of love. Of the few aspects of men in groups that bear any close examination, this one altruistic and absolute bond was far and away the finest and most admirable. A cop incapable of this bond was hated and despised as a traitor to something higher and older than a badge or an oath.

Do the job was the second rule. This meant do what was necessary according to the Code, do what was called for by the Book, and do the right thing, according to your experience. For instance, street cops know that all theories stop at the street. If you let theories and postulates about antecedent social injustices as a shaping force on aggressive patterns interfere with your readiness to fight, your will to kill if needed, then you'll die, or you'll choke when a citizen is counting on you to defend him. At the heart, a street cop needs to maintain the will to *act*, and this will depends to a great degree on his experience and his judgement. Academics may postulate that all criminals are guiltless, but the cop knows in his veins that some men are devoid of souls and the only way to stop them is to stop them by force. Not to back away from the necessary thing is the clearest statement of rule two.

Don't cross the border is the final rule. The street cop lives in a world of shades, grey into white, white into grey, grey into black. Criminals are the most skilled equivocators, the subtlest deviates, the silkiest apostles for the main chance. Opportunities to profit from his work, from the chances and coincidences of police investigations or pursuits, occur frequently. Suppose you have chased and caught a man with a deposit sack in his hand. Suppose you are alone when you catch him. There may be a great deal of money in the bag, and you may need money badly. Why not chase the man away, and claim not to have caught him? The money is yours. Or a prostitute informs you that a client of hers is a local politician rising to power on a platform of self-righteousness and religious posturing. Would he pay for your silence? How much? In a smaller scale, how many discounts can the used-car dealer give you before he has bought you? The policeman's power, in his own mind, derives from his deeply-felt desire to do the right thing, to prove worthy of the trust. If he stands by that principle then he has something real to hold onto in an infinitely shifting sea of guilt and innocence, of good and evil. If he lets go of that, he's lost. Few people are burdened with such a weight, and few people are blessed with such a clarity.

As far as I'm concerned, I was given a rare chance to travel on some very odd roads. I have made some friends and I'll undoubtedly make some enemies with this book. I know something about the policeman I didn't know before. I know he's neither a saint nor a brute, but merely an ordinary man doing something extra-ordinarily subtle and dangerous with all the skill and heart he can deliver. Some street cops fail. The wonder is so many do not. If, finally, this book and the stories in it have brought you closer to him, and made him more human for you, then the book was worth reading, and the street worth the walk.

Glossary

ABH —	Assault Causing Bodily Harm, a charge.
ANI - ALI —	Any Number Indicated Any Location Identified — a recent computer breakthrough allowing police and fire departments to immediately trace and identify the street address and precise location of any person calling in to a stationhouse.
B & E's —	Break and Enters: a crime of robbery.
THE BANKER —	In the drug-trafficking jargon, a man who takes and holds cash paid out for heroin; not necessarily the same as a SHOOTER or a DEALER.
BLOW —	Varies; usually Heroin, but now more often applied to Cocaine.
THE BOOK —	Not a formal entity, the book is best described as the sum total of all departmental rules and policies regarding the execution of a policeman's duty.
BUGS —	In police jargon, a criminal with a pathological disregard for life and a complete lack of empathic feelings.
CEEPICK —	The Canadian Police Information Computer, or ceepick, is a teletype information-sharing computer serving all police departments in Canada (and the United States, in some cases) on which information about any individual may be circulated. This information is limited to any arrest records or convictions, in any province, and any outstanding warrants in the individual's name.
CHOIR PRACTICE —	Originally an American term for semi-official police functions; later developed into a general term for off-duty recreation of varying degrees of wildness.
CODE SEVEN —	Radio code phrase for Officers on Lunch or Dinner.
COLLARS —	Arrests.
CROSS-TALK —	Most police radios are open to all calls from other units in the sector. The talk that is heard in this way is called cross-talk.
DOB —	Date Of Birth.
DOG CAR —	A squad car with an officer and a trained police dog, usually a German Shepherd, used to track and subdue fugitives.

234

FLACK JACKET —	A bullet-resistant vest worn by police officers in high-risk patrol areas; previously made up of steel plates but now being replaced with a DuPont fabric called Kevlar, which is a tight weave of fibreglass mesh capable of stopping high-calibre small-arms rounds. Ineffective against "varmint rounds" and Teflon-coated slugs.
THE FRUIT LOOP —	A section of Vancouver's Stanley Park favoured by homosexuals for the purposes of casual sex.
GFY —	Go Fuck Yourself.
HALF-AND-HALF —	Oral sex and intercourse.
HORSEMEN —	The Royal Canadian Mounted Police.
THE HYPES —	From hypodermic needles; heroin addicts.
KEEPERS —	Arrests that result in a prisoner being held and charges being formally laid against him.
'LUDES —	Quaaludes, a soporific; the world's most candy-assed drug, the breakfast of losers.
MITER —	The police walkie-talkie carried by officers not in scout cars.
MO —	Modus Operandi; literally, the method of operation employed habitually by a criminal.
159 SHEETS —	The monthly performance report, which includes arrests and demerits, prepared on each officer by division staff.
PCP —	Phencycladine Phosphate, a horse tranquiliser that causes severe perceptual and psychological distortions in the user. The effect of PCP is cumulative and frequently fatal to bystanders.
A PIECE —	Usually a weapon or a firearm; sometimes used to describe a woman.
REDS —	A spansule or gelatin capsule; usually dexedrine.
REEFER —	A uniform cold-weather car coat, usually blue.
SEMI-WAD-CUTTERS —	The standard Police cartridge; a modified wad-cutter slug in which the slug is still flat at the tip, but the shoulders of the slug are rounded into a flat-topped cone in order to insure the optimum combination of in-flight stability and energy transference to the target material. Usually a .38 Special calibre.
THE SHOOTER —	In the drug-trafficking jargon, a man who holds the capsules of heroin and who actually turns them over to an addict who has bought them.

SMASH-AND-GRAB —	A type of burglary in which a window is broken and property stolen without actual entry into the building or vehicle.
SOL —	Shit Out Of Luck; bad news.
SPOTTER —	An undercover Police Officer so placed as to be able to monitor illegal or suspect activities in a private or public place.
SUITCASED —	A method of concealing capsules of heroin inside a condom or balloon inserted into the rectum.
TAKE A FALL —	A conviction and a subsequent sentence to prison.
28 DAY REPORT —	Similar to 159 sheets.
WAD-CUTTERS —	A type of cartridge in which the slug is flat on the tip, which allows it to cut a neat round hole out of a paper target, making grading of competitions easier.
WANTS AND WARRANTS —	Literally, any outstanding Bench Warrants or other Court Orders requiring the arrest and delivery of an individual to the jurisdiction of a city or province in Canada.
A WIRE —	A battery-powered FM voice transmitter that is usually taped to the body of an undercover cop during a surveillance or arrest operation.